HITLER, MAO, & JESUS

HITLER, MAO, & JESUS

THE AUTOBIOGRAPHY OF
WERNER BÜRKLIN

WinePressPublishing
Great Books, Defined.

WinePress Publishing (PO Box 428, Enumclaw, WA 98022) functions only as book publisher. As such, the ultimate design, content, editorial accuracy, and views expressed or implied in this work are those of the author.

The author of this book has waived a portion of the publisher's recommended professional editing services. As such, any related errors found in this finished product are not the responsibility of the publisher.

Unless otherwise noted, all Scriptures are taken from the *Holy Bible, New International Version®, NIV®*. Copyright © 1973, 1978, 1984 by Biblica, Inc.™ Used by permission of Zondervan. All rights reserved worldwide. www.zondervan.com

Scripture references marked KJV are taken from the *King James Version* of the Bible.

Scripture references marked NASB are taken from the *New American Standard Bible*, © 1960, 1963, 1968, 1971, 1972, 1973, 1975, 1977 by The Lockman Foundation. Used by permission.

ISBN 13: 978-1-4141-2221-2
ISBN 10: 1-4141-2221-7
Library of Congress Catalog Card Number: 2011918149

CONTENTS

PREFACE

THIS MEMOIR HAD to be written!

As I grew older I sensed the need to leave something behind for my children and grandchildren. I do not have wealth nor do I have an estate. But I do have memories that I can leave behind and share, which sadly, are fleeting all too rapidly. To recall them, thank God, I still have letters, documents, journals, and volumes of newsletters that I had written in the process of my extended life's sojourn. This helped me immensely to pen these pages.

God has been good to me—very good.

My life has been a roller coaster, to say the least! However, the eighty plus years on this earth have been filled with amazing experiences and inspirations. They have been a proof to me that God is real; that He is good, and that it is worth following Him. In no way could I have attained all those glorious events without God's help, His support, and above all, His blessings.

I was born into a poor, yet godly family. I was raised in devout surroundings and educated in foreign countries. I was given direction by a host of saintly mentors. Yet, I also was challenged by demonic ideologies and depraved systems and almost succumbed to their wicked intrigues.

God intervened and led me on a triumphant path. This path was worthwhile to track and rewarding in its conclusion. I am eternally grateful to God who gave me a loving wife, God-honoring children, and an energizing and thrilling vocation.

It was good and rewarding to do God's work.

I tried my best to record the facts as I remember them. Some people, like Billy Graham, played a major role in my life. This is not name-dropping, but it shows my sincere appreciation for a man who has guided my thinking and judgment ever since my early years. It was his integrity more so than his preaching that inspired me most. There are of course others, including teachers and pastors, who have influenced me deeply, but most will not be named. I am profoundly grateful to all of them. They shaped my character and challenged me to achieve loftier heights.

You may be surprised how personal and intimate my descriptions are in some cases, but I was committed to tell it how it was. Therefore I am using many of my letters and portions of my journal. Reading them again, I noticed how lonely I often was while traveling the world. But God's Word sustained me. As an illustration, this is what I entered on October 12, 1988:

> Up at 4 a.m. Wonderful quiet time. What would I do without the daily spiritual food received out of the Word of God! The Bible truly has become my companion. The longer I live, the more I love God's Word and the more I depend on it. Even for smaller decisions in life! What a path to tranquility

and inner security! It gives me so much fortitude through correction and guidance.

It is my prayer that some may learn from my convictions, beliefs, and principles and that they will adopt them into their lives—especially those who are still young in age.

These pages were recorded to bring glory to my heavenly Father. All accolades received I place at the feet of my Savior whom I served and whom I love very much. All failures of mine, and there are many, I leave at the foot of the cross, knowing that they have been forgiven and forgotten. One thing I learned: God is the only one who can forget.

Hallelujah!

CHAPTER 1

CHINA—A LAND TORN BY CIVIL WAR

I T HAPPENED ON a bench under the only willow tree in the lush garden of our home on *Da Shi Lu*—Great Western Road—in Shanghai, China. Lois rested her beautiful face against my shoulder. We were in love—puppy love. I was seventeen, she two years younger. "Do you want to kiss me," I ventured. I had never kissed a girl. Films were rare in our Shanghai. The few I had seen were propaganda films of the German Nazi Party (NSDAP) and not flicks portraying scenes of love. "I do not know how," she whispered. I squeezed her hand. I wanted her to kiss me, was disappointed when she didn't, but then did not mind. I loved her no matter what. She was the only girl I had truly loved during my growing-up years. I could wait.

For us living in Asia, the Second World War had ended in August 1945. Two atomic bombings in Hiroshima and Nagasaki had brought about the sudden and final death to the most brutal war ever fought. It had cost more than 50 million lives worldwide. The Chinese had suffered greatly. Millions of them had given their all in their gargantuan struggle against the Japanese. Germany had succumbed three months earlier. My parents were interned as German missionaries by the Chinese Nationalists in the province of Jiangxi, also known as the revolution province, an important province for Communists in the interior of China. I had not seen them for over five years. China, siding with the Allies, had been at war with Germany. I lived in Japanese-controlled Shanghai and my parents in Nanfeng, a remote town in Jiangxi, some 1,000 miles away. I was free; they were not. There was no way to cross the front drawn arbitrarily between them and me. It was a tough time in my life.

After the war, Lois with her three sisters had come to live in the children's home, where my parents had put me so that I could study at the renowned German *Kaiser Wilhelm Schule* in Shanghai. Her parents were missionaries from the United States and had worked in the interior of China. Now that the war was over, the four children with her mother were on their way home, passing through Shanghai. Their dad, Loyal, had decided to remain in China, no matter what might happen under an imminent takeover by the Communists. According to the local police, he died on March 16, 1971.

Things did not run smoothly during the aftermath of the war. That's why they were stranded in the exotic city I called home, while working on their documents to enter America. I was happy for the time they were stalled, and thrilled to have Lois close to me.

Then she was gone. I saw her off at the Bund, the famous waterfront of downtown Shanghai. Her ship anchored close by. To see the ship eventually disappear down the Huangpu River tugged at my heart. Four years went by before I saw her again.

2

Finally, at that time, I got my reward when she stretched out her arms to embrace me passionately. Her kisses then meant a lot to me. I saw her only for a few hours in Wheaton, where she was studying at the prestigious Christian college, and then lost her forever.

God had someone else in mind for me. And what a girl she was! But this has to wait until later. Let me relate how and where my life started.

My German heritage—Mannheim and Reiherbach

My father, Gustav Bürklin, was born on a hot summer day on August 27, 1897, in Mannheim in southern Germany and my mother on September 19, 1895, in Reiherbach near a sleepy town, Sachsenhausen, on a remote farm in central Germany, close to Kassel.

Mannheim is an industrial town, famous for its unique squares of city blocks and her street names using the alphabet from A-Z. During the Second World War, the city was practically destroyed by Allied bombing raids, but only a relatively small number of civilians perished due to the foresight of its mayor. He had huge bunkers built before the bombs rained down on the city, obliterating everything in sight. Even though many innocent women and children were exterminated, most of the inhabitants came through alive.

The parents of my father died when he was a teenager. He became a believing Christian on the day of his confirmation. Children of Lutheran parents attend confirmation classes, but to most, those were just meaningless lessons. My father, however, took it seriously. When he was asked to repeat the vow to follow Jesus during the sacred ceremony, he meant it. As a teenager, he volunteered to join the army during the First World War. He served three long years. In spite of the many dangers he faced, he was sustained by his faith and decided, while battling the hardships and horrors of war and later as a prisoner of war of the British, to enter a spiritual ministry—if God would keep him alive. This led him eventually to China.

St. Chrischona near Basel in Switzerland, a theological seminary only a few yards across the border from Germany, trained him well. There he was confronted with the spiritual needs of a world. Werner Spohr, a missionary to China, who later became my godfather (*Patenonkel*), challenged him to consider China as his mission field. Some 300 million Chinese at that time had never heard about the saving power of Jesus Christ. Whereas most Europeans had been inoculated with the gospel of Christ, most Chinese did not even know that Jesus existed. My father rose to the challenge and after graduation and several months of religious practical work (*Praktikum*) in the Marburg area of central Germany, he was sent as a missionary to China. It was the year 1926.

Reiherbach is a winding brook through a picturesque valley at the foothills of historic Waldeck, south of Kassel. My mother's father, a farmer and enterprising shepherd, had built a modern farmhouse in that valley and named his farm Reiherbach. Germany's emperor Kaiser Wilhelm had dedicated the Edertalsperre with its huge dam before the First World War only a few miles away. The British torpedoed the dam a few months before the end of the Second World War and in the wake of the onrushing flood, hundreds, perhaps thousands of innocent civilians perished. The waters reached the outskirts of Kassel some fifty miles away. The dam was rebuilt and today the surroundings of the Edertalsperre with its gorgeous lake have become a tourists' paradise.

My mother, Lina Pfeifferling, was born on the farm Reiherbach. Her parents were God-fearing folks and she was raised in a good home, but it was a warmhearted seamstress who led her to Christ. She studied nursing in Kassel, attended the Bible School in Malche in the eastern part of Germany, and was drawn to China. The *Allianz China Mission* in Barmen, an associate mission of Hudson Taylor's China Inland Mission, sent her first to England to learn English and then to China. She arrived in Shanghai just before Christmas in 1925.

Both my father and my mother studied Chinese in the mission's language training schools, he in Anking, the school for men, and she in Yangzhou, the school for ladies, both on the shores of the majestic Yangtze River. As singles, they hoped to find their life partners among those who also had come to China as missionaries. My mother was featured in a mission magazine where a photo showed her serving Chinese kids at a birthday party. *Hmm*, my father thought, *a lady working with kids will most likely make a good mother.* So he set out to find her, and he did. It was an arduous trip covering hundreds of miles. In the days of no planes and few highways, he did most of his travels on foot. When he finally arrived in the town where she worked, he was told that she had moved on to a different city farther south. "To find what you set out to see, you have to walk a little further," the missionary in that city told him. So he walked on to Nancheng, another forty-five miles. It took him one full day. She was flabbergasted when he proposed. "I first have to write my parents and ask them what they think," she said. With a triumphant smile he reached in his pocket, pulled

5

out a letter from Reiherbach, and *voila*, the approval in writing. Soon thereafter, they married in Shanghai in 1928. One year later, their first son, Friedel (later, when he became an American citizen, he changed his name to Frederick) was born on May 22. I was born on November 2, 1930, and my sister, Gisela (she also changed her original German passport name during naturalization proceedings and changed her name to Joy) on July 23, 1932. I will use their various names in the sequence of events described in this book.

My parents had been introduced to China in a turbulent time. Western powers were competing for economic gains. Already in 1925 Lucius Porter had written in his book *China's Challenge to Christianity:*

> No Western power has been willing or able to allow the Chinese people to work out themselves either their own revolution or their own political development through modern constitutional forms of government. Even the least aggressively selfish of Western powers has been inclined to put its spoon into the broth that is brewing in China in the hope of securing more or less of special privileges for its own interests. Taken together, the Western powers have been more interested in a stabilized and an orderly China because of the advantages to them in carrying on trade and in developing concessions under such conditions, than in allowing the Chinese people time for quiet natural adjustment to new conditions and for essential self-development. Charges can be laid against every one of the Western powers and against Japan for interfering in China's internal affairs by urging some particular policy upon the Central Government; or by supporting some particular leader who gave promise of securing wide control in China; or by selling arms to revolutionary

groups; or by arranging with corrupt officials for loans that are a mortgage on the nation's resources.

It is impossible to estimate how much of the political confusion and anarchy in China today is due directly to foreign interference, open and secret, and how much is due to causes of an indigenous character and of Chinese origin only. Practically all of China's friends agree that her development would be far better assured if the Western powers and Japan could agree among themselves upon a complete "hands-off" policy, and could allow her full freedom to work out her own salvation along lines of political organization true to her own traditional and native genius. Lao-tzu's ideal "Development without Domination" has received no support from foreign governments.

Missionaries were mistrusted by many Chinese. They were seen as riding on the coattails of unscrupulous western businesspeople. So right from the beginning my parents had to grapple with those attitudes. Furthermore, the Chinese were proud people with a long cultural history. Most missionaries apparently were not capable of grasping what Porter saw and wrote about:

> Within recent years very much of the development has been in the hands of the Chinese. These changes have been not only "introduced" to the Chinese, but they have been accepted by the Chinese very quickly. Adaptability, one of the outstanding qualities of the Chinese people, is shown in the adjustment that has been made to the new economic environment. China has packed into the limits of a single generation the process of modernizing the physical environment of daily life in home

and street and office, which has occupied Europe through the last three hundred years.

My parents also struggled with learning Chinese. It is a very difficult language to master, very different from European languages with their alphabets. The Chinese use individual characters and you have to memorize up to 3,000 of them to be able to read a newspaper or a book. My father preached his first Chinese sermon in February 1930—some four years after he first arrived in China in January of 1926. On that Sunday he entered his sentiments into his diary:

> I took the free moments for final sermon preparation. Then I entered the pulpit with great trepidation to deliver my first sermon in Chinese. Many folks were present, unusually so. The Lord gave me freedom to open my mouth and I expounded the Scriptures found in Philippians 1.12-26. We ended the service with Holy Communion.

In the following three years he perfected his Chinese but earnestly looked forward to his first furlough where he could express himself freely again in his mother tongue. For them it had been a challenging and dangerous time in China. The Communists under such leaders as Chu Te, Chu En-lai, and Mao Zedong were battling the nationalists led by Chiang Kai-shek in the same province where they ministered. My father wrote in his diary:

> The streets are full of troubling news; often the robbers [Communist dissidents were called robbers] come by night and cart away hostages.

On Saturday, February 1, 1930, he entered this:

> Rumors are manifold. The hordes of robbers greatly harass and frighten the farmers. Today we packed to flee and at 11 a.m. the necessities were on board. What anxiety and nervousness!
>
> The streets are full of frightening stories about the situation in the rural areas. Robbers come by night and take hostages indiscriminately. Repeatedly you hear devastating rumors; the rural population is kept in constant fear. Today we packed a few things and by 11 a.m., a few of us were on a boat. Finnish missionaries Cajander, Ingman, and Hedengren were on one boat, and a larger boat lodged Mrs. Tyler, missionaries Weber, Nesland, and my wife Lina with child [Friedel]. What tension and restlessness!
>
> Once things quieted down in the evening, I retrieved my wife and son.

The reason for him to retrieve the nine-month-old son was his incessant bawling. Why would he cry his heart out? My mother insisted that she could not go on into an unknown future with a possibly sick child. So my father took them back to the mission station. This saved their lives. Here now some more excerpts from my father's diary:

> February 2. Early this morning the Finnish sisters departed for Changshu; the others returned from the boat. We try to normalize things; but what uncertainty! Soldiers everywhere. They seem to fortify the city.

> February 5. At lunch time Mr. Tyler brought disturbing news. Ming-Yong, our cook, is back with the tragic news that the

Finnish Sisters were taken hostage by the robbers. They were moved to a nearby temple. How dreadful to think that Lina with our son could have landed there as well. What wonderful protection! However, those poor Sisters! Our cook is back but with such terrible news.

February 15. Prayer meeting in our home. We pray for our three Sisters. What must they endure?

February 17. Situation worsens. Our trust is in the Lord, because change can take place momentarily.

February 18. No news yet about the Sisters.

While the political and military situation was extremely precarious, my parents kept on doing their missionary work—visiting the sick, preaching in churches, passing out tracts on the streets, inviting people to attend their services, holding street meetings, plastering gospel posters on street walls, studying for language exams, and trying to make sense of the horrors surrounding them.

February 20. All we hear are terrible rumors that the Sisters had been killed and were thrown into the river. My head is so tired; the exams [the forthcoming language tests] drive me crazy. Also my nerves are so fragile. Am depressed due to worries about our future. Nevertheless I keep trusting my Lord who will help.

February 22. During this week I was in charge of morning devotions. I love to do them, however, the preparation [in Chinese] takes so much time. On top of this I am so weary of the exams. But I must plow ahead. The news about the Sisters is getting crueler—they most likely were murdered.

February 23. I so much want to get close to the people, but haven't achieved that as yet. I would love to get involved with the young people. Everything seems so difficult. Also Lina dreads speaking in women's meetings. However, we have to conquer the new challenges thrust upon us.

February 24. Mr. Tyler now says that the Sisters are held by the robbers for ransom. There might be a chance for someone to act as a mediator.

February 27. Passed out tracts on the streets. In the afternoon, many came to hear the gospel and the local Christians are actively engaged. Tomorrow two people plan to look for the Sisters. May God be with them.

March 2, Sunday. Many folks attended the service. How I long to find the way into their hearts. Often so depressed with gloomy thoughts. My nerves are so raw.

March 3. This afternoon a man came to report that the Sisters have been shot in Shui-Nan. Soldiers were pressuring them [the robbers] and because they were convinced that no money would be forthcoming, they killed them. Even though this is dreadful news, we now are thankful to know what has transpired.

March 8. Now we hear that some people have seen the Sisters alive, and others say they are dead. If only we could know the truth!

March 16. Spoke at the large meeting. Well attended. The Lord helped me to articulate well. I was free and full of joy. Many women came to our home to see our son. We are so happy to have them come—one way of getting to know them better. We also visit them in their homes.

March 18. In the afternoon eight robbers were executed—four were shot; the other four were killed with knives and swords.

March 20. Forenoon on the streets to plaster posters on walls. People stopped, read, listened, and gladly received gospel tracts.

March 24. What will happen when northern [government] and southern [Communist] troops fight each other! What about the Sisters?

March 25. Plastering posters on walls on the streets; it is so hot! And I am so tired; all day long I felt on my left side as if my heart was tightening. While on the street a notice was posted that eleven robbers had been executed, one of them was the son-in-law of our Christian Tseng.

March 28. Saw a number of robbers being led to the execution grounds; what a terrible sight!

March 30. I have again the privilege to preach next Sunday in the main service; I am excited with fear; however, this way I get some practice.

April 3. Another eighteen people were executed.

April 15. Again over twenty people were executed. The preparation for my exam tires and upsets me. I feel a constant pressure in my head.

April 16. This morning two women were executed, and in the afternoon another six men and one woman.

April 18. Good Friday. I hoped for a quiet day of remembrance but it was a restless day and full of anxiety. I wanted peace and serenity for my torn heart and my wounded nerves.

April 20. Where are the Finnish Sisters?

May 2. More critical days; no rice reaches the markets. I again saw twelve men taken to the execution grounds, and in the evening another twenty or so robbers were seized.

June 8. Pentecost. Quite a few attended the evening service and some were very attentive. However, so many live in this big city and in this large country without knowing the living God and are without Christ!

During those frightful, horrifying, and unbearable days, my parents never gave up. My mother later told me how often she had been tempted to give up and return home but then said, "God had called us to China and therefore we stayed through all the horrors of war, upheaval, and loneliness."

Also in other ways life in China was challenging and difficult during those days. With little medical support, illnesses were rampant, and many children of missionaries were buried in China's soil. My parents were constantly in fear of losing their newly born children. I almost did not make it either. In the summer of 1931 my father penned this into his journal:

July 10. The doctor diagnosed pneumonia with high fever. After another anxious night worrying about the life of our Werner, we finally welcomed the breaking morning.

July 11. During the night, we again were extremely alarmed about Werner's condition. Both of us were up at 2 a.m. helping him to inhale. Now we thank the Lord for improvement and trust Him for complete recovery.

Furthermore, no one ever heard from those Finnish sisters again! Martyrs for Christ.

Germany in uproar

In those days, furloughs were permitted only after missionaries had labored seven years on the field. The second furlough would be granted after ten more years. My parents took their first one in 1933, and after a refreshing two years, they returned to China in 1935. Hitler had come to power in Germany and my parents did not know how best to interpret the new policies he introduced. Already in October of 1930, my father had expressed his concern about Hitler's rise. His diary reveals: "The Hitler-movement is very vocal back home. Their seats in the parliament catapulted from twelve to one hundred seven. This causes trepidation and unease within the ranks of the parliament and among the people in general. Is its goal dictatorship like in Italy [under Mussolini]?"

While at home, he wondered whether Germany would have to go through the same type of political unrest as they had faced in China. In the years from 1928 to 1933, they had suffered greatly because of the battles fought between Chiang Kai-shek's and Mao Ze Dong's troops. Often they had to flee the areas where battles were severe. I was born on one of those flights into the city Wuhu, on the banks of the muddy Yangtze in the province of Anhui, north of the province Jiangxi. My mother had complained often about packing, unpacking, and repacking again and again. She was so tired of moving from place to place, and it gnawed on the nerves of both of my parents.

During the two years of furlough, we kids had a great time living on our mother's home farm with horses, cows, sheep, pigs, cats, dogs, and chickens. I watched the farmhands milk the cows. I wanted to try it, but as a four-year-old was scared of those huge beasts. Those animals were too intimidating, so I chose a calf, not knowing what I was doing. She kicked and catapulted me into the manure. On another occasion, I fell into a cesspool. The stench was indescribable! I never milked cows again, nor did I go near a cesspool!

As we traveled back to China on the *MS Stuttgart,* a German ocean liner, during the summer of 1935, I enjoyed some of the incredible sights between Europe and Asia. In Suez, Egypt, I was captivated watching small kids dive after coins we threw overboard. They always showed off by extracting them from their mouths when they resurfaced. *What skill,* I thought, *grabbing them with their mouths! How do they do that,* not realizing that they were using their hands and then sticking the coins into their mouths before breaking through the water!

I started school in Shanghai as a five-year-old. We were placed into a children's home run by the mission. It was tough to see my mother leave after she had introduced me to my new teacher. When she said good-bye in the classroom, I clung to her and cried, knowing that she would leave me in Shanghai. I felt so insecure and abandoned! She, of course, had to return to the mission station in Jiangxi, and I would not see her for months. Only during the summer vacations was this possible. This is how she related that incident:

> It is not easy to have to leave children behind that young. But their future depends on what they learn when they are young. But at least we can keep the boys out here [in China, without having to send them to Germany for schooling as it had been done in earlier years], and thus we can see them at least once a year in their summer vacations...Werner, the younger one, could not comprehend why he had to part from his mother. He cried loud in his classroom and did not want to let me go. But then the little guy, not quite six, braced himself and said: "The tears want to flow, but I don't want them." After I departed [back into the interior], homesickness would overcome him in the children's home, but he seems to be okay now.

Once a year, I, along with my brother and sister, was taken to the interior to be reunited with our parents. Those were precious times but I dreaded when we had to return to Shanghai after those summer vacations. My parents were stationed in Chongren, where my father supervised the construction of a new house on the grounds of the mission station. Emmanuel Baumann from Switzerland helped him in this endeavor. He was good looking, athletic, and a daring kind of a fellow. He climbed up and down that building under construction without using the stairs. That impressed me as a little boy—*what a guy*, I thought.

Japan had started a war with China after the Marco Polo Bridge incident in 1937. Although the two countries had fought intermittently since 1931, total war started in earnest in 1937 and ended only with the surrender of Japan in 1945 (July 7, 1937 – September 9, 1945). The war was the result of a decades-long Japanese imperialist policy aiming to dominate China politically and militarily and to secure its vast raw material reserves and other economic resources, particularly food and labor.

For the next seven years, we now had to live through this horrific period. The Japanese overran and then occupied Shanghai while my parents ministered in the center of the province of Jiangxi, which was still under the control of the Chinese Nationalists. Only once did Japanese troops meet up with my folks on the hill Makushan near Nancheng, where missionaries had built summer cottages to escape those stifling hot summer months. The Japanese were surprised to see German missionaries live with American and English counterparts without any problem. However, they were beaten back by Chinese forces and all German missionaries were then put under house arrest when China declared war on Germany. We German kids had total freedom in Japanese-occupied Shanghai. We never saw our parents for over five long years. Only through occasional letters, we knew how they were faring.

I, along with my siblings, was stuck in Shanghai attending the German school *Kaiser Wilhelm Schule*, recognized as the best foreign school in Asia. I was not a good student. I would rather play soccer outside than sit in a classroom. I also was known for my pranks. On a school outing to the famous sightseeing

17

spot Lunghua Pagoda, our class climbed the six flights to the top. Reaching our objective, I was not satisfied. I wanted more. I wanted to climb higher. As I was hanging on to the top roof, trying to swing my body over the edge of it, my teacher, Amann, spotted me and yelled, "Bürklin, are you crazy? Get down! And that immediately!" After I was back safely on solid ground, he grumbled, "Typical Bürklin, 'Nearer my God to Thee, nearer to Thee.'"

In our German school we had teachers who opposed Nazism and others who were party members. Every young German had to join the Hitler Youth movement, called HJ. So was I. We were issued uniforms and on Fridays, we had two hours of indoctrination classes. They were boring, at least to me. Once our Nazi instructor asked, "Who is the founder of the NSDAP (*National Sozialistische Deutsche Arbeiter Partei*)?" No one answered because no one knew; neither did I. I had never heard about the founder. The chap sitting behind me whispered, "Karl Marx." Wanting to be a smart aleck, I saw my chance. In a loud voice, I blurted out "Karl Marx." Everybody laughed, even the Nazi instructor did. Then things changed dramatically. "Whoever said that, stand up," he demanded. Now he was serious, even frightfully solemn. "Get out! Run around the track twice and then report back." He now was livid. *How can a young Hitler youth come up with such a remark*, he must have thought. Communism, the ideology Karl Marx had initiated, was worlds apart from Nazism. In fact, Hitler threw Communists into concentration camps.

One week later, the entire Hitler Youth brigade of Shanghai was summoned to a special meeting. Wiedemann, the leader of the Hitler Youth movement in China, gave a rousing and patriotic address. "While our brave troops are waging heroic battles in Europe," he intoned, "a young German in Shanghai had the audacity to declare that Karl Marx, a Bolshevik, is the founder of our German Nazi Party. What nerve! Whoever made that comment, stand up and come to the front. Everyone here must take notice of him."

As I was making my way forward, he continued his tirade. Then I faced the large crowd and wondered what this was all about. *It was a joke, fellows, why this uproar,* I thought. At least to me! But they took it as a major event that required to be confronted with vigor and a stern rebuke. "You are lucky to live in Shanghai," he continued. "In Germany we have other means to deal with such scum." Now I realized that they really were serious. But there was nothing I could do further to remedy the situation. Incidentally and luckily, this the whole episode was forgotten. I never heard from them again. But it did scare me at the time and my brother, who was a leader in the HJ, was ashamed.

As a young kid, I did not care about school at all. My grades were bad, so bad that once I had to repeat a class. Later I learned that even Winston Churchill had to repeat a class, and that twice or even thrice. So, I was in good company. *I am not nearly as bad as he is,* I mused. I simply had no interest in learning until I reached my teenage years. And then I took off. I finally understood the necessity of learning and I began to love it. My grades accelerated to the top.

In the final days before Germany surrendered, the big incorrigible Nazis in Shanghai were still celebrating the fifty-sixth birthday of Adolf Hitler on May 8. His birthday actually was on April 20, but those fanatics had planned a sinister, not to say creepy, assembly in the darkened Deutsche Halle, which had been formerly used by the Kaiser Wilhelm Schule as its gym. Under the sound of rolling drumbeats and surrounded by flickering torches, hundreds of Germans sang the *Horst Wessel Lied* for the last time. It was the Nazi anthem.

Die Fahne hoch, die Reihen fest geschlossen,
S.A. marschiert mit ruhig festem Schritt.
Kam'raden, die Rotfront und Reaktion erschossen,
marschier'n im Geist in unser'n Reihen mit.

That was it. *Fini!* The war was over a few days later, at least in Europe.

The doors of our school closed on September 9. The German radio station XGRS shut down. A couple of weeks before, the Chinese-American radio commentator Herbert Moy, who had sided with the Axis powers, cut his wrists and threw himself down from the top floor of the school building. There he lay with a broken skull and blood pulsating from his arms. He did not want to be confronted by the American victors. We were sent home right away, and that day was the last day of my studies in that school building.

The US army moved into our buildings. Our teachers had to find other places where they could teach their students. Our children's home made room, even the Lutheran church was used for classrooms. But what about our parents? The war was over, but they were still interned. *The person who might be able to help was Madame Chiang Kai-shek, the wife of China's paramount leader*, I thought. So I wrote a letter to her pleading to release them. I do not know whether she ever read or even received my letter, but in the spring of 1946, they were set free and I, along with my brother and sister, made the long journey to China's hinterland.

CHAPTER 2

CHINESE RED ARMY IN CONTROL

THIS WAS ONE of the worst trips I have ever taken. Once we had to stay overnight in a vacated Chinese school. The beds were crawling with bedbugs even though the bedposts were resting in cans filled with petroleum. The bugs were smarter and found us by crawling up the walls, and then dropped from the ceiling on to our beds. We could not kill them fast enough, so we gave up, took benches out into the open air, straddled them, and carefully maneuvered our backs upon them. My, were they hard on our backs! We experienced a sleepless night in moonlight but free of bugs.

Finally, we made it to Nanfeng, the city where our parents dwelled. "*Lao haitse lai la,*" the sixteen-year-old kitchen hand or cook shouted. Without opening the gate, he ran to our parents with the good news. "The children arrived," he shouted. Our parents were overcome with emotion. At last, we were back together. More than five years is a long time for anyone, especially for loving parents. Before sitting down for a meal, our father took us around showing us their home and mission station. We ended up on the wrap-around veranda. On a wall, a poster showed in vivid painting a broad road leading to hell and a narrow road to heaven. "On which road are you?" he asked.

All three of us had made a commitment to Christ as teenagers while living in the Shanghai children's home. "On the narrow road," each one of us said. Tears filled his eyes as he whispered, "All we could do while being separated was to pray for you. God has answered our prayers."

It was an English missionary with a white beard who had triggered the desire within me to find Christ. Of course, the Christian children's home in which we were raised had laid the foundation for my faith. But I had never surrendered to Christ. One Sunday morning in church I turned to my friend and whispered, "This sermon is too boring for me. I will see you later after the service." The white-bearded gentleman spotted me as I was leaving the church. "Do you know Christ as your personal Savior," he asked. "No," I responded and while turning my back on him I heard him continue, "It would be wonderful for you to get to know Him. He will never let you down."

Somehow this struck a chord deep inside of me. As a young German I had followed Hitler. I had been forced to believe in him. I had been told that he was the greatest leader ever. I had been asked to swear allegiance to him. And then the debacle! He had committed suicide. His Third Reich had collapsed and with it my faith in him. I was a disillusioned young teenager. I went to church because I had to. But that morning something dramatic had happened.

For the next three days I pondered about what that Englishman had said. I knew about Christ. I knew the entire story of Christ. But I had not appropriated it into my life—into my belief system. Finally all alone, I knelt at my bed and said, "Lord, you know that I am confused. I followed someone who let me down. If it is true that you exist and that you can take over my life, then I want you to do that. Right now."

I got up from my knees as a different person and I never regretted to have surrendered my life to the living Christ on that fateful morning.

For close to a year I stayed with our parents in the back country of China. In August of that same year, after they had been set free, they moved to Ningdu, 130 km further south. My dad asked me to transport a number of trunks with their belongings to that city. I went to the bus station to see whether I could find someone to take the load south. Lo and behold, a large UNRRA truck (United Nations Rural Relief Agency or United Nations Relief and Rehabilitation Administration) stopped, coming from the north. Spotting an American driver, I took the courage and asked him whether he would be willing to load our baggage onto his vehicle. "Yes, I would love to help you," he said and off we went. There was no room in the cab, so I sat on top of his cargo and our trunks in the back.

It was windy and dusty on those unpaved roads, but I did not mind. Action accomplished! My father was thrilled because the driver did not charge a dime. Several hours later, I arrived in Ningdu with an aching stomach and terrible runs. I must have eaten something that had been contaminated.

Ningdu was a key city for the Communist Revolution. Mao Zedong had established his first Soviet republics in the southern part of Jiangxi in the period from 1929-32. Close to 10 million people were under his control at that time. When in

Ningdu, he resided in the mission station. In one of the rooms, later the bedroom of my parents, execution orders were signed, and the executions were implemented in the chapel next door. The mission house was used as one of the headquarters of the Communist Party. Now it accommodates a museum depicting the early period of those war-torn times. You can still see the revolutionary writings on some of the walls.

My parents stayed in Ningdu until after the "liberation army" of the Communists had moved into the city. This took place during the fall of 1949. A Swiss missionary couple with their two children had arrived to take over the responsibility overseeing the mission station. Their third child, Johannes, was born in Ningdu. My parents helped them get settled. Together with the new missionary, my father took extended trips on foot to the outlying districts, introducing him to Christian leaders.

The transfer of political power was relatively smooth except in cases where the new rulers displayed brute force. Ernst Wyss, the new missionary, experienced this firsthand. The husband of a dedicated church member had been a high official in the Kuomintang government. Expecting unpleasant, even brutal treatment from the new authorities, he sought shelter with some of his relatives in the countryside. After things seemed to normalize, he decided to return to his family in Ningdu. He did not make it. On his way back, he was arrested, tried, and executed.

Mr. Lai, one of the dedicated Christian men and a church member, was known as a respectable teacher. He was fifty years old and a close friend of the church's moderator, Mr. Li. His wife attended church, but she laughed when confronted with the claims of Christ. Her husband and her friends often urged her to put her trust in Christ. She only laughed.

Someone wanted to harm Mr. Lai and reported to the authorities that he concealed weapons in his home. This was forbidden and punishable by death. However, no weapons were discovered and Mr. Lai was exonerated.

A few weeks later Mrs. Lai appeared at the mission station weeping, "They have executed my husband! What shall I say? He now is in heaven. If they would have executed me, I would not be in heaven. I now want to hand over my life to Jesus!"

In order to do him in, his adversary had secretly deposited ammunition in a hidden spot during the first house search. With this he provoked a second search. Mr. Lai was unable to prove his innocence. He was rapidly convicted, sentenced to death, and executed.

His wife accepted Christ and became an ardent follower of Jesus.

Besides many hardships the missionaries faced, they bonded deeply with the locals and especially with the Christians. Ernst Wyss wrote about the final hours in Ningdu:

> Our helper in the home wept—a woman, who had given birth to sixteen children and none of them survived. "Why do you weep," one of the policemen scolded, "be glad that you don't have to leave with the foreigners." Nevertheless, tears ran down the cheeks of our friends and us, as our vehicle started to move away. Seldom in our lives have we felt as one and had such a close relationship with our brothers and sisters of faith in Ningdu. To us it was like home was torn from us.

Mao was the great liberator of China. In his early years he was a brutal and ruthless kingpin. He led his troops with an iron fist. He put into practice what he had learned from the German revolutionaries Karl Marx and Friedrich Engels:

> The revolutionary is a dedicated man. He has neither personal interests, nor affairs, nor feelings, nor attachments, nor property, nor even a name. Every part of him is absorbed by one sole interest, one sole thought, and one sole passion: the revolution.... Strict with himself, he must be the same with others. All feelings of affection, all the softening feelings of kinship, friendship, love and gratitude must be stifled in him by a unique and old passion for the revolutionary cause … this goal of pursuing coldly and without respite; he must himself be ready to perish and to destroy with his own hands all that which obstructs the achievement of this goal.

The Chinese Communists in the early days of revolution were ardent and devoted followers of the party line. Sydney Rittenberg in his book *The Man Who Stayed Behind* quoted one of the initial revolutionaries Qian Xing, later Mao's wife, saying, "When we came here [Yanan, the original base of Mao Zedong in northern China] we gave everything we had to the Revolution. We gave ourselves to the Revolution. We had to remold ourselves, to get rid of our subjectivism, selfishness, vulgar interest, anything and everything that interfered with our devotion to the cause. We put aside our personal problems and ambition, and we just became a part of the Revolution." Her fascination with Communism was pure, ascetic, almost that of the early Christians to their religion.

What dedication to achieve their goals! During the years in the late '20s and early '30s of the twentieth century, while ruling in large parts of southern Jiangxi, Mao had also confiscated the mission house in Ningdu and lived in it for several months. It was then when he used the chapel to perform heinous executions.

Now, while in Ningdu, I had a momentous experience which taught me a great lesson and later helped me in my ministry. My brother and I roomed together. One night I woke up to the noise of a horde of people running around the wrap-around veranda. *What's this,* I thought, *why would people visit our home at night?* During breakfast the following morning my parents explained what had happened. "Those were not real people, but evil spirits," they explained. "Ever since Mao and his cohorts lived here, this house has been haunted."

Not much is known in western countries about such issues. In fact, most people, even Christians, have no knowledge about the "other world" existence. It is not being experienced, unless you dabble in the occult, and therefore not believed by most. In countries like China, where some of the religious teaching is based on the occult, such macabre events are the norm. People are confronted with this all the time. The Bible, however, is full of its teachings.

However, on another occasion, this time in Germany, I faced the demonic power. I had hired a young man to serve as an evangelist in our ministry of *Jugend für Christus in Deutschland.* He was an ex-convict and had served a couple of terms in prison, once even in a penitentiary. After his second release he miraculously found the Lord through the Salvation Army. He was very intelligent, although not well-educated, and the Lord was able to use this broken vessel in an unusual and powerful way. He became a much sought-after youth evangelist, and I hired him. But at times his old nature perked up again.

"You need to come right away," I was admonished by our business manager. "Wolfgang Dyck is causing a lot of trouble within the team."

Inge and I hopped into the car and drove some one hundred fifty miles north to Hofgeismar, a lovely town near Kassel. That night after the evening service, we confronted him in the large, now-empty tent which was used for the crusade. We were alone with him and his team members. He vigorously defended his behavior, and the longer we pointed out his failures, the more he argued against us. It was getting out of hand and there was no way he could any longer justify the outbursts he unleashed against his team members. By then he was ranting at the top of his voice.

I stood there stunned and felt like the personified devil had entered our midst. It was like demons were encircling us.

"Stop," I said and started to pray aloud against those evil forces.

Slowly things calmed down and eventually a peaceful stillness pervaded the periphery of the tent. Wolfgang surrendered and asked us to pray for him. Together we laid hands on him, rejoicing that the Lord had given another victory.

Such phenomena were far more commonplace across a heathen-pervaded country like China. The city of Ningdu had been a hotbed of Communist activity.

On May 25, 1947, three days after my brother's birthday, the three of us—Friedel, Gisela, and I—were baptized with three Chinese believers in a simple ceremony by our father. With that we publicly declared that we were followers of Jesus and wanted to live for Him.

Shanghai—the city I love

In the spring of 1947, I along with my sister returned to Shanghai. My brother stayed on, teaching English in a Chinese middle school. Back in Shanghai, we attended the makeshift German high school. The next two were formative years for me. I was very active in our youth group, Ambassadors for Christ. An American missionary lady, Anna Swarr, was in charge. Some Chinese kids joined our group, but the rest were mostly German, American, Canadian, and British missionary kids. Bob Pierce preached at our church. Later he founded World Vision and Samaritan's Purse, the two evangelical organizations now with the largest budgets of all such ministries in the world.

Bob Pierce has a special place in my heart. As a teenager, I committed my life to Christ's service—full time—at one of his meetings in Shanghai. He had challenged us to go all out for Christ—one hundred percent. This Youth for Christ evangelist had just returned from Korea and poured out his heart as only he could do. His heart's cry came through loud and clear: "Let my heart be broken with the things that break the heart of God," he declared.

Just days before, he had walked along dusty rural roads as a fiercely hot sun beat down upon him. He had shared Christ with thousands of Koreans, and many had come to know Christ. Korea had just begun to recover from years of Japanese subjugation. Not many Christians lived there at that time. However, the harvest was great.

"Who among you is willing to go to win the lost?" Bob challenged us in one of the Shanghai YFC rallies. "If you will not go, who will go in your place? A lost world is waiting to hear the redeeming message of Christ. The Lord wants you."

29

I was so moved that I left my seat at the Free Christian Church in Shanghai and walked to the altar. I was willing to go. The time had come for me to dedicate my life to His service. In the anteroom, I knelt in prayer beside Dick Hillis, a China Inland missionary, who later founded Overseas Crusades, who had come to counsel with me. I handed over my life to God. I shall never forget that sacred moment.

Dawson Trotman, founder of The Navigators, visited Shanghai and showed me how to mark my Bible with his developed unique "ladder." With it, one can find the books of the Bible much quicker. He introduced his topical memory system. I started to learn verses of the Bible. This eventually led me to memorize entire books—Gospel of John, Philippians, James—and hundreds of verses, also hymns. The Bible became real to me.

During this period of 1947-48 amazing evangelistic meetings took place all across China initiated by Youth for Christ leaders. It was the period when Mao Zedong was conquering northern provinces one by one. Many Christians were concerned about his anti-God stance. Missionaries encouraged and even urged the Chinese to accept the Lord before he would shut down every religious activity, which he actually did during the Cultural Revolution later in his regime. *We must reach China for Christ before it is too late,* they said. Let me quote from the book *Developing a Heart for Mission* written by Roy Robertson:

> The meetings where David [Morken] ministered in South China, enroute from Canton (Guangzhou) to Shanghai, met with a response far beyond what anyone has ever experienced or anticipated. The YFC team recorded more than 10,000 professions of faith in South China.

After these fruitful meetings in South China, the team took a plane from Amoy (Xiamen) to Shanghai for the opening of the Shanghai Mission. Not only did nearly all Christian groups cooperate, but the mayor of Shanghai, K. C. Wu, with his dedicated Christian wife, added their support.

But this was not all. The YFC evangelistic team continued for another four months of "great harvest and blessing." They preached in Suzhou, Hangzhou, Nanjing, Xian, Hsien Leng, Tianjin, Tsingtao, Tsimi, and Chongqing. In Xian alone, 25,000—some say over 30,000—attended each night.

In those dramatic days of 1947, just prior to the Communist takeover, Chinese people of all classes responded in unprecedented number to the claims of Christ. Numerically nothing like this had ever happened in Asia, even in the great revivals of Evangelist John Sung. YFC recorded about 30,000 decisions for Christ in a one-year period, as multitudes flocked together to hear the Gospel.

During the latter parts of the '30s and the earlier parts of the '40s of the twentieth century, Hubert Mitchell and David Morken had been missionaries in India and Indonesia respectively before they were forced out because of the Second World War. Back in the United States they were prominent in establishing YFC centers in southern California. But the burden to reach the masses in Asia never abandoned them. After the war, they left the comforts of their homes and started YFC rallies in India, Indonesia, China, and Japan. The most impressive evangelistic crusades happened in China just before the Communists moved from northern parts of China to the south.

I first met them as they spoke to our little Ambassadors for Christ group in Shanghai. Dick Hillis was another one, who, as a CIM missionary, linked up with the other two in arranging and preparing for evangelistic crusades across China. In the evenings I would go to the headquarters compound of the China Inland Mission, where they stayed, and joined the missionaries playing volleyball. There I met David Morken. "Would you mind kicking a football with me?" he asked. I had kicked a soccer ball around but never seen the quaint ball called football. I learned to throw and kick it, and many an afternoon I spent some time kicking the ball with him. This was his way of exercise.

These were spiritual men! Once I came a little early, went up to his room to fetch him, and knocked at his door. When I opened the door I found him kneeling at his bedside praying. I was awestruck to see this. This, more than anything else, helped me to follow his example for the rest of my life. Some of the most moving and uplifting experiences in life I spent on my knees.

CHAPTER 3

EUROPE—ANOTHER WORLD TO GET USED TO

THOUSANDS OF FOREIGNERS were forced to leave China. Passage on ships was hard to come by. Finally, my brother Friedel, fellow student Hans Werner Wehmeyer, and I found room on the *SS Rena,* a 2,000-ton ship that had previously been used as a ferry across the English Channel. To me it looked more like a boat. I was told that boats are put on ships, but this one actually transported people! And they were many! Every crook and cranny was used to accommodate them. People were willing to take what they could get, no questions asked.

We shared a large section in the very front of the ship with some fifteen Chinese Catholic theological seminary students traveling to Rome. This was not a stateroom or cabin. It was a large hole! Our bunks were rudimentary and installed to make room for as many passengers as possible. The dining room was pathetic. Everything on the ship was pitiful! And we had to live six weeks on that vessel! But we were glad to get out of the country.

We left on March 4, 1949, and arrived in Marseille six weeks later on April 15. It was a monotonous and dreary time onboard ship. Six long weeks! There was absolutely nothing to do on the ship as it tuckered along the ocean. The English Admiralty used to say, "Join the navy and see the world." We experienced what their sailors had already learned, that the reality is different. The sailors added the slogan, "What did we see? We saw the sea." No games, no swimming pool, no library, no recreational activities—nothing but the sea! And nothing to do!

I finally went to the purser for a job. He assigned me to the kitchen to wash dishes. After one week, the cook asked me whether I had received my pay. "You have to demand it on a weekly basis, otherwise you will never see it," he cautioned. The purser was surprised when I asked but then reluctantly paid up. Later I found out that this was a gangster ship full of crooks. They never landed in the intended harbors. They never paid the harbor fees. They never wanted to play by maritime rules. Just before reaching the Suez Canal, however, a plane buzzed us a number of times. We were caught and were refused to pass through. Negotiations took a couple of days until things were settled. Authorities finally let them go after the captain promised to pay up. He had to return to the Suez to do so.

The final days through the Mediterranean were rough. Storms hit us, and we hardly made it from our quarters in the front to the dining room in midship. We had to climb up some outer stairways to the deck, and run across it before reaching the dining area. We took many showers that way as the sea washed over us!

From Marseille we took the train to Basel, Switzerland. What impressed me now traveling through Europe were two things: Cleanliness and smallness—everything seemed to be so tiny compared to China. Europe is a small continent compared to the vastness of Asia. The river Rhone looked like a rivulet. The spaces between towns were so short. However, everything looked organized and clean. People seemed to take care of their properties. Not so much in France, but Switzerland was gorgeous. In France the buildings looked run down, whereas in Switzerland they were well kept. I soon found out that the French considered gourmet food as their priority and the Swiss put their money into buildings. We were housed in St. Chrischona, the theological seminary on a beautiful hill close to Basel, where my father had received his theological training.

Germany with all the bombed-out cities could not cope with the millions of refugees that fled the Red Army. We had to wait two months before we received the entry permit to Germany. While living in St. Chrischona, we worked in the fields as all students did. Every student had to work a number of hours per week for his room and board. The first day we showed up with white shirts and ties. We had never worked manually and did not know better. We became the laughingstock on that hill.

We had the privilege to attend a conference in Winterthur put on by the Alliance China Mission. We had to catch a train in Basel for the two-hour trip. As usual, we were late. We ran down the mountain, then we heard a command given by a Swiss border control officer, "*Stop, bei Fluchtversuch wird geschossen!*" (If you try to flee, I will shoot). He took us to the border control station where we had to verify that we were Germans from China living at the theological seminary. One of us had to go back up and get the required papers. The embarrassed border control helped us find the schedule for the next train to Winterthur.

After months of waiting, we finally got the permission to enter our homeland. Crossing the border into Germany was a devastating experience. City after city still lay in ruins. I became depressed and wondered whether I had made the right choice to move back to my home country, Germany. *Was not China my real home country? Was it not my real home? Should I not have stayed there?* While in China, I had played with the idea to go to college in the United States. But that did not work out.

Staying in Reiherbach with my uncle Gottlieb, however, brought new hope. He had a farm in a charming valley—so tranquil and peaceful. This was the location where my mother grew up. We helped in the fields. The summer was harvest time. When not in the fields, I shepherded cows. What a boring, yet necessary job. I herded them from pasture to pasture. To add some thrill to this enterprise, I took along my Hermes typewriter to write letters. Once I fell asleep and when I awoke, all the cows had disappeared. I finally tracked them down as they were making their way through a forest to greener pastures beyond. What a job to get them under control and herd them back to the stable.

My uncle gave us some pocket money. It was not much, but we had free meals and shelter while earnestly waiting for our parents to relieve us. They were still stuck in China. They had to prove to the authorities that they had not done any harm to the Chinese before they could leave the country. It took months for them to get the exit permit. So we had to wait.

Kassel—where things changed

One day my other uncle, Friedrich Pfeifferling, with his wife, Emmi, visited the Reiherbach. He had a thriving blueprinting business in Kassel. After visiting their relatives, aunt Emmi wanted to say good-bye and found us on our knees in the bedroom praying the morning they were leaving to return home. This was our habit before starting our day. She thought we were under distress and promptly offered me a job in their business. They had no children and wanted me to eventually take over their company.

But what about my commitment to serve the Lord! Hadn't I dedicated my life for His service in a YFC rally in Shanghai? I reasoned, as many young men would probably have done, that in business I could make much money and then support others who could take my place in the ministry. *Instead of one on the field, there could be ten,* I surmised. Wouldn't that make sense? *Lord, you called me, but with this arrangement I can enlarge the troupe of your servants,* I rationalized. So I moved to Kassel in the fall of 1949.

Uncle Friedrich's business operation had been bombed out during the fierce bombing raid by the Allied forces in 1943. Eighty percent of the beautiful city of Kassel had been leveled. On that particular night, my aunt sat with others in the basement as bombs rained down, fearing for her life. After the bombers had left, she crawled out of the hole then enveloped with blazing, fiery rubble. The entire neighborhood was aflame. Covered with a wet blanket she dodged falling debris and made it to safety.

At that time, my uncle was a soldier in occupied France and later was detained as a prisoner of war in one of the US infamous prisoner-of-war camps, where up to 10,000 German soldiers were kept on open fields. No housing, not even tents. Prisoners dug holes in the ground to shelter from rain and frost. Food was trucked in occasionally, dumped, and then as the starving men rushed to retrieve it, the food was doused with gasoline and set on fire. The guards gunned down women from nearby villages as they tried to throw bread across the fences. Prisoners died like flies, hundreds of them. My uncle could never forget those deeds and voiced his disdain this way, "The Americans came with Bibles under their arms and then treated us worse than animals."

I remember him uttering his contempt—even hatred—when I stated that Hitler was responsible for the flattened city as I was clearing rubble from a bombed-out building he had bought for DM 50,000 (ca. US$ 12,000 at that time). He said, "It were the Americans who bombed and destroyed our homes and businesses and murdered hundreds of thousands of innocent civilians—in Dresden alone 30,000 plus, and that in one night! Get it? Your aunt hunkered down in our basement when they firebombed our home and miraculously was spared as she fled out of the devastating inferno. Don't tell me that Hitler did this. It was the Americans and British!" He was livid.

Of course, any war brings out the immoral and dishonorable. The atrocities implemented by Hitler were far worse—gigantic, cruel, and inexcusable and different from those committed by the Allies. Never before had anyone gassed several million Jews. The first were done from the top down, those by the Allies were done from the bottom up. The Nazi massacres were ordered by leaders of the government, those done by the Allies were done by individuals without the approval of its government. But barbarism took place on both sides.

In his book *Patton's Last Battle,* Charles Whiting wrote, "Revenge had to be taken. In his diary Patton noted that five hundred SS prisoners were shot in cold blood…" The Russians entered and moved across eastern Germany raping up to 2 million women between the ages of teens to seventy-year-olds. This was not the general behavior of Americans, but even they gave way to such brutalities. Whiting wrote, "But looting was not the only problem in Third [Army] and other armies now sweeping across Germany. The more serious crimes—desertion, murder, rape, assault with intent to commit rape—sharply increased now. The upswing in rape was particularly marked." He continues, "Naturally there were not the virtually organized mass rapes indulged in by the Red Army as it swept through Germany's eastern provinces; or the terrifying orgy of arson, pillage, and rape carried out by France's colored colonial soldiers in the Black Forest area...Or the village of Rohrbach, for instance, where every female 'between twelve and eighty was raped.'"

Some tried to excuse those raping soldiers by stating that they committed those crimes only as revenge. But the facts are that soldiers away from their homes became sex maniacs, and on the battlefield they felt liberated from traditional or conventional moral standards. So they raped blatantly and shamelessly—not out of revenge, but to gratify their sexual passions.

Later, when I lived in the United States, the pastor of our church related the confession of a former US soldier that, while serving in the occupation forces in Germany, he had fallen in love with a German girl. She was engaged to be married to a local, so he made up his mind to get rid of him. He lured her fiancé into his Jeep, drove him to a nearby forest, and put a bullet into his head.

This is what I call bottom-up atrocities. Individuals in any nation, whether citizens or soldiers, are capable of committing horrendous crimes!

It took some time for my uncle to forget and forgive what others had done to him and his wife. He was aware of the atrocities Hitler had perpetrated across Europe and agreed it was far worse than what he had experienced. It was some of the most atrocious crime ever committed in the world's history.

Once a week I would go swimming at the newly built indoor swimming pool. A distant uncle ran a small restaurant just around the corner. I often would visit him for a drink. One evening two American GIs in uniform entered for a meal. The minute he saw them, my uncle started to shake. "What's wrong," I asked. "I was a prisoner of war in an American camp. I was interrogated and in the process I was beaten so badly that one of my legs had to be amputated. An American in uniform scares me. It is difficult for me to forget," he replied.

Nevertheless, my uncle and aunt were kind people. They were non-believers, yet compassionate folks. With no children of their own, they took me in and offered me an enticing future. Blueprints were in high demand, as the city was being rebuilt. Factories and business establishments shot out of the ground no matter where you looked. The *Wirtschaftswunder* (economic miracle) was in full swing. With the help of the US Marshall Plan, amazing "miracles" did take place. My uncle profited in a big way, and I was one of the beneficiaries. Life was good and the future was bright.

Yet, I had a problem—a big problem. In my subconscious mind, I battled with the disobedience to my Lord. This had affected my health. My doctor diagnosed my malady correctly—stomach ulcers. He said, "Something is wrong in your life, and I cannot help unless you correct what went wrong." This felt like a four-by-five hitting me. I was stunned, but I knew he was right. And I knew what it was.

I went home, fell on my knees, and asked God to forgive me. Then and there, I recommitted my life to God anew. I shared this with my parents in a letter.

During this time, Bob Hopkins visited me. Dawson Trotman, founder of The Navigators, had sent him to represent his mission organization in Germany. He lived in Frankfurt. As a teenager in Shanghai, I had been dramatically challenged by the biblical principles of this movement. I had learned how to study the Bible and the importance of Bible memorization. Discipline is one of the key virtues for a Christian. Making Christ known through witnessing should be on every Christian's agenda. Bob came for a few days to encourage me in my daily walk with Christ. On the day of his departure, I handed him some tithe money, which I had saved. "I don't believe this," he exclaimed. "I have no money left and did not know how to return to Frankfurt. I was going to hitchhike, but this money enables me to buy the return train ticket. I prayed for a miracle, and now this!" This fortified my conviction to continue with my tithing.

I had learned to tithe as a young boy in Shanghai. Leni Wink, the missionary lady who helped raise us, had taught us the biblical principle of tithing. I took it to heart, tithed the pocket money I received, and became the "richest" kid in the children's home. It was a principle I never lost in all of my life. I had started giving away ten percent. Later I upped it to twenty percent. When Inge and I got married, we decided to give away twenty-five percent of our income to the Lord's work. On this particular occasion, it was my great thrill to see how God had answered the prayers of Bob Hopkins in such a dramatic way. This was one of the many lessons I learned on my Christian sojourn: Obey the commands as spelled out in the Bible! Someone once said: "Shovel your tithes to the Lord and He will shovel right back. The only difference: His shovel is so much bigger than yours."

In Kassel I was burdened for the many around me who had no idea what it meant to be a follower of Jesus. For instance, my uncle and aunt were upright and honorable people. They had been baptized and as teenagers confirmed into the Lutheran church; practically all Germans had. However, they were far removed from any spiritual experience and a personal relationship with Christ. Often I explained the gospel to them. They listened kindly and let me have my beliefs.

My uncle sent me for additional training to Wiesbaden. I spent a couple of weeks learning the trade at the headquarters of a large paper company. Wiesbaden was close to American army bases. Soldiers meandered through the streets. I wondered whether some of them might attend Youth for Christ rallies, which had sprung up around the world where GIs had been sent. I was a shy person but mustered enough courage to ask the next one I saw.

"Do you know whether YFC rallies are being held in Wiesbaden?" I asked. He shrugged his shoulders and as he turned away, he spotted three others on the other side of the street. "Ask them," he said, "they might know." I walked across and sure enough, one of them said, "Yes, I regularly attend them. In fact, next Saturday the national director of *Jugend für Christus in Deutschland* (JfC or YFC) will be the featured speaker." This was the beginning of a close relationship with this movement in Germany.

My passion for lost people and God's call

How about asking JfC to hold an evangelistic crusade in Kassel, I pondered. Soon after, I wrote a letter to Hans Rudolf Wever, the German director. I got a prompt reply stating that one of their coworkers would come to talk things over with me. They dispatched Anton Schulte, a twenty-four-year old fellow who later became the founder of *Neues Leben,* an evangelistic organization in Germany. (He died on December 25, 2010, as an eighty-five-year old). We did not have an extra room for him to sleep in, so he slept on the couch in the living/dining room. We walked the streets making plans how best to publicize and promote the coming event.

Having just migrated to Germany from China, I did not know the religious landscape of the city. I had attended a Lutheran church but was a stranger in town. So I ventured out in faith, contacting churches of different denominations, their pastors and Christian leaders. It was a hard sell. No one knew me. *What in the world is this upstart doing? Who in the world does he think he is,* they must have thought.

Then I heard of a brand new auditorium that had just been constructed by a Christian organization, called *Entschiedenes Christentum* (Christian Endeavors). It lay in the middle of mountains of rubble caused by the Allied air attack in October of 1943. Eighty percent of the city was pulverized into rubble. This newly constructed building was a symbol and a foretaste of what Germany might look like in the years ahead. It was modern. It looked appealing. With the help of JfC I rented it.

The time of the crusade approached but I did not know where to house the members of the Canadian team—the evangelist Bill Sifft with his interpreter Anton Schulte, trumpeter Jack Will, and the organist of the famed People's Church in Toronto, Frank Trenchard. I was told of an air raid shelter, a massive bunker, which was used by the city for refugees and homeless people. The team arrived in a VW bug and were ushered into this, their "home." Bill was shaving just before the first evening meeting and without him knowing, I heard him share his feeling with one of his team members: "Well, this is some place; however, considering what our Lord had to go through when He came from His glory to this miserable world, this is not too shabby." After the meeting we found a few Christians who volunteered to host them. My, I never saw a happier crew.

Not too many showed up the first night. The head of Christian Endeavors, Rev. Schmiedinghoff, watched the proceedings from the balcony. After the third night he approached me. "The preaching is biblical and solid, so we decided to throw our weight behind you." From then on the crusade took off. The attendance grew rapidly each night, and we ended with a packed and overflowing hall. I, along with many, had so sit in the staircase, marveling as multitudes of young and old decided to follow Christ. Many years later Rev. Schmiedinghoff told me, "We have had many crusades following that one in Kassel, but the JFC crusade was the best, resulting in spiritual fruit that will last for eternity." God had used that Canadian YFC team in an amazing way. Germany was hungry for truth after having been lied to for twelve years under Nazi domination. This whetted my appetite for evangelism. But I was stuck working for my uncle.

I became restless. In my prayers I sensed the Holy Spirit prompting me to leave my uncle's business. The argument that by becoming a well-to-do Christian, I would be able to support ten missionaries overseas, which would be so much more advantageous compared to having only me for that task, did not hold. No, this argument definitely did not hold. God had something else in mind for me to do. As I struggled, I asked my parents for help:

Kassel, Annastrasse 5
17. June 1951

My dear parents!

You will be surprised to receive such a long report from me. But it is a very nice report, and you will be as happy to read it as I am now as I write it. I would like to tell you off-hand: I have heard the Lord's call into full-time ministry and to serve Him with my whole life!

Now you are probably shocked. But let me tell you in detail how everything happened in such a wonderful way. I also would like to tell you that I have not said anything yet to uncle or aunt, because I first want to hear your opinion in this matter. (Please read this letter with prayerful hearts, because here I am with so many ideas going through my head, what and where I should start, and yet I only want to do the Lord's will and follow Him wherever He leads me). It all happened like this:

You can hardly imagine how very happy I am on one side, and yet how sad on the other, since I have to say good-bye to my dear ones here. But the Lord's command is for us (for me) a holy duty to do that which He commands us (me).

As you know I took it as God's will to regard this work here as my life's work, and I have acted and worked as such, although I have had a hard time adjusting to life here, especially since uncle and aunt are non-believers. But with God's help I was able to do it and was quite happy here lately. Sometimes aunt Emmi opined that maybe later on I might still be called into God's work, but I always answered: "I don't know that, but I believe God led me here and that this is my life's work."

But now it is truly happening that I am to renounce the world to serve Him directly... and I love to do it!

Maybe the time in England and especially the Swanwick conference [CIM conference] to which I had been invited by its president, Bishop Frank Houghton] contributed to my decision, or prepared my heart for this without me noticing it.

Anyway, one night late, as I was preparing for bed, unexpect- edly the director of the "Brethren Volunteer Service" in Kassel and the lady of the "Brethren Church" visited me. She is the lady I talked to once for two to three hours about "faith in God" and "assurance of salvation" (mother, I told you about this, when you were here for a visit). They told me after a long introduction that I was one of six young people, both young men and girls, they would like to send to America as volunteers for free.

I would get two months of training and would then work with poor families. They had chosen me because I was the only one that lived his Christian life not only by habit, but took it seriously on a daily basis. I was the only one of the six. The director told me that most of these don't have this deep Christian commitment, even the people in their circles in America, and so they wanted to send this young German to America to "shake up" some young people to real, dedicated faith in the Lord Jesus Christ.

Naturally I told them that I could not decide alone, but had to ask first uncle and aunt, and also you of course, my dear parents, to find out, if this was God's will for me. They understood this, but said that they had to know by next noon (in sixteen hours, no less), because the program is running under the exchange program of HICOG, and the deadline would be noon the following day. I promised I would do that and wanted to ask uncle and aunt first, and if they agreed to it, they could put me on the list, however, with the stipulation to take me off the list, if they did not agree with it. I told them also that I would take either a yes or no as God's will. They were very happy about this and said, then I would never hold my uncle responsible even after four or five years, should he not concur, but take it as God's will. I asked them to pray for me that I would make the right decision.

How long I stayed on my knees that night you can probably imagine. The next morning I talked to aunt Emmi about it, and she had nothing against it, but uncle Friedrich had a different opinion. When I asked him around noon about his decision, he said the following: "Twenty-five years I worked for my business to bring it to this level, and in those twenty-five years I only had the luxury of going to Edersee twice for a fortnight. Other than that, I never took a long trip, although I would have liked to. And now you are here and have taken over most of my work, and if I allow you to go, I will have to do all the work alone again, and that is too much asked. Werner, I leave it up to you as I told you many times: you can tell us if you want to leave us, and you are not bound here, and I would not hold it against you if you want to go, but then don't come back anymore! And I would like to explain it like this: Aunt Emmi told me this is something religious, and if I let you go for one year into this work, you will want to do something like that again in two or three years, and that I cannot tolerate, and will not tolerate. If you want to stay with us, you have to put yourself totally into the business...it's either this or the other... Nobody can serve two masters."

Quickly I told him, "Okay, then I will stay." I called the Brethren and told them they would have to do without me. So the America trip is cancelled.

But that was not what made me listen to God's voice. That was only the preliminary (I mean regarding America). But a sentence of uncle Friedrich kept coming back to me, because it came really from God: Nobody can serve two masters. And that came from the mouth of an unbeliever! That really struck me! Nobody can serve two masters—it's either business or God. Had a pastor or you said this to me, I would have answered, I can serve God by being in business. But an unbeliever had to say something like that to wake me up! And when I stood at the machine my eyes filled with tears and I fought a battle—a wonderful battle really, because it ended with a victory for God. Nobody can serve two masters…and I had the breakthrough. I will serve God and God alone for the rest of my life from now on.

But I did not say anything yet to uncle or aunt, because I wanted to write to you first. Please write back and tell me what you think and what I should do now. Please don't write to uncle or aunt yet, because I want to tell them myself, after I have heard from you.

I do not know yet for what God is calling me: missionary or preacher or whatever, but in this He will guide me too.

When I was in England a Swiss missionary asked me if I wanted to be a missionary, and I answered: I have not heard the call of God yet. And she said again: "Have you not heard it yet, or don't you want to hear it?" and I answered: "I would like to hear it very much." And now I have it. Hallelujah!

Now the question: What shall I do? Bible school? Which one? Chrischona, Beatenberg, or a school here in Germany? To be honest, I would like to go to Beatenberg (Switzerland), but I don't know the requirements. Please write what you think about that… and please pray much about this.

I waited a few days before I wrote to you, to see things clearer, but the longer I wait, the stronger the voice gets in me: your life is all for God, and only for Him.

And so I write to you with the hope that you will see God's will in this also.

Another thing I want to tell you, something wonderful, which came back to me. Three years ago exactly on June 12, 1948, I asked Dick Hillis after a sermon by Bob Pierce to go with me into the vestry and pray with me, which he did. On my knees I said: "I want nothing for myself, I want God to have it all." When Dick asked me if I felt God calling me, I answered: "He is calling me into His work, possibly as a missionary." And then this all faded away, life took its turn, and for three years God let me go through His school, until I was ready to really completely give myself to Him. And exactly three years later on June 12, 1951, he gave me the "go ahead." And here I go!

Well, my dear parents, please write to me soon. I am so very happy!

Awaiting your soon reply, lovingly, your Werner.

CHAPTER 4

SPIRITUAL AWAKENING IN CALIFORNIA

S O THAT FALL I left my uncle and aunt to sign up with
the Brethren Volunteer Service, a department of the Church
of the Brethren, one of the three major peace churches (the
others are Mennonites and Quakers). I moved in with a group
of American volunteers and started to deliver used clothes to
refugees and homeless people. It was quite interesting to engage
with those volunteers in conversation about their spiritual affairs.
I remember only one who had made a definite commitment
to follow Christ. The others were kind and easy to work with;
however, they had no clue how to address the spiritual needs of
the people they were trying to help. Food and clothes, yes, but
spiritual matters, no.

By the end of the year, a special amnesty program of the US
Congress would be coming to an end. Refugees, or displaced
persons (as they were labeled) from Eastern Europe would no
longer be allowed to immigrate to the United States under
that policy. I was sent to München (Munich) to accelerate the

procedures to assist as many as possible to get their US visas. Thousands were being processed and only a few more weeks were available. For the first time I experienced firsthand, how desperate people were for a new home. All of them wanted a new start in life. America to them was the golden opportunity. But there were too many of them! There was no way to accommodate everyone. In desperation, and besides my regular routine, I picked one young man in his early twenties. I moved him quickly through the various stations. His eyes beamed with joy as he saw what I was doing. When he held the documents, including the visa in hand, he was thrilled and I rejoiced with him. I often reminisced about him later and wondered how he had fared in his new home country.

In February of 1952 I took the train from Kassel to Bremerhaven and with great anticipation boarded the *SS America*. Many of those we helped in Munich were on board as well, and along with them I gazed with admiration as we passed the Statue of Liberty a week later. To me it was a sightseeing event. To the others the statue meant liberty.

As I walked down the gangplank, I pondered if anyone was there to welcome me. "How much is it to pick up my trunk," I asked one of the porters. "A buck a piece," he answered. I was shocked, because I had only a couple of bucks in my pocket. One US dollar was a fortune for me at that time! I grabbed my piece and walked off.

Hundreds of people were milling around. "Are you Werner," a stranger asked. He was my uncle, my father's brother. He just bumped into me. My father must have written him about my arrival, and off we went to his home in New Jersey. The first thing he did was buy me a bottle of Old Spice aftershave.

"People here want to smell good," he explained. After the war most Europeans had never seen such items, including deodorant sticks. I remember Billy Graham later mentioning that when he first traveled through England in the late '40s, the people were too poor to buy such perfumed stuff. Even today, with many immigrants from Eastern Europe now living in Germany, you wonder why they do not use such pleasant inventions.

For me it was a good start in the US. My uncle and my cousin Norma drove me around and showed me many sights. He introduced me to his fellow workers in his factory, and his daughters, Ilsa and Norma, along with his wife hosted me royally. He had immigrated to the United States in the early '20s when things looked bleak in Germany. The First World War had devastated his home country. Tens of thousands of Germans were looking for a better life in America, just as the one I had helped in Munich.

New Windsor in Maryland was my final destination. This was the little town where the headquarters and training school was located. I joined twenty-two other young volunteers coming from several churches of that denomination and from different states, even as far as California. Seventeen boys and five girls. Two of the fellows were black, and one of them was my roommate. This was the first time I had encountered black people. Previously I had known only Chinese and Caucasians.

We were all young; even the director was in his twenties. We had a lot of fun and played pranks on each other. Sometimes those went too far and I did things that were foolish.

One morning I found my door bolted solidly. After repeated knocking and hearing just laughter on the other side, I got angry. With my body weight behind me, I knocked down the door, just as I had seen policemen do it on TV. It came off its hinges and lay fragmented before me. Later I was ashamed and apologized

In the mornings we had classes about denominational beliefs, doctrines, and history. The Church of the Brethren denomination was founded in Schwarzenau, Germany. In the afternoons we sorted clothing, which was shipped to Europe, mainly to Germany. I was hungry for good evangelical fellowship, which I did not readily find. I contacted the Navigators in nearby Washington and asked their representative to minister to our group. On the first day of our schooling the teacher questioned the validity of the Scriptures. I was stunned. Asking for permission to say something, I ventured to give my testimony. I told them how I became a believer and ended with, "I believe the Bible to be the Word of God. I believe it from cover to cover."

After the session one of the volunteers, Ken Francis, approached me. "Thanks for speaking up. I believe the same way you do." Immediately I set out to recruit those who would join us for an early prayer meeting. Five young men signed up, and from then on we met every morning at 6:15 a.m. for prayer. We were burdened for those who had not yet become followers of Jesus Christ. I vividly remember meeting with one of the five girls in our unit who did not have the assurance of salvation. She hailed from Key West, Florida. I explained the gospel as best as I could. Then we knelt down and I prayed for her. Following the prayer I saw tears running down her cheeks as she left the room. She had not prayed audibly and I did not know whether she had repeated my prayer silently in her heart. But God had touched her soul.

Toward the end of our two-month training, the husband and wife, Mr. and Mrs. Rodney Davis, who directed the program, arranged a weekend retreat for all of us. Each one of us was put into the middle of a circle of the volunteers. We were challenged to speak up about anything that came to our mind about the person in the center—good or bad. This kind of therapy should help us later in the ministry not to take ourselves too seriously. Even the director and his wife were scrutinized. The minute Mrs. Davis settled in the center, she began to cry. All of us were stunned, because none of the others had shown that kind of emotion. "Ever since the few of you met for prayer early in the mornings," she blurted out, "I felt insecure. I do not know what caused this, but I felt something is missing in my life."

This was some confession. I was saddened and thrilled at the same time; saddened, knowing that she still had not made peace with God, and thrilled that our sincere witness had brought her to the realization that there is more to life.

During the time at New Windsor, we made field trips to the US Congress in Washington, DC, attended a Youth for Christ rally in Baltimore, and visited the Navigators chapter in Washington, DC, but I longed to be active in His service.

The New Windsor experience was good for me. I was confronted with liberal theology, which helped me crystalize my convictions about biblical truths. In fact, it was the first time I had encountered the difference between conservative and liberal Christians. However, I did learn the importance and positive side of social involvement as represented by members of the so-called Peace Churches (Mennonites, Friends or Quakers, and Church of the Brethren). Many virtuous and honorable ideas are put forth by those well-meaning people. Moreover, Bob Pierce, for example, the founder of the humanitarian organization World Vision, exemplified an even better way that social enterprises can be linked with biblical evangelism.

But I was glad to leave New Windsor behind me. I was assigned to Van Nuys in California. On Friday, May 2, I left for Washington to meet with the Navigators representative Don Rosenberger, spoke in one of their meetings, and from there on to North Carolina to speak on radio at Billy Graham's radio station, not knowing at the time that it was his station. I still do not know why I had been invited to speak that Saturday night. And then again on Sunday! Furthermore, one of the New Windsor volunteers had invited me to preach at a couple of churches in that area, and he probably had arranged that event.

I had to meet Rodney Davis in Elgin, Illinois, who had arranged to deliver a new car all the way across the country to California. To save the $300 cost of shipping cars, the car companies offered $35 gas money to travelers who were willing to drive them free of charge to the West Coast. This was a win-win situation for both parties. On the way to Elgin I stopped in Wheaton to see Lois, my Shanghai girlfriend. We spent a few hours of bliss together. She took me to some classes at the Wheaton College, the school I had originally wanted to go to. Time went by too fast, as I was picked up at 3 p.m. to continue on to Van Nuys, California.

One of the highlights of the trip was driving through Las Vegas. I had never heard of that city before, but chauffeuring through the sparkling city at night took my breath away. After having lived in a war-torn country with bombed-out cities and its massive ruins, Las Vegas to me was spectacular and overpowering. I thought back to the ragged looking displaced persons and refugees in their hovels back home and was overwhelmed by the wealth now being displayed in this country. Wow!

Rev. John Coffman and his wife, Roxanna, welcomed me warmly in Van Nuys in southern California. He was the pastor

56

of the Church of the Brethren on 14517 Osborne Street. All of the houses around were newly built in the late '40s and early '50s. The church was erected as an outreach to this new community. "I believe in the Scriptures from cover to cover," I told the pastor's wife while helping her with washing the dishes after our first meal together. I wanted to get this off my chest right from the start. She spun around from the sink and exclaimed, "We do too!" What a surprise and blessing this was to me. Now I could feel at home and was assured that my ministry was set on a solid Bible-centered basis. I was ready to tackle any assignment given to me.

I set out to build up the youth group. The church had only a few young people. In a letter to my parents I wrote on June 2, "One of my main goals here is to lead young people to the Savior." And this passion pursued me the entire year I spent in the San Fernando Valley.

The year went by in a whirlwind. I taught Sunday school classes, arranged big parties for the young people, took the kids to YFC rallies in Los Angeles, attended a Navigators conference in the San Bernardino mountains, went from house to house inviting people to our church, preached in neighboring churches, was in charge of Sunday evening church services, led singing in the main services, assisted the pastor in many ministry functions, and spent much time mentoring the youth. It was an exciting and a mind-and-heart-enlarging year. During that year I drew closer to my Lord and received a burden never known before for my home country Germany. Here just a sample of letters, this one written on June 8, 1952, I sent to my folks in the Black Forest:

I have a plan [for Germany]. We need young men, filled with the Holy Spirit and the love of Christ in their hearts, with a goal that goes beyond the normal, with an inner fire that removes all barriers in the way, and that with faith and obedience. And I believe that God wants to use US—me, you, and anyone who has been purified and infilled by the Holy Spirit.

On my knees I saw millions of people passing by, who do not have Christ, and I wept and wept for those who still live in darkness. Loved ones, please understand me, this is not anything emotional going on within me; it is a reality and I feel God in me. It is a desire which grows deeper day by day, a desire to serve Him and to proclaim the message of Christ. Often I feel being propelled forward, and I see and understand things which I have not seen or understood before. I need HIM more than ever before!

During the summer Mrs. Coffman surprised me. "Werner, the Lord laid something on my heart. A friend of mine sent me $100 to attend a Church of the Brethren conference. I am urged to give it to you for the YFC conference you so much desire to attend in Winona Lake, Indiana." I was speechless but then thanked her from the bottom of my heart. This had truly been my great desire, and now it was made possible!

At 10:30 in the morning of Saturday, June 28, I boarded the plane in Burbank for Chicago. It was my first plane trip, and I was excited to have that chance. From there I took the Greyhound bus to Winona Lake and checked into the Inn Hotel, an old and shabby place. But the conference was terrific. 3-4,000 young people attended, and the Billy Sunday Tabernacle was filled each night with 8,000 visitors appearing from surrounding villages and towns, hearing men like Bob Pierce, Stuart Hamblen, and Bob Cook. I saw hundreds make commitments for Christ. This whetted my interest for evangelism even more.

Bob Evans, founder of Greater Europe Mission and the European Bible Institute in Paris, France, counseled me about signing up as a student in his school. It was amazing to run into him during this time—he all the way from Europe and I from Germany now living in California. This sealed my resolution to become a student in that institution.

Bob Evans (1918-2011), an American citizen, was born in Baltimore, MD, to missionaries who served in Africa, where he grew up. During the Second World War he was a chaplain of the US forces, and during the battle in southern France was severely wounded by an exploding mine. His skull was torn open. This was the end of his military career. He finished his studies at Wheaton College, where he befriended Billy Graham and Torrey Johnson, pastor of a Chicago church and founding president of Youth for Christ International.

Having been raised in a francophone African country, he moved to France and became a representative for YFC there, preaching all across the country. At that time he saw the need for biblically trained young people to reach their own people in France with the gospel. So he encouraged young people to become his students and founded the European Bible Institute. The same was true for the other European countries, and so he also founded Bible schools in Germany, Greece, Great Britain, Portugal, Spain, and Sweden. I set my eyes on the Institute Biblique Européen in Paris (the school was actually located in a suburb called Chatou).

After one week of incredible inspiration, I flew back to California and dove into my ministry responsibilities. Mondays were my days off. I was given only a little pocket money, so I decided to earn some more money. One of the church members hired me to help him on his chicken farm. It was hard and dirty work, cleaning out the coops and wringing the necks of sick chickens. But I earned money! With it I could buy a car. It was an old Plymouth and needed some work. Rev. Coffman liked to tinker with cars, so that was a big help. The price: $70!

Having a car, I now could travel around. I drove to Los Angeles to visit Dawson Trotman, founder and president of The Navigators. He had encouraged me to memorize Bible verses during his visit to Shanghai in 1947. "How is Bob Hopkins doing in Germany," he asked. "Roy Robertson was our first representative overseas—in China, and later we sent Bob to Germany." He was glad to hear that I planned to attend the European Bible Institute in Paris, because one his other representatives was a teacher there. "You and Hans Wilhelm need to get together for fellowship and Bible study," he concluded.

Hans had been a close friend of mine in Shanghai, going to the same *Kaiser Wilhelm Schule*. Off and on he came to Van Nuys for Bible study, and on May 31 he preached at our church.

What is this? I wondered as my bed was moving from side to side. It was 4:52 a.m. on July 21, 1952. "Get out of your room," Rev. Coffman shouted, "we have an earthquake." As I stumbled in my pajamas onto the street, I saw the power lines swinging back and forth and cracks opening up on the pavements. This was California's most powerful earthquake since the 1906 quake in San Francisco, where 28,000 buildings and 500 city blocks were destroyed, costing $8 billion in today's dollars. It was scary, yet electrifying to watch an earthquake in Van Nuys. To see the power of God's nature was amazing.

On October 26, Bob Richards came to our little church to preach. He was a celebrity in the United States. He had won gold medals as a pole vaulter in the Helsinki (1952) and Melbourne (1956) Olympics. His message was to the point, and after he had given the invitation to come forward to the altar to receive Christ, he stepped back to his seat while the congregation sang the first stanza of "Just as I am." Unexpectedly, at least to him, one young person left the seat to come forward, then a second, then a third, so he quickly moved back to the pulpit and encouraged others to take the step. Nineteen altogether made open professions that morning!

Afterwards at lunch he told us, "The last few weeks I have crisscrossed the country preaching in many Church of the Brethren churches, and in none of those churches even one person made a commitment. Therefore I did not expect anything to happen here. Your church," he continued, "is doing something right. The folks here had been well prepared for this occasion."

I was exhilarated. What we had been praying for just happened. All of the efforts over the last few months were validated. Our pastor and Roxie—that's what we called his wife—were overjoyed. And I thanked the Lord for having answered my earnest prayers in such a dramatic way. Mrs. Coffman asked me whether she could include something in a letter to my parents I wrote two days later. Here it is:

Today I have an inner urge to write you a few lines about Werner. Last Sunday night as he led our group in singing, I thought of you folks and wished you could have seen him. With his joyful enthusiasm and sly humor he gets us all to singing, or at least we make a loud noise. We all love him so much! Three different parties said to me last night, "Won't you miss Werner, when he leaves?" I assented with a pain in my heart. He was and is just what we need here, and we feel very definitely he is God's gift to us, as a church group, I mean. I wished you could have seen him as he knelt by Wesley at the altar. I was so thankful he was there to help Wesley in his need. Werner's big party did catch young people and they are accepting Christ. I do not think he is getting enough sleep, although I approve heartily his devotional periods. I think he should sleep in the afternoon, since he does not get enough at night. May God bless you for giving such a son to the world.

The young man she was referring to, I had visited in his home a couple of weeks before. I explained the way of salvation to him, and just as I was ready to lead him in prayer, one of his friends walked through the door. This interruption stopped me from going on. I had to leave. Sunday night he was struggling, sitting in the last row of the church. I had asked the congregation to stand while singing the invitation hymn. He did not. He sat with his head bowed. During the last stanza he suddenly stood up, turned to the side, slipped out of the row, and walked forward. Immediately I left the pulpit to meet him halfway. My arm around him, I walked the final steps forward with him, where he dropped on his knees sobbing. I prayed with him, and then led him to a side room where he asked Christ to come into his life.

It was one of my most cherished experiences at the church.

It is true that I was tired. I always got up early in the morning, before any of the others did. I studied my Bible and wrestled with God in prayer. I had a deep burden to serve my Master well, but recognized my sinful nature. I wondered *am I the only one with such struggles?* I was determined, however, to battle on; for not being victorious, how could I be an example to other young people?

I thought of the letter Bob Evans had written me when I was deliberating whether to sign up as a student in his Paris school. He wrote:

> How we pray that God will raise up another Luther or perhaps a number of them that will call their German people back to the faith of their fathers, that they might truly bless Europe and the world." He continued, "It is not impossible that He can use you to bring this about and I have thought of this again and again.

But what really got my attention was his next sentence, "There are so few true biblical Christians who have a thorough understanding and whose life is pure enough for God to use in Germany today. For that matter, there are few in any country."

This is where and why I struggled. Do I have a "thorough biblical understanding" and is my life "pure enough"? While battling in my mind these matters, I wrote to my parents:

> I agree with him that even I could be a Luther, but only if found faithful. He mentioned a "pure life" which I still do not have. Oh, how hard it is to toss Satan a NO each time he confronts us. And Friedel [my brother], you brought tears to my eyes when you said that you feel so unworthy being called a child of God. That stunned me, because I also feel

so unworthy. So often we—or rather I—think of myself to be quite respectable, but oh my goodness, how far removed I find myself from purity in thought and action! So many around me marvel at the wonderful life I live. Standing in the pulpit preaching how a Christian should live but then being caught red-handedly sinning like all the others. The feeling of disparagement overcomes me, yes; in reality I truly am insignificant and weak. So small!

And then pride rises its ugly head. God cannot use such people. Only as we live in deep humility and total purity and in full obedience to God and His Word can we be used by God. I constantly pray to be filled with His Holy Spirit as experienced by His disciples. We also can experience this!

Bob Evans also wrote:

As we talked about the great problems and possibilities of Germany in the European situation and/or the present crisis and our Lord's return, I felt strongly that the Lord has called you to Germany to serve at least in the immediate future. It is so true that Germany has always led Europe in recent generations, and so, no doubt, once again her destiny is to have a great effect upon the course of history.

Those were challenging words. Of course I knew it was preposterous to be compared to Luther, but those words invigorated me greatly in my days of *Sturm und Drang Jahren* ("storm and stress" years; more than a bucket list)! *What had God in mind with my life,* I often mused.

The one struggle I had was with my sleep patterns. I worked hard during the day, went to bed late, but had made a commitment to rise early around 5:30 a.m. for prayer and Bible study. I had read that Wesley got up every morning at around 4 a.m., so I thought 5:30 a.m. was a good time for me, not realizing that in Wesley's days, people did not have electric lights and were accustomed to retire early in the evenings. On October 9, I vented my frustrations in a letter to my parents:

> In so many areas I still need to win victories but sometimes it appears I am failing. Every morning I get up at 5:30, but just this morning, as I heard the alarm clock go off I thought to myself, *Werner, just imagine that you have made up your mind to always get up early—every morning of your life—always; always every morning. Give it up; you do not need to be a fanatical Christian. Stay in bed and just be normal. Let someone else do the work in Germany.* Satan tries with all his might to destroy the vision I have for Germany. The more we are willing to fight for our Savior, the more Satan will try to bring us down. Pray for me. I am praying daily for you.

As the time for departure got closer, I thought about the situation the world was in. The Cold War was in full swing and the results of the Korean War (1950-53) were on everybody's mind. I was wondering whether the Soviet Union would enter the war and that this could possibly mean an extension of the war into Europe. Germany was especially volatile, being bordered by Warsaw Pact countries. *Will I ever get the chance to minister in Germany,* I pondered.

On January 3, 1953, I wrote to my parents of such concerns:

Yes, now we started another New Year and who knows what it will bring. Will another war start or will our Savior return? Nobody knows. But all of us wish that we may utilize the time in which we still live and in which we still have freedom to lead people to the Savior.

CHAPTER 5

INSTITUTE BIBLIQUE EUROPÉEN, CHATOU/PARIS, FRANCE

A T THAT TIME I was anxiously awaiting the visa for France. I did not know whether it was a hindrance for the French to let a German citizen in those years study in their country. My country had been at war with them and their sensitivity towards us was still delicate. But I prayed that God's will be done. I also was yearning to get closer to the Lord. I was restless and decided to spend more time in solitude with my heavenly Father. My mother sent me a letter of encouragement at that juncture of my life. Finishing off my assignment in California and looking forward to a different challenge studying for the ministry—His service—was thrilling and exhilarating.

I shared this in a letter:

Do you know that I now need your prayers more than ever? Satan tries to overcome me with all of his might. I do not have as close a communion in prayer with my God as I used to. It is tougher for me to get up early. However, I need

67

those times; otherwise I will not be able to grow spiritually. It seems to me that shortly before my departure Satan tries to block my vision for ministry in Germany. But I also know that Jesus is stronger and you can assist me. Each step we go backwards will make it doubly hard to regain. And to remain stationary is wrong!

On New Year's Eve I decided to spend the night alone with my Lord in prayer. At 11 p.m. I took my car and drove into the mountains, where I could find tranquility. As I was prayerfully driving into the night, I was battling with Satan and ordered him to let me alone. I reached the ridge of the mountains and looked back across the valley below; how spectacular to see thousands or even millions of lights sparkling and penetrating the darkness. You know, at such a moment you feel drawn to God. And in my car I prayed to God and asked Him to help because I am so weak. I slept a little while, then prayed, slept again and prayed. And then I let the entire elapsed year pass by in my thoughts and realized how the Lord had wonderfully led me. But I also recalled the hours in which I had let sin overcome me. God, forgive me! And then I drove deeper and deeper into the mountains, all alone, no other soul around—only God and I. It was a great experience. I got back home at 4 a.m., because we wanted to watch the Rose Parade in Pasadena that day.

The Rose Parade—the official title is Tournament of Roses Parade—was first held January 1, 1890, in Pasadena, California. John Coffman and his wife took me to view it that morning. We left at 5 a.m. to secure a good spot from which we were able to see the floats go by. They were all decorated with flowers, mostly roses. We waited for three hours to see the first float come down the road. It was spectacular. I had never seen anything like it and it was over by 11 a.m.

The parade is held every year on January 1, except when the first day of the year falls on a Sunday; then it will be moved to Monday. Every year hundreds of thousands of people view the spectacle, and millions watch it on TV. I was impressed.

As a young twenty-year-old I had many girls drooling over me. I did not know whether it was my looks or the novelty of being a foreigner that caused them to feel that way. However, before heading for California a year earlier, I had made up my mind that I would not be involved romantically with any girl. True, some of the girls were attractive. Once I was conversing with the pastor in front of the church building after the Sunday evening service. We had said good-bye to all the congregants except one. She was the prettiest girl within our church. She kept talking on and on, and finally the pastor withdrew. At that moment she asked me to go with her behind the church. "Why?" I asked. "I will show you something," she replied. "What is it?" "Well, come and see." I really did not know at the time what she wanted but I got suspicious. I demurred.

Later I asked the pastor about it. He said, "Come on, Werner, did you not get it? She wanted to kiss you!" At that moment I was doubly glad about the commitment I had made before. It was so easy to fall into temptations that might lead to fornication. In all of my years I kept pure before the Lord. I had one main goal in my growing-up years. I wanted to enter marriage as a virgin and succeeded. But it was only with the help of my Lord, to whom I was committed, that enabled me to stay virtuous.

Naturally I was not blind about things happening around me. I saw and met many suitable girls. I knew that someday

God would show me which girl would be mine. But I had to be circumspect in this regard. I did not want to make any mistake.

At the YFC conference in Winona Lake I volunteered to sing in the huge youth choir. I met a petite and pretty girl singing in the soprano section. I was drawn to her and started to pray whether she might be the chosen one. Traveling back across the States to board the *SS America* for my return voyage, I stopped to see her in La Paz, Indiana. I knew that Phyllis liked me, and she welcomed me into her home. She wanted to introduce me to her parents.

It was an extremely cold night that February day. In the middle of it, it must have been around 3 a.m., she entered my room to spread another blanket over me. That's all she did. I was impressed with her courage to enter, but more with her concern. We of course had talked things over the day before, whether we should pursue our relationship. I told her about my call to minister in Germany and that it was my paramount conviction and goal, superseding every other issue, in planning my future. I suggested to further pray about it and to write each other once more—I from Paris and she from Moody in Chicago, the Moody Bible Institute, where she planned to attend.

The following day she drove me to the Greyhound station. Both of us had a hard time saying good-bye. I never forgot what she said before I stepped aboard: "I know you would like to remain in the States for my sake, but something else is pulling you away which weighs heavier on you. It is the burden you have for Germany." She was right.

Many years later I was scheduled to preach at a YFC rally in the city she then lived. She had read about me in the newspaper and contacted the YFC director. He arranged a visit. Both of us were happily married to partners we first met at Bible schools—she to a pastor whom she met at Moody in Chicago and I to my German sweetheart whom I met at EBI in Paris. God had answered both of our prayers for the good of His work.

On a cold February afternoon I was picked up at the *Gare St. Lazare* train station in Paris by Belgian EBI student (European Bible Institute) Samuel Liberek. He recognized me easily with my brand new beige suit and my light brown Samsonite suitcase. I looked like an American. I had bought both of those items with the money I had made from the sale of my beloved Plymouth car. I had disembarked in Le Havre, France, and taken the train to France's capital instead of traveling on to Bremerhaven, the final destination of the ship in Germany. This was faster and cheaper for me.

Early in life I learned that I needed a support group, especially as I entered my theological studies at the European Bible Institute (EBI). My family was it. I was in constant communication with my parents and also with my siblings Friedel and Gisela. Letters went back and forth from and to the United States and now from Paris. My last letter from the US was written on February 26, 1953, from my uncle's home in Marlboro, New Jersey. I was deeply concerned with the physical condition my parents were in, especially my father. I wrote about my worry for him:

> After receiving your loving letter, I want to write you a personal letter. I am deeply disturbed reading your lines. But do you know what I think? The labor in the Black Forest is too strenuous for you. For someone who toiled over twenty years as a missionary in China, your work now is too demanding. You rob yourself of your health which you desperately need

71

for your ministry. It might be better for you to transfer to a different city from which you don't have to travel so much. Don't you know of any other location where a preacher or pastor is needed? Mother was deathly sick and you are not well either and it would be best to relocate to a different place. Perhaps the Lord is waiting for our prayers in this regard. What do you think?

In another letter written earlier to the one above, I revealed my appreciation for his welcomed counsel:

Dad, I am always thrilled to receive your counsel because I am aware that I still have to learn so many things. And a much experienced father is the one who can help the best. I am now memorizing three new Bible verses each week because I know that this will be useful for my later service. However, I still have some difficulties with meditation on the Word of God which is so very important.

My folks, especially my mother, were concerned about my wardrobe. They constantly asked me whether I had enough to wear in view of the coming years I would spend in theological studies. I wrote before leaving California for France:

Dear parents, you don't have to be worried about my attire. The Lord will supply all of my needs. I plan to buy here a new suit and other items, whatever I need. I trust Him. He called me into His service and He will not abandon me. The money you offer is yours and you can use it well for yourselves.

The studies at EBI took all of my attention. It was exhilarating for me to be immersed in the Bible. Some of the courses I took during the first semester were Old Testament, Christian Education, Christian Life, Romans, Church History, and Bible Doctrine. My fellow students came from Greece, Lebanon, France, The Netherlands, Belgium, Spain, Germany, Great Britain, Austria, and even the United States. It truly was an international group. We slept on bunk beds but enjoyed the French cuisine. Every afternoon we were served French bread—baguettes—with chunks of dark chocolate. But portions at meal time were small, and I quickly lost weight. "What's the matter with you," a friend of mine from Germany quipped, "you look like one from a concentration camp!" All I knew was to concentrate on my studies.

I quickly befriended Gottfried Lauth from Germany. He was a tall guy, and to me he looked like a foot taller than I. When Dawson Trotman saw him, he asked, "How is the weather up there?" His father had been a pastor in a Lutheran church in Wiesbaden. Gottfried told me, "He preached in the pulpit but in reality did not know Christ. His profession was the pastorate, but he was not a believer." Often he and I went for prayer to an island in the Seine River, which ran close by to our school. Later on both of us joined the Youth for Christ organization as evangelists.

Now living in France, I immediately went sightseeing in Paris, the famous "city of light." In reverence I stood in the Pantheon where great heroes of France, such as Voltaire, Rousseau, Victor Hugo, Louis Braille, and others are entombed. Then I visited Les Invalides with the tomb of Napoleon (1769-1821). Initially he was interred on Saint Helena but in 1840 his remains were brought back to France, and he found his final resting place in the tomb under the gorgeous dome in 1861. The historian Pieter

Geyl compared him to Hitler because of his ruthless rule, when the press was muted, his critics imprisoned and killed, and his murderous wars fought, in which millions were slain. He was finally brought down by European allied forces. In fact, Hitler did visit his tomb after his victory over France on June 22, 1940. He idolized Napoleon and made many of Napoleon's dictatorial traits his own.

France is a beautiful country. I fell in love with Paris. During the years of study at EBI, I made many visits to that historic city. I also entered *Alliance Française* and later *Sorbonne* (University of Paris) to take the course *Cours de Civilisation Française*. Even though courses at our Bible school were being taught in English and French, and the messages at the daily chapel services were interpreted into both languages, I felt the need to learn proper French. For a couple of years I traveled from the suburb of Chatou to downtown Paris three times a week in the afternoons to augment my skill in French. It was a twenty-five minute ride by train to *Gare St. Lazare* and another thirty minutes by subway to *Quartier Latin* on the left bank of the river Seine where the Sorbonne University is located. It is well known for its student life and its charming and lively atmosphere with its quaint bistros. In the summer of 1955 I lived for three months downtown studying French and helping a US chaplain run his meetings at Bleriot and SHAPE (Supreme Headquarters Allied Powers Europe).

Back to the spring of 1953!

I quickly got used to the routine of theological studies. I took them very seriously, and my grades showed that. We were asked to form student teams to evangelize in different churches in and around Paris. I loved that. Living in a new culture was stimulating and motivating, especially in view of my approaching years in Germany. But I wanted more.

One day Bob Evans asked me whether I would be willing to help a US chaplain run his meetings. "I would love that," I said. Colonel Kirkpatrick was a career soldier. Ordained as a Southern Baptist, he loved the Bible and preached the gospel clearly—well, as long as he had the regular army GIs before him in Bleriot. But as soon as he saw stars on the epaulettes of those sitting at SHAPE, he changed his tune.

General Clark was a famous four-star general who fought under General Eisenhower during the Second World War. He ordered the bombing and total destruction of the monastery Monte Cassino in Italy, surmising that German troops were using it for observation. He later found out that this had been a false assumption. In fact, German officers had evacuated all monks, with its valuable library and other artifacts. These are the facts reported by the monks:

In the course of the battles, the ancient Abbey of Monte Cassino was entirely destroyed by bombing and artillery in 1943. Two German officers, Captain Maximilian Becker, a surgeon in the *Hermann Göring Panzer Division* and Lieutenant Colonel Julius Schlegel of the same unit, with singular prescience proposed the removal of Monte Cassino's treasures to the Vatican and Vatican-owned Castel Sant' Angelo before the war would come closer. Both officers convinced church authorities and their own senior command-ers to use the division's trucks and fuel for the undertaking. They had to find the materials necessary for crates and boxes, identify skilled carpenters among their troops, recruit local laborers (to be paid with rations of food plus twenty cigarettes per day) and then manage the "massive job of evacuation centered on the library and archive" a treasure "literally without price." The richness of the Abbey's archives, library and gallery included "800 papa; documents, 20,500 volumes in the Old Library, 60,000 in the New Library, 500 *incunabula*, 200 manuscripts on parchment, 100,000 prints and separate collections." The first trucks, carrying paintings by Italian old masters, were ready to go less than a week from the day Dr. Becker and Schlegel independently first came to Monte Cassino. Each vehicle carried monks to Rome as escorts; in over one hundred truckloads the convoys nearly depopulated the Abbey's monastic community. The task was completed in the first days of November 1943. "In three weeks, in the middle of a losing war, in another country, it was quite a feat." After a mass in the basilica, Abbot Gregorio Diamare formally presented signed parchment scrolls in Latin to General Paul Conrath, to *tribuno militum Julio Schlegel* and *Maximiliano Becker medecinae doctori* "for rescuing the monks and treasures of the Abbey of Monte Cassino." After the war Schlegel spent seven months in an Allied prison as a suspected looter but was freed after favorable testimony from the Monte Cassino monks.

General Clark was one of those who attended our services. I was especially flattered when, after a rendition of Handel's Messiah I directed, Mrs. Clark warmly shook my hand and said, "Well done. Thank you so much." He, a typical macho guy, just grunted. But such individuals with four stars on the epaulettes struck fear into the hearts of cowards like our chaplain. But I liked the chaplain. He was a good guy, dressed immaculately and getting his weekly Marine-style short—very short—haircut.

He also paid well, at least I as a poor Bible school student thought so. This was another blessing I experienced throughout my sojourn in Paris.

A married couple at the Brethren church in Van Nuys had told me before leaving for France that they wanted to help me. Len Frederick's father had come from Germany. Len was born in the Midwest. His family was poor, so he decided as a teenager to move to California. He climbed aboard a slow-moving train traveling west as a stowaway. He made it all the way. He did not have much schooling but made it big in the food marketplace. He married Marylyn and both lived very well. They took a liking to me, and once they found out about my evangelistic passion for Germany, chose to support me. But I did not know how.

One sunny afternoon I was working in the garden of the school, when Bob Evans looked out the window on the top floor and shouted, "Werner, I have something for you." A piece of paper floated through the air. It was a check of US $25—a fortune for me at that time. It was exactly what I needed each month. *Money floating down from heaven,* I mused. Month by month I received a check until my graduation. God had come through once more.

Finally my chance to be involved with evangelism arrived. YFC Germany (*Jugend für Christus in Deutschland*) had invited me to help out in evangelistic crusades during my summer vacation. While in Bielefeld in northern Germany I wrote to my parents on September 7, 1953:

I am kept busy all day long. Preparations for the evangelistic meetings are plentiful. At noon we show Christian movies in schools, then the noon meal, prayer meeting, meetings for children, and then the evening meetings. You see, the day is full with activities. But that's the way it ought to be. Are we not doing the most important work in the world, namely leading the lost to Jesus? This brings so much joy to my heart.

I wish you could attend and hear the singing! Yesterday 1,000 people filled the tent. And this already *in* the first week! Next Sunday we plan a large closing rally at the Oetker Auditorium which holds 1,700 – 1,800 people. Please pray for this great undertaking so that the Lord may do great things by leading many to Him.

In the fall I was back in Paris. My theological studies were a great blessing to me. I wanted to be well prepared for my ministry in the future.

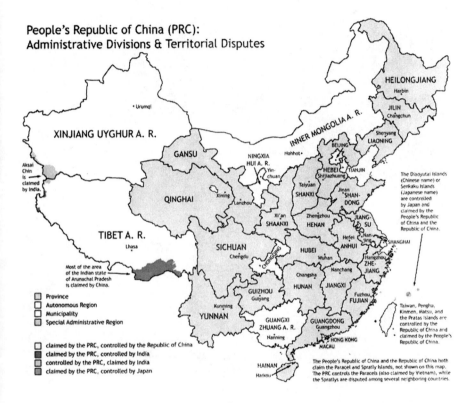

People's Republic of China (PRC):
Administrative Divisions & Territorial Disputes

HEILONGJIANG
Harbin

JILIN
Changchun

XINJIANG UYGHUR A. R.

· Urumqi

INNER MONGOLIA A. R.

Shenyang
LIAONING

GANSU

NINGXIA
HUI A. R.

Hohhot ·

BEIJING

Aksai
Chin
is
claimed
by India.

QINGHAI

Xining

Yin-
chuan

Lanzhou

Taiyuan
SHANXI

HEBEI
Shijiazhuang

TIANJIN

Jinan
SHAN-
DONG

The Diaoyutai Islands
(Chinese name) or
Senkaku Islands
(Japanese name)
are controlled
by Japan and
claimed by the
People's Republic
of China and the
Republic of China.

TIBET A. R.

Lhasa

Xi'an
SHAANXI

Zhengzhou

HENAN

JIANG-
SU

SICHUAN

Chengdu

CHONGQING

HUBEI

Wuhan

Hefei

ANHUI

Nan-
jing

SHANGHAI

Hangzhou
ZHE-
JIANG

Most of the area
of the Indian state
of Arunachal Pradesh
is claimed by China.

GUIZHOU
Guiyang

Changsha

HUNAN

Nanchang

JIANGXI

Fuzhou
FUJIAN

□ Province
□ Autonomous Region
□ Municipality
▨ Special Administrative Region

YUNNAN

Kunming

GUANGXI
ZHUANG A. R.

Nanning

GUANGDONG
Guangzhou

Taiwan, Penghu,
Kinmen, Matsu, and
the Pratas Islands are
controlled by the
Republic of China and
claimed by the People's
Republic of China.

□ claimed by the PRC, controlled by the Republic of China
■ claimed by the PRC, controlled by India
□ controlled by the PRC, claimed by India
▨ claimed by the PRC, controlled by Japan

HONG KONG
MACAU

HAINAN

Haikou

The People's Republic of China and the Republic of China both
claim the Paracel and Spratly Islands, not shown on this map.
The PRC controls the Paracels (also claimed by Vietnam), while
the Spratlys are disputed among several neighboring countries.

China

My Love

Gustav and Lina Bürklin, nee Pfeifferling, on furlough in Germany 1935

The mission station my father built in Chongren, Jiangxi, with my sister Gisela

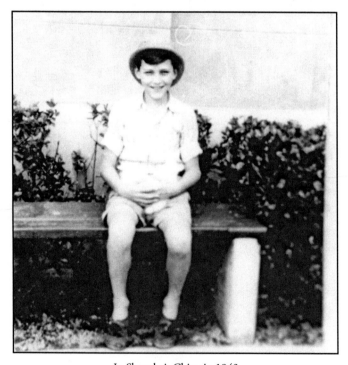

In Shanghai, China in 1943

SS Rena, the gangster ship that brought me back to Europe in 1949

YFC team at the first crusade I had arranged in Kassel in 1950

Jugend für Christus (YFC) Rally in Frankfurt, Germany, 1957

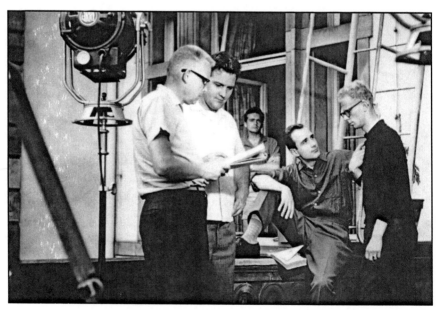

Producing the first evangelistic film in Germany *Aufruhr im Jugendheim* in 1965

YFC Teen Team that we sent to South Africa and Rhodesia (Zimbabwe)

YFCI world leadership meeting in Geneva, Switzerland

CHAPTER 6

REVIVAL IN GREAT BRITAIN

B ILLY GRAHAM HAD become very famous throughout
Europe. In the spring of 1954 he was holding a large
evangelistic crusade in London, England. We received word that
on a Saturday 30,000 people wanted to enter the Harringay Arena
[built in 1936 and torn down in 1958] which could seat only
11,000. In order to accommodate the crowds, three services had
to be held. And each night people by the hundreds made decisions
for Christ. As people traveled home after the meetings, they kept
singing in London's tubes. Graham had never experienced anything
like this before. The meetings had to be extended for three months.

In the middle of April all students of EBI traveled to London.
Billy Graham, a good friend of Bob Evans, had invited us for
one week to experience God's doing. It was a life-changing
experience for me. The Billy Graham Evangelistic Association
(BGEA) paid 50 percent of our traveling expenses. Two weeks
before, I had written to my parents:

Each evening the hall with 11,000 seats is overflowing. On Saturdays they had to schedule three meetings. Last Saturday 70,000 people wanted to attend, so four meetings were scheduled and the other 30,000 people had to be sent home. People are coming from all over England. Many come to faith in Christ. Hallelujah!

YFC Germany sent me a nice letter inviting me to work this summer again with them. I am looking forward to this summer. Pray for our poor Germany—pray much—so that revival will also begin there.

But now I was in England, staying at the headquarters of the China Inland Mission (CIM) in Newington Green, London. My friend Gottfried Lauth and I met each other at the arena each night of our London visit. The first night there, all of us students were given front-row seats. What a thrill to see Billy Graham close up and then marvel at all those people who walked forward to make decisions for Christ. How I longed for Germany to have the opportunity and experience this kind of awakening.

After the meeting Bob Evans took us backstage to meet Billy Graham. This, of course, was a great honor since just a handful of those who flocked to the meetings were able to shake his hand. We did. Billy then introduced us to his wife, Ruth. I was struck with her beauty but even more with her graciousness. Billy had fallen in love with her when both of them had studied at Wheaton College. She was impressed with his integrity and with his prayer life. And he was attracted by her love for Christ and her desire to serve the Lord in a far-away place like Tibet. But now they served together in London.

The next evening Gottfried and I did not find an empty seat until we spotted a couple of them in a box reserved for special guests. We assumed to qualify; after all, Billy Graham had invited us to his crusade and even paid for half of our tickets. We were some of the very few who had been invited to shake his hand! So we took those seats. One of the ushers came over and told us to move out. "These seats are reserved for guests who hold a special invitation card," he warned. We grudgingly accepted his snub and wandered around not knowing where to sit. But then we ran into Dawson Trotman of the Navigators, who was in charge of counseling.

Remembering me from the meeting I had with him in Los Angeles and again from the time he saw both of us during a visit he made to EBI in Paris, he took out his name card and scribbled a short note on it. "Go up to the stage and show them this card and you can sit up there," he said.

I never will forget the bewildered look on the face of the usher who had chased us away. *How in the world did those guys manage that,* he must have pondered. Gottfried and I waved kindly at him from the stage sitting behind Billy Graham. We knew he had done his job—and that graciously, yet firmly.

I had been busy memorizing Scripture. I finished the Navigator course, which included 108 Bible verses. To keep them solidly fixed in my mind, I had to continuously review them. In view of my later ministry in Germany, I switched from English to German. Someone had challenged me to memorize the book of Philippians. Once this was accomplished, I tackled the Gospel of John. Every morning before breakfast I walked out into the school garden and went through my memorization routine. On June 7, 1954, I wrote this to my parents:

Just imagine I finished memorizing the entire Gospel of John. To be able to quote it fluently, I need another two months or so. It is so wonderful to know another book of the Bible by heart.

Furthermore, in my prayer time I increasingly felt the need for fasting. In the past I had omitted a meal now and then. But I wanted more. I wanted to fast for an entire week. I recalled a wonderful blessing I once experienced many years past, while visiting the *Diakonissen Mutterhaus* in Aidlingen, a little town close to Stuttgart in southern Germany. This originally had nothing to do with fasting; however, it reinforced my desire to do it.

My brother Friedel and I wanted to see something of Germany after we had arrived from China in 1949. We did not have much money, so we decided to hitchhike across the country.

This was a tough feat. We never expected such a difficult yet rewarding experience as we traveled from place to place. For instance, in Frankfurt we bedded down in a bunker for homeless people left over from the war time. Before reaching our bunks, one of the employees ordered, "Open up your collar." Not knowing why, I asked, "What's this for?" "This DDT will kill all of the pests on you," he retorted. I had never experienced such intrusion before, not even in China! I knew I needed a bath but to rid me of fleas or whatever other pests were on me was hard to swallow. I was shocked but then realized what many had to go through just to sleep somewhere.

Soon after that awful experience we arrived in Aidlingen near Stuttgart in southern Germany. Gerda von Viehbahn, one of the German missionaries in China whom I had met in Nanfeng when I saw my parents again after a five-year long separation, had told us about the amazing ministry of German *Diakonissen* (deaconesses). She was a member of this "sisterhood" then serving as a missionary alongside my parents. She impressed me with her genuine kindness. These women vow not to get married but to spend all of their lives in total submission and service to Christ. Most of them live in communes, wear uniformed garb, spend many hours in prayer and meditation, and often work as nurses in hospitals or as missionaries in different parts of the world. They are known for doing good deeds.

This Christian organization or rather ministry had been founded by the daughter of a famous German general turned evangelist, Georg von Viehbahn. Christa (1873-1955) started this as a fifty-four-year-old in 1927. After having hitchhiked for several days, we were warmly welcomed by her, given a bath, and then slept between snow-white bed sheets. There we did not have to be debugged! What a treat and something I will never forget!

This *Diakonissen Mutterhaus* also had a beautiful retreat center in the Black Forest close to St. Georgen, where my parents lived. I had asked my parents to reserve a room there for a week of fasting, meditation, prayer, and Bible study. Once there, I took long prayer walks through forests that made the Black Forest famous. Every new fasting day became a greater blessing. It was an incredible week of reflection. God was very near to me. The fellowship with Him was intense. This was exactly what I had been yearning for. But then I got a shock I was not prepared for.

On the day of my departure, Satan came after me with unbelievable force.

After having paid my bill and said my good-byes to the kindhearted deaconesses, it appeared like a host of evil spirits ascended upon me. As I left the premises I was driven by an unseen force to walk faster and faster to distance myself from the location of my hallowed encounter with God. When I finally arrived at the train station, I was overcome with a rare and intense craving for food. I sat down at a restaurant nearby and gave in to that craving.

What's the matter, I mused, *why this sudden and intense craving which I did not have during the week of fasting!* I was confused and felt defeated. *Why fast and then not be able to control your hunger?*

I felt attacked like I had never been before. Earnestly contemplating this during the time of utter confusion, I gradually realized that I had been engaged in spiritual warfare. This was a new revelation I had to deal with, which then I never forgot. With prayer I had entered Satan's territory, and he was out to challenge me. Satan with a host of evil spirits were out to reclaim control over me, and through this occurrence those evil spirits became real to me—I had been attacked by real beings! I thought back to my encounter with such spirits in the haunted house in Ningdu, China, except now they were attacking me spiritually and that personally. In China I just heard them, now I was attacked. In Ningdu I only had learned that such spirits exist. Now I was under severe and explicit assault. It was the gravest encounter I have ever had in all my life. If someone says that believing in evil spirits is foolishness, I know they are wrong. This was real. This was traumatic and hurtful. This showed me that I was living in a world ruled by the principalities and powers of evil.

I was thankful to have learned that lesson.

Back in Paris I was told that some ten thousand otherworldly mediums live in this capital city of France. Missionaries, who lived here to study French before moving on to francophone countries in Africa also encountered such spiritual battles. They talked about living under a cloud of darkness they had not experienced back home.

For me it was a worthwhile experience. It strengthened my resolve to withstand the evil forces when thrown at me. To do this, I immersed myself in the Word of God and put on the whole armor of God.

Often I have been asked what I do in a practical way to shield myself from such fiery darts of the devil. *How do you overcome temptations,* they ask.

For one thing, I learned that the greatest battles in our lives are being fought in our minds. Before we do anything evil or before we succumb to any temptation, the battle in our minds begins. When this became clear to me, I reflected about what kind of weapon I need to overcome this. The Lord disclosed it to me and I have used it ever since. Here it is:

Whenever I am tempted, I immediately reflect on what Jesus Christ did on the cross for me—and for mankind. I concentrate on His death and the blood He shed. I concentrate on the nail-pierced hands and feet. I observe His wound on His side and the crown of thorns on His brow. I deliberately focus on the blood of Christ that was shed for me, knowing that the blood of Christ puts Satan on the defense. More than just believing this, I then claim the blood of Christ to "cover" me. In fact, I know when I do this that Satan has to flee. He simply cannot stand up to the power of the blood of Christ. He will have to leave. And he does.

We often sing the hymn composed in 1899 by Lewis E. Jones (1865-1936), who was a classmate of Billy Sunday (1862-1935) and a graduate of Moody Bible Institute. He based this song on the Scriptures found in Revelation 7:14:

Would you be free from the burden of sin?
There's power in the blood, power in the blood;
Would you o'er evil a victory win?
There's wonderful power in the blood.
There is power, power, wonder-working power
In the blood of the Lamb;
There is power, power, wonder-working power
In the precious blood of the Lamb.

Already as a teenager I had sung this in Shanghai at our Ambassador for Christ youth meetings. But I had never really understood the true meaning of this truth. I had never put to use the power of this truth—not consciously. But I finally embraced it and started to use it. It became a powerful weapon of defense!

Besides memorizing Scripture, I also memorized hymns. One that became popular during that time was "It Took a Miracle." I loved it and was inspired by its powerful words:

It took a miracle to put the stars in place;
It took a miracle to hang the world in space.
But when He saved my soul,
Cleansed and made me whole,
It took a miracle of love and grace!

Later when visiting my parents in their Black Forest home, I used to sing it while doing my chores. My mother, who felt that I had become too Americanized during my stint in that country, confronted me one day, "What's this all about your singing, 'It took America, to put the stars in place. It took America to hang the world in space.' This is sacrilegious!"

Finally my dreams realized—the call attained

In the summer of 1954 I was back in Germany assisting John Thiessen in YFC crusades. He had been a Dutch missionary in Indonesia but now was working together with Youth for Christ doing evangelism in Germany. He was married to a lovely American lady who always accompanied him. I served as the master of ceremony and directed the choir.

Before the crusade in Gelsenkirchen, a city in the Ruhr area *(Ruhrgebiet)*, Thiessen invited me to spend a few days of relaxation with his family in Den Haag, Holland. His son showed me the sights all over the country. We traveled north to Friesland, and on the way stopped in Amsterdam to visit the Rijksmuseum. Rembrandt's (1606-69) famous painting *"De Nachtwacht"* (The Night Watch) intrigued me greatly, especially spotting his self-portrayal (as assumed by some) on the right side of this huge masterpiece. We were on the road for twelve hours.

The Gelsenkirchen crusade thrilled me greatly. The size of the meetings grew steadily until over 1,000 people overflowed the 650-seat tent night by night. We had to move into the *Hans Sachs Haus* with a seating capacity of close to 2,000 people. People were so eager to get in that they stood outside long before the meetings began, waiting for the doors to open. When opened, I saw some ladies using their umbrellas to fight their way in to get good seats. I had managed to recruit between 150-180 youth for the choir. Man, did they sing! In a letter to my folks on September 10, I wrote:

Again I see here, how people have a great hunger for God. If only we could have a few good and genuine evangelists who preach the Word clearly. I sincerely believe that this will come

95

and that the Lord will use us three [us three Bürklins] in a special way. I have an inner conviction and look forward to the day when this will occur, here in Germany and across Europe.

We had to extend the meetings for four days as the crowds reached 2,500 people. It was an amazing experience for me. I saw how people were anxious to find God. My prayers for revival were being answered. I was thrilled. However, I had one concern which I shared with my parents in a letter written on September 17:

> The only sad thing is that we do not have many decisions due to the fact that the evangelist, a missionary who had worked in Indonesia, is not as decisive as he could be [in giving a clear-cut altar call]. Too bad, otherwise many people would come to know Christ.

On the final night of the crusade I invited all of my choir members to join me for a banana split in a local Italian ice cream parlor. The day before I had gone to the owner and forewarned him of what was coming. "Get ready to buy two hundred bananas," I told him. "For what?" he asked. "Well, you will see tomorrow up to two hundred kids converge on your place who all will be asking for banana splits." He had never served banana splits before. Recognizing great business, however, he offered banana splits for the first time. He was ready and what a blast we had.

Several months later I was back in the town and went to his place for a banana split. On the menu I found a new item I had not seen before. It included "Banana Sprit." I chuckled because Germans use the word *sprit* for gasoline. The owner had misspelled the word split and I wonder how many of his clients ever ordered it because in their minds ice cream does not go well with gas! Pfui!

Before returning to Paris, I spent a few days with my parents in St. Georgen. Even though I had been separated from them so often in my youth and once for a period of over five years, we were an extremely close-knit family. I always wanted to know how my siblings Friedel and Gisela were doing, whether they had enough money to pursue their dreams and when they would join me in theological studies at EBI. I was concerned about the health of my parents, knowing what they had gone through in China. For several months my mother had been hospitalized in Mannheim with an illness the doctors were unable to treat until finally a potent medication was brought in from the United States that helped her survive. She lived to be eighty-four years; my father died of cancer as a seventy-two-year-old. We deeply loved each other. In St. Georgen it was always a great time of togetherness. After receiving a heart-wrenching letter about physical separation from my mother, I answered on October 15, 1955:

> Yes, Mom, you are right to say that it is not easy to be separated. But do you know, this is a cross that we have to bear. One day we will be able to see each other eternally and that will be so much lovelier. At this time all of us as—our entire family—have surrendered to the Lord and we decided to live only for Him. That's why we have to live with those inconveniences! But those inconveniences are nothing compared to what Jesus had to cope with when He came to this world. He left everything and lived on this wretched earth for thirty-three

years being separated from His Father. That's why it should be easier for us to take [the separation].

On November 28, 1954, I shared with my folks some other struggles I had; these were with my French lessons:

My French courses keep me busy. Three times a week and two hours each time generates six hours of classes. On top of this I have to travel six hours to Paris and back, which then results in twelve hours in all. Furthermore, I have to spend much time to do my French homework. So I need a total of close to twenty hours per week just for my French studies.

The first hour at the Sorbonne [University of Paris] was terrible. I hardly understood anything because the lecturer spoke very fast and that about French literature! It was terrible. However, now I am able to follow very well. Well, I hope to be able to converse comfortably by next February.

Over the New Year I had the thrill to spend a long weekend with my parents in the beautiful Black Forest. It was a real winter wonderland. Mountains of snow everywhere! The streets were cleared but all the authorities could do was to push the snow to its sides. In order to cross streets they built tunnels through the mounds, something I had never seen before or since.

On the way back to Paris, we made a quick side trip to Basel in Switzerland for some shopping our driver wanted to do. Robert Munn was our professor at EBI and he also wanted to exchange many US dollars his coworkers had given to him into French francs. The exchange rate in Switzerland was extremely lucrative and far better compared to France. All foreigners living in France used to travel to Switzerland only for the sake of changing money.

We did not get away from Basel until 5 p.m. As we got to a mountainous area it was snowing heavily. We made some progress but then had to slow down because of the snow turning into ice. As we were coming down a slope, our car slid from side to side, hitting the sidewalks. We then decided to stop; it was getting really dangerous. We tried to book some rooms in a small village hotel but everything was taken. So we had to sleep in the car. After an hour or so Mr. Munn tried to move on but only succeeded in going one hundred meters. After another hour just sitting and freezing, one more try. But this lasted only six short kilometers, and now it was 1 a.m. We tried to reach the next village to find a hotel but as we were trying to ascend another incline, even us trying to push the car, we failed. We were stuck and had to wait until 7 o'clock in the morning to proceed. It took us twenty hours to reach our destination that otherwise would have taken only six hours.

While in St. Georgen I shared with my parents about my attraction to Juliette Bouchard, the prettiest girl among the students at EBI. Her home town was Bordeaux on the western seaboard of France. Once walking through the living room at the school, I saw her looking at me with a longing in her eyes that touched me. We fell in love. The school had a strict rule of the so-called "eight inches." We were not allowed to get closer than that. Well, eight inches are not hard to overcome when you are in love. We took that hurdle quite easily, no matter what the rules were.

My parents were not happy with this development. They felt I needed a German girl to become my life partner, not a French girl. Juliette had taken two years of German in high school, but this would not be enough to carry on a conversation with them. Neither did my parents speak French, so the only way to communicate would have to be in English. Well, this seemed too much of a hurdle for them. But I made every effort to learn her language.

The entire summer of 1955 I lived in the center of Paris studying French. I passed an important examination at the Sorbonne, which helped me later in my further college studies in the United States. My final semester at EBI ended in February of 1956. I had to return to Paris for graduation in June of 1956. However, the conviction for further studies grew stronger from day to day. I felt increasingly that Bob Jones University in the US would be my next destination. But I also was determined to enhance my skills in French, which led me to take a night job as a receptionist in a Parisian hotel. What an opportunity to improve my French! What a challenge to check in guests and answer the phone—all in French! Now I had to prove my skills in French.

The relationship with my French girlfriend suffered more than I had anticipated. She was saddened to hear about the apprehensions my parents had about our bond, and after struggling with this, she concluded it must be better to dissolve our relationship. We took a long walk in the beautiful and fancy park *Bois de Boulogne* on the western side of Paris. Numerous times before, we had traveled by metro to *Porte Dauphine* to spend time together in prayer and bliss. The expansive park had been built under Napoleon III, nephew of Napoleon Bonaparte, in the later part of the nineteenth century. On the edge lies *Roland Garros*, the site of the French Open, known to tennis players around the world. Both of us prayed, embraced one last time, and together decided to call it quits. This decision weighed far heavier on her than me. I realized then that girls take relationships much more seriously than boys. She never pursued another relationship and never married. This was the last long walk we had taken together. However, we stayed friends and even after having married my sweetheart, Inge, we again met in Frankfurt, Germany, and Paris—but just as Christian friends.

From then on I resolved never to start another relationship until I was absolutely sure that God is in it. I never would kiss a girl again until then!

On Friday, March 23, 1956, I checked into the St. Georgen hospital in the Black Forest for one week of restoration. I had struggled so long with my duodenum that I had finally chosen to try a cure to rid myself from this affliction. It certainly helped, but it was not until years later at the Mayo Clinic in Rochester, Minnesota, that I was encouraged to have part of my lower stomach removed. I had it done by a renowned lady surgeon in Frankfurt soon thereafter. Today such ailment can easily be taken care of by Prilosec—no more surgeries are necessary.

Amazingly, God spared me from a long drought of oscula-tion. Bob Hopkins, the Navigator representative in Germany, had alerted me about a beautiful German girl.

Inge was born in Memel [now Klaipeda], a remote town on the Baltic Sea in the most northeastern part of Germany, now Lithuania. In 1944 her pregnant mother was evacuated with her two children, Hannes and Inge, to Uelzen, Niedersachsen, in the central part of Germany to escape from the advancing ruthless Soviet Army. The German women were horrified to hear about those raping soldiers—a British historian later published his surveys that during that time up to two million German women between the ages of twelve and eighty were subjected to rape. So everyone who could flee to the West did so.

On a Saturday night I preached at the Frankfurt YFC rally, which at that time was run by American GIs. Sitting on the platform, I saw a girl with her younger sister enter the high school auditorium. She wore a striking black felt coat. This was Inge. This was the same girl I had met briefly in the *salon* (living room) of EBI two years before. That encounter had been very short, but I recognized her. We met again. Wilfried Zibell, an evangelist with *Jugend für Christus*, later invited me to come along in his car, traveling to southern Germany. I grabbed this opportunity to visit my parents in St. Georgen and was amazed to find Inge sitting in the back seat of the car. I sat next to her and for some reason was strangely attracted to her and remembered Bob Hopkins raving about her. Now I was able to find out more about her on the two-hour drive to Karlsruhe.

"When you said good-bye to me while I was sitting in the car to travel on with the Zibells, you gave me a penetrating look that I shall never forget," she told me later. "You almost 'burned' me with your dark brown eyes!"

It was true, she had slain me. A spark had been ignited that over the next few weeks developed into a passionate flame. She traveled on with Wilfried and his wife, and I took the train to St. Georgen. At that moment I knew that she was to be my companion for life.

CHAPTER 7

FINDING THE LOVE
OF MY LIFE

I HAD BECOME an official evangelist with *Jugend für Christus* (YFC). My dream had come to fruition. I loved to evangelize.

One of my first tent crusades took place in Hiddenhausen in northern Germany. I shared my initial experiences in a letter to my parents written on May 29:

> The ministry here is being blessed just as I had prayed for and expected it. However, the streams [of blessings] are still missing. But the Lord can still make them available. It began slowly. In the first week it started with seventy attendants, then eighty, one hundred, then one hundred eighty and finally three hundred sixty. The tent can accommodate 350 people.

One week later I wrote:

Yes, the Lord marvelously helped in Hiddenhausen. The tent got fuller from day to day and then it overflowed. We had to add more seats. For the final night we decided to move out to a sports field. We placed the seats onto the field, erected the platform with flood lights, and then looked forward [to what God would do]. We had prayed for good weather; however it started to rain in the afternoon. In the evening the sun broke through the clouds and we had an open sky. After the message I asked all those, who, during the past three weeks had decided to follow Christ to come forward along with those who still wanted to make a commitment. Between eighty to ninety people moved forward to stand in front of the podium. Forty-three of those accepted the Lord that night. It was marvelous. God had worked. Yes, Mom, you are right that I need to stay humble. You have to pray for me. It is a huge danger, and if I would come to the point of thinking that it is my doing, then God will put me aside.

Back in Frankfurt I visited Inge, who had become the bi-lingual secretary at the German Bible Institute in Bensheim. I used the occasion on a gorgeous summer day to take her for a drive to a castle up in the hills of the *Bergstrasse,* the *Heppemheimer Schloss.* The castle lay in ruins amidst beautiful surroundings. It was the perfect spot to pop the question. This was the first time I had ever done this. I had other girls in the past, but never got to the point to ask this all-important question. But now the time had come.

"Du kennst mich doch gar nicht!" she exclaimed. In English: "You don't know me!" She was totally surprised and stunned. We had dated a couple of times, but true to my vow we never had kissed. So this came as a total surprise to her. "I can wait," I answered, when she explained that she was in the middle of

plans to enter the Moody Bible Institute in the United States. But I was so sure that she was going to be mine that I let her embrace and kiss me. This was the first kiss and the beginning of myriads of others to follow over the years. To me this was the kiss that sealed it.

I went back to an evangelistic crusade in Rixfeld, constantly praying that Inge would get the assurance that we belonged to each other. Rixfeld was a tiny village with about three hundred inhabitants. Only one family had invited YFC to hold evangelistic meetings in their hamlet, and I was staying in the home of the mayor, Honorable Ritz. It was tough going. Once taking a prayer walk with sermon preparation through the surrounding forests, a farmer accosted me, saying, "You lazy dude! Taking nice walks throughout the day while we have to work hard. Nice going!" I was deeply hurt, but I did see his point of view. After all, the farmers were in action from daybreak to sundown working manually extremely hard, and I had the privilege to stroll through the woods meditating and praying.

"Ich bin dein!" Those were the words I had been waiting for. "I am yours." Those were her words when Inge called me early one day in Rixfeld.

I immediately sat down and wrote to my parents on June 22, 1956:

> Today I have to write you because something huge has occurred! You have no idea what happened and that's why I have to write you right away. I found my life partner! Bong!!! We will announce our engagement within two weeks. I can't wait for that day to arrive. But let me tell you first what transpired and who this girl is.

She is a German girl! *Da fällt Euch sicher ein Stein vom Herzen, nicht wahr?* (This, no doubt, will lift a load off your mind, right?) Two or three years ago I saw her for the first time in the American Chapel [in Frankfurt]. Then she came to Paris—to EBI—in 1954 and I met her briefly. Now in March she attended the Frankfurt YFC rally where I spoke. Bob Hopkins had already thought for quite a while that she would be the right girl for me...but she planned to move to the States on March 22. A couple of times I met her at Bob Hopkins' place and then I had to enter the hospital [in St. Georgen].

We then began to correspond with each other and I heard the news that she would not be able to go to the States because shadows on her lungs were detected [by the US Consulate]. Nothing serious, but the Americans are very stringent in such matters and will not accept a person so diagnosed.

I have prayed about her since I thought she might be the ideal girl for me. Her father is not a believer and many are praying for him. However, she has led her mother to Christ. They are very kind and noble people from East Prussia.

When I saw her at a [YFC] conference in Gießen, it "clicked"! We did not mention anything to each other, because I wanted to see unmistakably how the Lord would lead her. She still planned to go to America but the Lord kept closing the door more and more.

Following the Hiddenhausen crusade I visited her in Bensheim and at the *Heppenheim Schloss* I asked her whether we could not work together in serving the Lord. She asked for some time to think about it, because everything had happened so suddenly for her and she wanted to consider it in prayer before the Lord.

Yesterday she received news from the consulate that for the time being she cannot emigrate. She phoned me early this morning and said, "I am yours."

My parents responded promptly and expressed their approval. My mother was especially glad to learn that Inge would be a "good German housewife, sewed all her clothes, could cook well, and was willing to learn how to cook Chinese meals, such as delicious noodles and rice." She did! Their approval was extremely important to me, because I always had heeded their godly counsel. I loved them very much and had a desire to please them as much as I could.

Death rattle of the church in Germany or a new beginning?

The Youth for Christ organization is a para-church movement, and on occasion it was problematic and challenging for us to work alongside the State Church in Germany. In Rixfeld, for instance, I was not permitted to give an open invitation for people to receive Christ. Many Lutheran pastors see their pastoral duties simply as a profession and not as a spiritual exercise. They were trained to be custodians of a religion that for them happens to be Christian in Germany. Many of them had never committed their lives to Christ. One of them told me once, "Even today I still have to cope with the poisonous philosophies that were planted into my thinking during my university studies."

Of course, as so often in the past, even today there still is a remnant of strong and committed believers among the State Church clergy. In several cities those were not only strong supporters of our evangelistic endeavors, but also instruments of blessings and encouragement to me personally.

In many cities across Germany, evangelical believers could no longer worship in churches where the gospel was not preached. They formed churches of their own and developed into so-called Free Churches. A host of other denominational church bodies developed from this, such as Baptists, Brethren, Mennonites, Methodists, Free Evangelicals, Pentecostals, and others. Those were the ones we usually could work with very well.

On Sunday, August 12, 1956, I attended the closing meeting or rally of the *Deutsche Evangelische Kirchentag* (literally interpreted: Church Day) sponsored by the State Church, which in that year was held on the outskirts of Frankfurt. About 300,000 church people from across Germany attended. It was a huge performance but with little evangelical or biblical substance. No doubt, during the week's meetings some positive declarations were made, but only a few evangelicals were asked to express their biblical beliefs. The subject of evangelism was hardly addressed. One of my friends said it was the death rattle of the State Church. I was not so sure because I knew some strong believers in it.

The *Deutsche Evangelische Kirchentag* had its origin in 1949 (*evangelisch* in German means Protestant, not evangelical as it is often depicted). The purpose was to "draw together Protestant Christians in Germany in order to strengthen them in their faith, to prepare them for responsibility in their churches; to encourage them in witnessing to the world; and to have solidarity with those in the world-wide community of Christendom."

Since 1954 it was a biennial event; previously it took place once every year. Some say that history was made in Berlin in 2003 with the first-ever Ecumenical Kirchentag, jointly planned and organized by the Protestant and Roman Catholic churches in Germany. This alone made it more difficult for evangelicals to work with the State Church, even though it is clear that there are pastors within this group who are solid in preaching the Word of God as Martin Luther did hundreds of years ago.

However, as I said above, evangelism plays hardly a role or none at all in it. Liberal theology based on biblical criticism takes central stage. The website "Religious Tolerance" explains it this way: "Biblical criticism originated with anti-Christian writers who valued reason and logic over faith and revelation. Their goal was to discredit and ridicule the Bible and Christianity. Their analysis techniques were picked up by some liberal theologians and initially used to explain away and discount Biblical accounts of prophecy, miracles, personal demon infestation, etc."

And this is where we in YFC had to overcome the hurdles of rationalism everywhere we evangelized.

But in spite of it, God blessed our ministries. Hardly a day passed without people—young and old, male and female—committing their lives to Christ! For instance, after the crusade in Neustadt in the western part of Germany I wrote to my parents:

> As I already mentioned before, the evangelistic ministry in Neustadt was tough, yet blessed. Quite a number accepted the Lord as their personal Savior. Many of them were young people.

Often during this period I struggled with financial penuries. My salary was very low and my parents were unable to support me. However, my trust was in the Lord and I knew that He would never forsake me. I remember spending much time in prayer as I struggled financially. I was yearning for a closer walk with Christ and wanted to learn how to totally depend on Him. Also financially! Hadn't Christ promised, "Look at the birds of the air, for they neither sow nor reap nor gather into barns; yet your heavenly Father feeds them?"

I then decided to live by faith and would give twenty percent of my income to the Lord. I would forfeit my salary. Men like George Müller (1805-1898) and Hudson Taylor (1832-1905) had inspired me greatly in this regard. George emigrated from Germany to England and started an orphanage, exercising total faith in his God through prayer. He took care of thousands of orphans and would never let his needs be known publicly through aggressive fundraising techniques. Hudson had a similar conviction and would never go into debt leading his China ministry. From these men I learned to put my trust in the Lord alone and in His provision as He saw fit.

Herrman Schulte, President of *Jugend für Christus in Deutschland* at that time was surprised to learn that I would not accept any salary anymore. However, he was sympathetic to this idea, since he belonged to the Brethren Assembly in Wetzlar and was aware of the principles of the men described above. He consented.

"God's work done in God's way will never lack God's supplies," a quote by Hudson Taylor, became my conviction as well. I also resolved never to spend money I do not have. From then on these became principles I lived by. Inge and I passed them on to our children.

Of course, it is one thing setting your mind on those convictions and another to live out the consequences. Yet quickly the Lord honored my resolve. In a letter to my parents on August 22, 1956, I wrote:

> The Lord supplies wonderfully. A few days ago I did not have any money and so I knelt down and mentioned this to the Lord… I asked the Lord for DM 50. I got up and went to the office to find a letter for me with DM 20. The following morning I received another letter with $10 [DM 42] and with it I had a little more than DM 60. It was a marvelous answer of prayer. That's the way the Lord helps me through.

Years later while working in China I had a different and far greater—even an earth-shattering experience. Chen Enai, the elder of the church in Linchuan, the city where my mother started her ministry, had the vision to build a new church seating 1,800 people. With some substantial help from China Partner he finished it. When I visited him a few months later he invited me to dinner and asked, "Can you please help me some more?" "What's the matter?" I retorted. "Well, it came out to be more expensive than first assumed. We still need $114,000. Can you help?"

I then told him that we have the principle never to spend money we do not have. "I would like to help lift your burden, but we just do not have the money," I explained.

"How about helping with part of the money needed," he ventured. "$30,000 would tide us over. The contractor knows that we trust God and he is willing to wait." I wanted so badly to lift this financial burden off his shoulders, but I was going to stick to my principle.

"I cannot help because of the above-mentioned reason but I can do one thing," I expressed. "I will promise to pray for a miracle. That's all I can promise now."

Back in my hotel room I dropped on my knees and prayed for that brother with his burden. Throughout the following days as I traveled through China, I kept on unloading his burden that had become mine as well in prayer.

On my return flight from Shanghai to San Francisco I was upgraded to business class. I had stuffed my luggage away and was ready to sit down, when the flight attendant approached me saying, "Would you mind moving to another seat on the other side? A passenger would like to have your seat."

I really did not mind to change over; I had often done this on my travels. Once I even earned a bottle of wine for doing so. But on that day after having stored my stuff away I must have looked a little apprehensive. "Well, don't mind. Stay where you are," she said. I was relieved not to have to unscramble everything and sat down.

At that very moment a passenger came down the aisle and seeing me blurted out, "So good to see you, Dr. Bürklin, you are doing a wonderful job in China."

I did not know who he was. I had never seen him before. In a loud voice he began to tell me about the "great things you are doing in China." Everyone in the cabin could hear him.

"As a former colonel in the US Army I have started a ministry amongst the Chinese military using the same methods you have by doing everything openly and above board," he continued. I was a little embarrassed but when the doors were being shut, he proceeded to find his seat in the back of the plane.

"How wonderful to hear about your ministry in China," the Chinese lady sitting next to me said. "I am also a Christian."

For the next nine hours or so, all we talked about was God's work in China. Shaking my hand as we said good-bye to each other she whispered, "I would like to help you a little with your China ministry."

Four days later back home I received a letter from her with a check for $100,000!

That's how the Lord answers prayer in unusual ways. Sometimes He blesses in little ways and other times in big ways. I had not known that lady before, nor have I seen her since. But she came through at the right moment. That's our God, and He enjoys responding to our prayers.

"We had tears in our eyes, when we received the check," Elder Enai from Linchuan wrote me after he received our check.

Back to 1956. After our engagement in June, we agreed for Inge to attend the European Bible Institute in Paris. She started in the fall and I continued with my evangelistic crusades. Following a YFC conference in Frankfurt, I started a monthly rally in the *Cantate Saal* located next to the *Goethehaus* on the *Große Hirschgraben*. It was a brand new city auditorium seating 600 people. In a letter to my parents I wrote:

> The YFC rally was fantastic. Over 600 attended and two-thirds of them were young people. After the message more than twenty people, most of them young, came forward to accept Christ. The Lord answered our prayers. Financially He gave what was needed. Members of our committee were amazed and said, "we should have had more faith." And guess what else happened. Someone sent us another DM 200, which will take care of the expenses for the next rally. God is faithful; all we have to have is faith. Please pray for our next rally scheduled for January 5 next year.

Month by month we held those rallies and we concluded the season with a super rally in the *Stadthalle*. I had invited Anton Schulte, a former YFC evangelist and founder of *Neues Leben* to speak that night. Over 2,000 attended and many responded to the gospel. This took place just before our wedding.

Wedding bells

On June 15 the great day arrived. Wedding bells were ringing.

Inge had returned from her studies at the European Bible Institute in Paris, and I just had directed the largest YFC rally in Frankfurt. We were ready to tie the knot.

It was a hot summer day. Some of the candles in the church bent delicately. The church where Inge had found the Lord was decked out and ready. As I stood at the altar seeing my sweetheart covered by a veil and dressed in a beautiful white wedding dress being led by her father down the aisle towards me, my heart raced. I almost buckled; was it the heat or was it love gone wild? Whatever it was, it felt fantastic but I know it was the latter.

Reverend John Parschauer, a missionary from Canada, officiated; Bob Hopkins and Hans Martin Wilhelm were my best men, and my sister Gisela and a Bible school friend of Inge, Wendy Hill, were her attendants. Following an unexpected and impromptu reception in downtown Frankfurt that some of our friends had arranged, we were ready to jump into the red Audi I had rented the day before. Her parents and mine were thrilled to see such a happy couple. We were looking forward to our honeymoon. But we did not know where to go. It all depended on the money we would receive as wedding presents. Our desire was to spend it in Italy, but if the finances would not be sufficient for that, the second choice would be Holland.

We drove off toward Bad Homburg counting the money as we traveled that friends had given us as wedding gifts. Italy won out! We checked into the most prominent and ritzy *Ritters Park Hotel* in Bad Homburg. Our room was still occupied by a Pan American captain. We settled down in the gorgeous dining room for a delicious dinner, holding hands with a sparkle in our eyes.

Finally we were alone. Both of us were thrilled to have waited for this moment, and that with great anticipation. We were not only thrilled that very night, but all the fifty-plus years to come. Later we often said to each other, "We were so grateful that we had shown the will power and commitment to stay sexually pure during our dating period and also before, having had other parties we dated. This is so satisfying to know."

Some may ask: *Why were you so extreme in following through with your commitment? You were engaged and knew that eventually you would be 'one flesh' anyway. Why wait?*

Well, the Bible is very clear about fornication (1 Cor. 6:18, among many other passages). Scripture prohibits fornication. Obedience to God's Word requires that sex be reserved for one's spouse. If both have waited until their wedding night, the intimacy begins with a solid foundation. If one gives in to moral temptation before marriage, what's to stop him or her from giving in to moral temptation once married? Sex outside of marriage also damages the relationship between the persons involved. Trust is the main issue here. If two people do not cherish sex enough to wait for a marriage commitment, how can they trust one another with fidelity later on?

Both of us entered holy matrimony as virgins. And both of us now know what difference it will make in marriage and to know without a shadow of doubt that abstention pays. The longer we were married, the stronger this conviction became. God honors those who live by His Word.

Today much is being said on this issue. It reaches even further—into the gay controversy. Here again I stand by the teachings of the Bible. I am for the ideal that only a man and a woman should be united in holy matrimony. I am against gay relationships and same-sex marriages. Let me give several reasons. First, the Bible condemns homosexuality (Romans 1:24-27). Secondly, gay relationships are abnormal based upon the unique physiology between man and woman. Thirdly, God's command to "multiply and fill the earth" (Genesis 1:28) can only be achieved when a man and a woman enjoy the ecstasy of sexual intimacy. This is not possible with homosexual performance; a same-sex couple cannot produce offspring. And fourthly, such intimacy outside of wedlock is fornication and is denounced in Scripture.

The next morning we were off to Italy. Traveling south through the Black Forest we detected a street sign "*Bürklin Strasse*" in Offenburg. We couldn't believe our eyes but thanked the city for honoring our wedding in such a conspicuous way. The second night we stayed in Küssnacht, the town Schiller made famous with his play *Wilhelm Tell*. I quoted the line we had memorized in high school, "*Durch diese hohle Gasse muss er kommen, es führt kein andrer Weg nach Küssnacht.*"

Driving along the Mediterranean coast we spotted a village that attracted us. We stayed in Deiva Marina for two weeks of heavenly ecstasy. The weather was gorgeous, the food was good, and the intimacy was exhilarating. Often we prayed that the Lord would bless and make us a blessing to others. Both of us were anxious to serve the Lord no matter the cost. We had to learn this in a hard way in the weeks to come.

My father once quoted an adage that I never forgot, "*In jeder großen Freudigkeit auch ein Tropfen Bitterkeit.*" In English: "In every great joyfulness, there also is a drop of bitterness." We also experienced this one day during our time of enjoyment. We had had our first argument. Nothing earth-shattering; just a minor disagreement! This, of course, is not unusual, but we did not expect it during a time where everything was so rosy and cozy. Reality had settled in. I was devastated. I walked out on the balcony confounded, wrestling with this actuality. Inge followed me and asked, "What's wrong, darling?" I answered, "You are too strong for me."

At this moment I came to the realization that we were two individuals with different personalities. We loved each other deeply, but we had to learn how to cope with our different dispositions. *The sooner we learn this, the pleasanter it will be*, I thought.

We were off to a challenging life. Through later times of problems, struggles, and tears—we made it. We always succeeded to meet at the foot of the cross. Jesus Christ, our Savior and Lord whom we followed, made it possible. The longer we lived together, the greater our love for one another flourished in spite of many disagreements we had.

Back from our honeymoon we settled into our new home—a one-and-a-half room apartment one of our friends offered us for a minimum cost. Our landlord was a young captain with the German airline *Lufthansa* and was single. He also played the Hammond organ at our Frankfurt YFC rallies. It was located in

Sachsenhausen across the river Main running through Frankfurt. The buildings were uniquely built, and the residents named it *Zickzackhausen*. We were happy to settle down.

However, there was one problem—in fact a huge problem. When we arrived home, we were broke. The rent for the first month was due and we had only a few cans of food in the cupboard, but no money. Nevertheless, we had many gifts that our friends had deposited in our apartment while we were on our honeymoon. We unwrapped them one by one and were about to chuck all the wrapping papers into the garbage dumpster when Inge exclaimed, "Stop, there is an unopened envelope." Opening it we retrieved a US 50-dollar bill, a fortune for us at that time! This exchanged into DM 210, a one-month salary I used to get from *Jugend für Christus* before having opted to live by faith. Again the Lord took care of us in a remarkable way.

But then the daily grind began. I was off holding evangelistic meetings while my sweetheart had to cope with running our home. I was staying with families who housed and fed me; she had to get by with whatever we had. And that was not much; to the contrary, often there was nothing left.

Once back at home, I found out what it is like to make do without money. Inge exposed in her diary what really went on:

> Werner had to return old bottles to have enough money to buy a street car ticket to get to the office. How he can get back home, he does not know! And then he is back. Did he walk the long way home? Did someone drop him off? No, he came by street car! God had answered prayer. The IRS returned some tax money—DM 16 [about US $3.80] using our old address Oederweg 74 [YFC office]. Praise the Lord. Now we can buy a few items.

However, those were also exciting days. Yes, many challenges, but wonderful breakthroughs with the help of our Lord.

One day a car drove up and out stepped a committee member of our YFC rally ministry. His father owned a noodle factory on the outskirts of Frankfurt. Theo Frank, a dark-haired and handsome young man, greeted us warmheartedly, holding a bulky carton under his arm. "I brought something for you to eat," he declared. We could not believe our eyes! We had nothing left and here he came with packages of noodles under his arm. For the next few days all we ate were noodles with red cabbage. Again the Lord had provided just in time.

Together we held an evangelistic crusade in Waldshut on the border with Switzerland. Inge was in charge of afternoon children's meetings, and I preached in the evenings. During the week I suggested an all-night prayer meeting. The pastor agreed and we had a great encounter with our Lord. My experience in holding such meetings always has been that the first couple of hours, I find it to be strenuous. However, the more time is spent in prayer, the more relaxed and blessed it becomes. God then starts pouring out His blessings. And this is what we experienced. The meetings were significantly blessed, people found the Lord, and we rejoiced.

Soon after that crusade, we traveled to Copenhagen, Denmark, to participate in the World Congress of Youth for Christ International. I had the privilege to be one of the main speakers, and after my message many came forward to accept the Lord. David Barnes, my former professor at EBI, observed the proceedings from the balcony and later said to me, "This was one of the best presentations of the gospel I heard all week." Such words, spoken by a mentor, were for a young guy starting out on an evangelistic career enormously encouraging and reassuring. I thanked the Lord, and both Inge and I were overwhelmed. God had answered our prayers.

Inge and I passed out tracts on the streets and ran into a well-dressed young businessman. When he read what we passed out he said, "I am tired of life. I am ready to leave this life. Suicide is the only way out." We were stunned. Never before had we heard anyone making such a statement. We counseled with him. It was apparent that in his innermost being he was searching for understanding and love, yet he was not willing to turn his life over to God. Tragically, many such people are struggling but are not willing to surrender to a loving and forgiving God. So we had to let him go his way.

After a blessed and successful congress, we returned to Frankfurt to face some more challenging days. Coming from a solid and financially secure background, Inge had a hard time to deal with the uncertainties of life. She felt like a failure when she, due to lack of funds, was not able to put ample food on the table. Often I had to comfort her. Often we went on our knees in prayer, and I saw tears streaming down her face. But she always recovered and was willing to battle on. Just to give a little insight how she overcame her mêlées and spiritual struggles, hear some of her words. Several months into our marriage she wrote the following into her diary:

[Before he leaves] Werner and I pray together for the last time—gone for two long weeks! The Lord has to answer. Then the farewell has come. Again I have an infinitely heavy heart.

Gisela [her sister-in-law] will leave tomorrow morning. And then I will be alone without a dime and with very little to eat. Shame on you, Inge! How fainthearted and little of faith you are! Don't you put your trust in the promises of God? Did the Lord ever leave you? No, but the "life of faith" has to be learned! No trial, when offered, is easy to bear; the apostle Paul even said this. And yet, how can the Lord send deliverance when we are so fainthearted?

Yet, hot tears flow in bed this evening—my darling is so far away. I feel like I am being smothered.

A day later she wrote this:

Gisela has left. Now I am alone with the Lord. Another hard day lies before me! When I got up I found DM 2 which Gisela left behind...Seldom have I been fortified and encouraged so much by such a small amount and this has filled me with prodigious thanks...The money will do for milk, a quarter pound of butter, one roll, and one stamp for a letter to my darling.

I am overwhelmed and weep for happiness and shame. My reaction is typically feminine! Women always tend to cry! Thank you, Lord, for proof of your love!

However, in the evening I am again gripped by immeasurable longing. I find rest in prayer.

Two days later:

During my "quiet time" God gave me a marvelous promise found in Exodus 14:13-14. "Stand firm and you will see the deliverance the Lord will bring you today." In my prayer I firmly claim this promise. Soon after, I receive a letter which realizes this promise: Werner, my darling, had been given DM 10 and enclosed it in his ardently awaited letter. The Lord keeps His promises. The workings of the Lord are enormous.

She also recalls another of God's provisions. Being in the early months of pregnancy, while I was often gone, she felt she was not getting enough vitamins through nutritious food. She was concerned. One day a man delivered a food package mainly with fruit and vegetables from a nearby supermarket, which were just coming to Germany. Shocked, she refused to accept, knowing she had no money to pay. "No, no," the man said. "It is all paid for." From then until our baby was born, the packages arrived every week. An unknown donor and a God who provided!

During the next few months I was heavily involved in evangelistic crusades all over Germany. To me they were exhilarating; this is what I had hoped and prayed for. Now they had become reality. On May 22, 1958, I wrote to my parents from Eickhorst in northern Germany:

The Lord is also blessing here. Evening after evening the tent is full. We are expecting even greater things from Him. Please pray for us, especially for the YFC rally in the Frankfurt *Kongresshalle*, scheduled for June 14.

In the same letter I expressed my great joy about the birth of our first-born, Erik. He was born on May 3, barely three weeks before my crusade in Eickhorst started. On the final night we had to redeploy to the soccer field; the tent was not able to accommodate the ever-increasing crowds.

> Yes, we are proud of our *Schatz* (treasure)! Above all, we are so thankful to the Lord, who has entrusted to us such a precious child. And we want to raise him in such a way that he will learn to love the Savior early in life. He is such a *Prachtkerl* (great kid) and Inge such a loving and good mother. I am likewise grateful to the Lord for having given me such a magnificent and lovely gal. Please pray much for her to remain strong; it is not easy for her to do without me at this time.

Wim Malgo, a Dutch evangelist living in Switzerland, spoke at the YFC rally in Frankfurt on June 14, one day prior to our first wedding anniversary. Again the hall overflowed with more than 2,000 people, and over fifty decisions for Christ were recorded that night. Looking back, it was so rewarding for me to have started and directed the monthly rallies and to have witnessed thousands of young people attend and hundreds of them find the Savior. God had answered my prayers; and the burden I have had ever since my time in California was repositioned into reality.

Just one example of what was accomplished with those exciting youth rallies. Worfelden is a tiny town south of Frankfurt. Elmar Rühl was a teenager in a small church who along with a group of other teens attended those rallies. Their pastor said, "This is what our young people need. Let them go and attend." One by one accepted Christ, and many of them are now active in the Lord's work somewhere in the world. Elmar is now working at the head office of *Jugend für Christus in Deutschland*. His brother-in-law, Horst Bausch, became a successful farmer in Canada and is a financial contributor to mission organizations in different parts of the world. Another convert is a medical doctor in Mörfelden, and her sister became a missionary in Laos. God had vitally used those rallies in thousands of lives over the many years in which we were involved.

CHAPTER 8

A NEW CHALLENGE IN "GOD'S COUNTRY"

O N JUNE 16 I relinquished my leadership to pursue a new goal the Lord had laid on my heart. On that day, members for a new local YFC committee were put forth and elected. I handed the directorship over to a competent young man, who had found Christ in Berlin. Olaf Holznagel had joined the YFC staff and now was ready for such a demanding task. He did a terrific job.

Inge and I with our newly born son went to the US Consulate and applied for a student visa. I felt the need for more academic training. The best place to get it was in the United States.

The day before we departed, the doorbell rang and a young handsome fellow entered. "I bring greetings from my mother," he said. "She and my sister Miriam met you at the YFC World Congress in Copenhagen. She told me that if I would ever get to Frankfurt I must go see you," he continued. He was John Huffman, a nineteen-year-old teenager, later to become the outstanding senior pastor of St. Andrews Presbyterian Church in Newport Beach, California. This was the beginning of a long-standing friendship. Fifty-two years later, he wrote me this letter:

What a joy it was to be present with you for the wonderful 80th birthday party planned for you by your loving family! When Erik many months ago invited me to attend, I was not aware he was expecting me to speak. I immediately responded "yes" to attending in honor of you. I would not have missed this event for anything. And I was so thrilled to be one of the few non-family members asked to speak!

I am sitting here in a hotel on Key Biscayne preparing to leave on a one week preaching ministry to Cuba in just a few hours. I want to take this opportunity to say what a joy it has been to be your friend since we met that summer night of 1958 in your Frankfurt apartment! How shocked I was to discover you were leaving for Winona Lake the next morning and I would be there the next night. Out of all the places in the world, what chance? And what if I had disregarded my mother's request to look you up or had arrived in Frankfurt one day later? Would we have ever met? Fortunately, God's timing is best!

Space does not allow me to recount the many joyful ways we have shared our friendship. But let me simply list a few:

Meeting in Frankfurt; working in the travel business together; traveling around the world together the summer of 1960; sharing times at my three churches (Key Biscayne, Pittsburgh, Newport Beach); having you and your children in and out of our various homes; working with you on "Generation '79" in Brazil; doing the Billy Graham Europe staff retreat on

Lake Zürich in the early '80s; participating in Amsterdam '83 & '86; watching your vision for China take wings in China Partner; helping Heiko get that Graham scholarship to Gordon-Conwell; joining you in the teaching team in 1995; watching your children grow up, marry and start families so well; watching Heiko in Lake Wales, Germany, and now North Carolina ministry; observing Erik fill your big shoes with a future oriented vision for China ministry; having frequent visits and conversations through the years; being honored by your presence at my farewell from St. Andrew's; and most of all just having a good friendship!!! Anne and I love you and Inge so much!

As I said at your party, you are a "global evangelist," a "great family man," and a "wonderful friend."

Please note that I have not referred to your "retirement" but only birthday. You will never truly retire from these three important functions and many more.

God bless you my friend! Perhaps we will both be around for your 90th and my 80th ten years from now. Here's to many more great times together!

The *SS Maasdam's* foghorn was blasting deafeningly as we were leaving the harbor of Le Havre on August 22, 1958. The day before, our family had boarded this Dutch vessel in Rotterdam, Holland. My sister Gisela and her Dutch husband, Bill, had come aboard to say farewell, but now we were on our way to Southampton to pick up more passengers. I was the second of the Bürklin family to move to the United States for further studies. My brother Friedel had gone earlier to study at the same college and then at Grace Theological Seminary.

Two months before, I had performed the wedding ceremony for my sister in Antwerp. She and Bill were YFC workers in Belgium. Belgium is one of the most hardened countries in Europe towards the gospel. In her memoir *Joy in Living* she gives a vivid description how the Catholic hierarchy was dead set against Protestants who were involved in missionary and evangelistic activities. A few years later she followed in our footsteps to receive further training in the US.

But now it was our time to go. It was a long ten-day voyage to Montreal, Canada. Our son was the youngest passenger on board—just four months old. He, of course, was the center of attention whenever we carried him around. And we were proud parents!

"Joyce will meet you at the pier," was the radiogram we received on board between Quebec and Montreal. And there she was, Joyce, whom we had never met before. Of course, it took quite an effort to spot her amidst the hundreds of people at the landing-stage. My brother had met her at Grace College and had married her soon after on June 8, 1957, one week prior to our wedding. As an alien student he was not allowed to enter Canada without a visa, but to finally meet him again on the border a few hours later was a joyous occasion indeed.

He had arranged an apartment for us in the basement of some very kind Christians. But it was damp. However, we moved in. Then I remembered John Huffman who had urged us to look him up in Winona Lake. He had said his parents have a home on the lake front. Walking along the lake, I passed a huge and lovely mansion and lo and behold the sign on the mail box stated the name I was looking for: Huffman.

I rang the bell, and out stepped an elderly gentleman. "Sorry for disturbing, I am looking for John Huffman," I said. "John Huffman is my brother, but he lives on the other side of the lake," he answered, "but come in to see if I can help you."

And what a tremendous help he was! "Why don't you come and live in our house," he asked. I couldn't believe my ears! The house was huge with six bedrooms and large living and dining rooms with a big round oak dining table. Right on the lake. He owned a couple of radio stations and was well off. He also was a committed Christian. "You know," he continued, "we only come here for a few weeks in the summer time. We need someone to take care of it the rest of the year."

This was a fantastic proposition for us. We of course had some hesitancy because of the other Christian couple who had been glad to have found in us someone to rent their basement apartment. However, after thinking everything through and praying about it, we accepted this marvelous offer. And we never regretted it. We only had to pay $65 per month for rent, and this included all utilities. During the summer months we did not have to pay anything! Inge took care of the rooms that were rented out to summer guests. What a deal! That's where we resided the two years while going to college.

To be back in school as a 27-year-old was not so easy, yet invigorating and refreshing. Besides that, I also had to earn money; our family was growing and the tuition took its toll. The first few weeks I worked in a factory in a nearby town, manufacturing movie screens. I worked from 4 p.m. to midnight, getting back at home at 12:30 a.m. Then my home studies began. After a few hours of sleep I was off to my 7:30 a.m. classes. It was rough going. But nothing like John Calvin had experienced. The rigors of his student life were far more taxing: [T.H.L. Packer, *John Calvin* (Herts, England: Lion Publishing plc, 1975), 9-10.]

> Up at four o'clock for the morning office, followed by a lecture until six, when mass was said. After mass came breakfast, and then, from eight until ten, the *grande classe* with a discussion for the ensuing hour. Elven o'clock brought dinner, which was accompanited by readings from the Bible or the life of a saint and followed by prayers and college notices. At twelve the students were questioned about their morning's work, but from one to two as a rest period with a public reading. Here our sources skip an hour, and it may be that the students were left free until afternoon class claimed them from three until five. Now vespers were said, and after vespers a discussion on the afternoon class took place. Between supper, with its attendant readings, and bed-time at eight in winter or nine in summer there was time for further interrogation and for chapel.

It was one of the most boring jobs I have ever held. With a spray gun in hand, I squirted black paint onto the edges of movie screens. This I had to do hour after hour—just pushing the spray gun back and forth—back and forth and that hour after hour, while a machine monotonously forwarded screen after screen. First I thought by doing this I could use the occasion for studies. What a delusion! After a few minutes, my brain went blank. All I saw were those stupid movie screens. Eventually I recited *Stumpfsinn, Stumpfsinn, oh du mein Vergnügen; Stumpfsinn, Stumpfsinn, oh du meine Lust!* (Dullness, dullness, oh, what a delight; dullness, dullness, oh, what an enjoyment.)

But I made money; not much, but enough to pay our bills. Then I met John Huffman, Sr., who had his summer home in Winona Lake, but whose main residence was in Wheaton, Illinois. He was the father of young John Huffman, my acquaintance from Frankfurt. After a few weeks working in the factory, he called me up and asked, "Would you be interested to work in my travel agency?"

What an offer! First, the office was within walking distance from where we lived; secondly, I could work in the afternoons; and thirdly, I would get away from the stupefying job I held and detested. Furthermore, when business was slow I could hit the books while on the job. Later on, Inge joined me filling the hours when I had to be in college. It was a "win-win" situation.

On November 11, 1958, we wrote our parents:

Now we have big news. The end of March Erik will have a sister! Well, we hope that it will be a girl. We are thrilled. Our boy has brought so much joy into our home and perhaps our second child will do the same. Inge is doing fine, in fact much better than awaiting Erik…The next semester we will have to adapt, but we have no fears; the Lord will help us.

Off and on I preached on the weekends. A German Lutheran church invited me to Milwaukee, Wisconsin, some 300 miles away; one service was in English and the other in German. The church leadership asked me to commute every weekend and to become their pastor. It was tempting, however, due to the distance we declined.

The weather was something else. The winter broke forth with fierce winds and deep snow. Living right on the edge of the lake made it even worse. The lake froze over and to the delight of teenagers; some of them raced their cars across the ice. Sometimes we had to slog through snowstorms. Often Inge had to push the baby carriage through deep snow drifts to deliver Erik to a babysitter when she had to stand in for me at the travel agency. At that time we did not have a car. But we made it.

Studies went well. The discipline to combine the studies with work and family was valuable for my future.

On April 28, 1959, our second son was born in Goshen, Indiana. "What name do you want to give him?" the nurse asked. "Heiko," Inge answered. "Heiko," the nurse exclaimed, "is that Japanese?" Well, it's true, Heiko is an unusual name, even in Germany, but we liked that Nordic forename. My father came up with an interesting explanation as he tried to rationalize or explain our choice. During that time the German president was Heinrich Lübke and the chancellor Konrad Adenauer. "Now I understand," he said, "you just combined the first part of their given names: Hei(nrich) and Ko(nrad). Heiko. Excellent idea!

Now with two kids it was tough to subsist. There were times when we wondered whether we would make it. In fact, one morning heading off to college, Inge told me she had nothing to feed our baby with. We prayed together. "God will take care of us," I said. It sounded flippant, but I meant it.

She told me later that after I had left, she placed our six-month-old baby on the couch, knelt, and cried out to God, "Lord, you promised to take care of the lilies of the field and the birds in the sky. Please take care of my baby now. I can't." A few minutes later we received $20 in the mail from a friend who had never sent a gift before and none thereafter. Immediately she went to the store to buy food for our baby and some for us. God again proved true to His promises.

During my quiet time once, the Lord had spoken to me through a Bible verse. On that spring morning in September 1958, just after having arrived in Winona Lake, God encouraged me with Psalm 81:10 "I am the LORD thy God, which brought you out of the land of Egypt: open your mouth wide, and I will fill it."

Egypt for me at that time was Germany. Now a new day had opened up before us and the Lord promised me that He would fill our mouths when we were willing to open them. And that is exactly what we experienced. It was tough at times, but faithfully doing what He had led us to do, He would stand with us. Again and again He proved Himself to be true to His promise.

During the next winter, we drove with our old Buick to attend YFC's Teen Congress in Washington, DC. It was an arduous trip with extremely cold weather. Our two little boys came along. We did not have much time traveling to and from Washington so we stopped only for emergencies. "How do we warm the bottle for our baby Heiko?" Inge asked. "No problem," I said. Stopping the car on the roadside, I opened the hood, placed the bottle securely next to the hot motor, and drove on. In a few short minutes the bottle was ready to be served.

Thousands of teenagers, in fact, about 10,000 of them, converged on America's capital city. Billy Graham was the keynote speaker. We met his daughter Gigi, a fourteen-year-old at that time and later became a close friend. A few years later Inge and I were invited to her wedding held at a romantic looking chapel in Montreux, Switzerland. She was only seventeen years old when she said yes to Stephan Tchividjian. In fact, our son Stephan later lived in their home as a high school senior, and she with her husband became his surrogate parents.

Stephan T. was the son of one of the richest men in Switzerland, I was told. He found the Lord reading the book *Peace with God*. With all of his wealth, he had been a miserable man. Billy Graham was holding a crusade in Lausanne, Switzerland. A maid of Tchividjian had pity on him. She was a believer. "Why don't you read this book, I just received it this morning," she asked him, "The author is a world-renowned evangelist." He did and was converted to Christ. A few weeks later, he entered the bedroom of his son Stephan. Getting off from his knees, his son said, "Dad, what you did earlier, I just did now."

Later when I was back in Germany as a youth evangelist with YFC, we met for the first time. One day I received a call from the YFCI's overseas director, Sam Wolgemuth. "Could you go to Switzerland and meet with a teenager who has contacted us for some help? He lives near Lausanne."

As I stepped off the train in Lausanne, young Stephan Tchividjian met me. He ushered me into his white Mercedes. *First time I am riding in a rich man's car,* I mused. In Montreux the iron gates to a huge estate opened automatically. Another thing I had not seen before. He introduced me to his father, a kindly looking man. He had migrated to Switzerland from Armenia in the wake of the Armenian Genocide initiated by the Ottoman Empire in 1915. Thousands had been massacred by the Turks. A huge ceiling-to-floor window opened on a spectacular view across Lake Geneva. *No doubt, this surely must be a rich man,* I thought. That evening I spoke at a small church they attended and Stephan interpreted for me. After the service they drove me to the Park Hotel, the ritziest hotel in Montreux.

There is no way I can pay for this; I panicked as I entered my room. The lobby was enormous but the exquisiteness of the room

134

was breathtaking—at least for me as a budding poor evangelist. Then I was reminded of the envelope Mr. Tchividjian had given me while we chatted in his home earlier in the afternoon. Opening it, I found one single 1,000 Swiss Franc banknote. I was stunned. I had never seen so much money in one single banknote. This represented four months of salary I used to receive before I started to live "by faith." I fell on my knees and thanked the Lord for His wonderful provision.

The final months in Winona Lake went by quickly. However, the money we made would not enable us to travel back to Germany. So I was looking for another job. Someone suggested a job as a salesman. For that, however, I needed a car. So far we managed without one. Now it was obvious that we had to get a car. A college friend and a wizard on cars took us to a used car lot and finally we found one—a dark blue Buick, year 1950.

First I tried my luck selling encyclopedias. No one in the rural area was interested in such sophisticated literature. *What do you need that for?* people thought. It was tough going, but wow, I finally sold one set! That's it.

"Why don't you help me sell china," a fellow student asked me. "It is good German-made porcelain," he said. This intrigued me, being proud of my German heritage, so I ventured into it. Inge set up appointments during the day and I went out in the evenings. At first I did not know anything about porcelain, yet seeing what kind the families I visited had, convinced me how vastly superior my product was. *Rosenthal* is the most famous brand in Germany, and this company sold their merchandise in the US under the name "Stonegate." Once I was convinced of my product, I sold like crazy. It helped me to pay for our return trip to Germany.

Years later my good friend Larry Rybka told me that he also had sold "Stonegate" while going to college. He was known as the best salesman of that company. Both of us did very well.

Something better yet! "As employees of a travel agency," our boss told us when we inquired about travel opportunities, "you only have to pay twenty-five percent of the tickets' value." So Inge and the two boys were given first class tickets by *Lufthansa,* the German airline, back to Frankfurt. Imagine—first class tickets!

I had always wanted to make a trip around the world. This was my chance. After saying good-bye to my loved ones at the airport in Chicago, I set out for California, spending some time with my benefactors Len and Marilyn Leonard. Then on to Hawaii, where in those days I was still greeted with garlands put around my neck. John Huffman, Jr., the now twenty-year-old who had visited us the day before we left for the US, joined me in Tokyo. His father had asked me to accompany him. "At his age he needs a chaperon," he said. It was a fun trip. Both of us were young and full of mischief. When flights were taking off late, we demanded steak dinners. In a Manila hotel we were accosted by a prostitute. She called our room and John picked up the phone. "What?" he exclaimed, "Why don't you talk to my evangelist friend!" Handing me the phone, I did not know what she wanted. "My services come with the room," she responded. Disgusted, I slammed the phone back on the receiver.

From there we traveled to Hong Kong, Bangkok, New Delhi, and Benares and visited the Taj Mahal in Agra. This mausoleum is one of the most beautiful buildings in the world. It was built by the Maghal Emperor Shah Jahan in memory of his third wife. 20,000 workers labored from 1632-53 AD and used 1,000 elephants to transport materials to the site. Every person should try to see this gorgeous structure. It is a must-see!

Benares, also known as Varanasi, was a different story. Hundreds of Indian pilgrims converge on the river bank of the Ganges every day. Then they immerse themselves in the polluted river believing their sins will be washed away. It is the holiest place in the world for Hinduism and the center of the Earth in Hindu cosmology. I watched them for quite a while, feeling sorry for those pitiful souls with no hope, yet rejoicing in the fact that we as Christians don't have to travel anywhere to have our sins washed away. Believing in Christ is the answer. Our sins are forgiven and our hope is spending eternity with our loving Heavenly Father, no matter where we reside!

Then I flew on to Teheran, Baghdad, Beirut, Jerusalem, Cairo, Ankara, Rome, and finally Frankfurt.

In Jerusalem I took time out to travel to the Dead Sea. What a remarkable yet odd experience to walk into the lake; relax in the water by simply lying or even sitting in it without going under. The heavy salt content makes that possible.

More exhilarating was the visit to the tomb of Jesus. I stood in the tranquil garden in front of the grave and was overcome with reverence realizing that from this grave our Lord arose. No other religious leader throughout history has experienced such a feat. He truly is the living Lord. I was overcome with emotion; stood, prayed, and worshiped Him with a grateful heart. In a letter to my parents on July 15 I expressed my overwhelmed and worshipful sentiment: "This morning I stood at the grave where Jesus was buried 2,000 years ago. Hallelujah, He arose from the dead! We do not have a dead Savior."

Cairo was another of my highlight experiences. Here in Egypt Jesus had spent part of his childhood.

I stayed at the famous, historic, and luxurious Shepheard Hotel without cost due to my status as a travel agent. Few hotels in the world can claim such rich history. Built in 1841, it became Cairo's leading hotel and one of the most celebrated in the world between the middle of the nineteenth century and 1952, when a devastating Cairo fire demolished it. As its website quotes, "It was famed for its grandeur and opulence and where the day's international aristocracy and celebrity elites sipped tea on the terrace, to see and to be seen." It was rebuilt in 1957 overlooking the Nile River, and I enjoyed every moment of my stay.

I visited the world-renowned pyramids in Giza on the outskirts of this metropolis. It is the only one of the Seven Wonders of the Ancient World still in existence.

In Cairo you have the very rich and the very poor, as in so many places in the world. But what shocked me most was the garbage city I visited. I had never seen anything like it, not even in China.

During the night hundreds of garbage collectors roam through the city collecting garbage. Some of them carry what they find on their back, others have little carts drawn by ponies, and still others are more sophisticated with their little motor vehicles. But all of them finally end up in the garbage city. Some of the structures—more like huts—are actually built on top of garbage that cannot be used. Imagine the stench! The collectors go through the garbage carefully picking out things that are still useable and sellable. With this they make their living.

For years, no one cared for them. In fact, the people in the garbage city themselves do not want anyone from the outside see where and how they live. But these are people created in the image of God and have the right to be reached and helped.

A Presbyterian pastor in Cairo eventually was challenged to do something about it. He won the confidence of a few collectors. Step by step he introduced the gospel in that "suburb" of Cairo. I first was apprehensive, and then thrilled, to be taken to a small church in the middle of the garbage city. The cleanliness and neatness was something to behold! One of the elders proudly showed me around. I was impressed. No wonder, people were finding the Lord and the little church community is growing! The pastor is doing a great work in the hearts of many Egyptians.

It was wonderful to finally get back to Frankfurt. I had been gone for some two months. The two little boys were adorable and Inge was glad that I had returned. It was like a honeymoon all over again!

In Frankfurt I took leadership once more of the monthly German YFC rally. We invited well known evangelists to preach, such as Werner Heukelbach. He was famous among Christians all across Germany. I had heard about him already as a teenager in China. He produced tracts and mailed them to anyone who was willing to pass them out. He sent them free of charge and depended only on freewill donations. My father was very fond of him and used his tracts liberally.

Out of the blue I received a letter from an unknown fellow in Spain. George Verwer had moved there as a graduate of the Moody Bible Institute after having done some missionary work in Mexico. He was the founder of Operation Mobilization, I learned later. He had heard about our successful Frankfurt YFC rally and wanted to preach. I invited him but was not in town when he spoke. When I returned, I was told that he had made a booboo. He had made some disparaging remarks about YFC in the USA. I was miffed thinking, *why would he do that as my guest?* He could have told me personally about his concerns, but not while preaching publicly.

Later he sent teams to Germany using old jalopies that someone had fixed up. On numerous occasions our YFC office received SOS calls from his coworkers when their cars broke down. Once I received a phone call at 3 o'clock in the morning from someone who was stuck on the Autobahn near Frankfurt. "Can you come and pick us up," was the request.

It even got worse. We wanted to help his ministry when asked. We offered a team of his to utilize an apartment YFC rented in Frankfurt. "What's going on?" neighbors phoned, "Water is leaking through the ceiling." My staff ran over and found no one in the apartment, however everything in a mess. The kitchen sink was full of dirty dishes while water was flowing over the sink. They had left to "serve the Lord" and didn't think it to be imperative to first clean the mess they had left behind.

We even had offered OM to use our office to put in some retractable beds for their crew. I was stunned to find some of the wallpapers torn off and things left in disrepair while they were out on the streets ministering to people.

Over the years we became good friends. George and I developed a warm relationship, but in the beginning of his ministry he had to learn how to do things properly. They have, and now it is a fine organization and hundreds of his staff are doing an exceptional work around the world.

CHAPTER 9

CRUSADE AT THE BERLIN WALL

AFTER MY GRADUATION we had accepted an invitation by Canadian evangelist Leo Janz to join him as his associate evangelist. For years he had ministered with his team with great success in German-speaking Europe. Thousands of people flocked to their crusades. He needed an associate evangelist to take over the preaching in case of illness. So he asked me to join his team.

"This is a great loss to us," the president of Youth for Christ International, Sam Wolgemuth, told us when we shared the news of our decision with him. But I felt led by the Lord to try something different. My first assignment was to be the MC (Master of Ceremony) at a crusade he held in the *Hallenstadion* in Zürich, Switzerland. Already there I noticed that this relationship would not last too long. The crusade was a great success. The final meeting was held in the soccer stadium with Billy Graham preaching. However, those meetings did not give me an inner satisfaction. Furthermore, Leo never got sick!

We spent one year of a blessed ministry with the Janz team but then were called by *Jugend für Christus in Deutschland* (JFCD), to become president of this youth ministry. We accepted wholeheartedly.

And years of blessings and enormous challenges commenced!

Challenges, yes. For one, *Jugend für Christus in Deutschland* was in debt—in deep and momentous debt! I will never forget how I felt burdened because saddled with a debt of over DM 100,000. This was a lot of money to me. It was far more than YFC's yearly budget. As comparison and as an example, the yearly salary for a JFC evangelist at that time was DM 3,000. It would take more than thirty years for one evangelist to soak up DM 100,000! To me such a staggering amount was almost unthinkable and beyond belief. But I had to face it. When I was voted in, all past board members resigned. They were glad to have been set free of all their former and heavy responsibilities.

Who would be willing to shoulder such a burden and responsibility with me as the new president, I pondered. I needed help from some competent and spiritual people.

I turned to three men of my age who I had gotten to know in JFC ministry. Two of them resided in Rüsselsheim, Max Bernard Kneusels and Albrecht Hofmann. Max was a leading engineer and a department head in the Opel motorcar company, a subsidiary of General Motors. Albrecht was also a key employee of the same company. The third was Theo Frank, a co-owner of a noodle factory in Frankfurt. All three of them were ardent believers and knowledgeable people in business matters and were willing to tackle the apparently insurmountable financial challenges facing us.

With their help we eliminated the debt within one year and added a number of new staff. I upgraded office equipment and streamlined the procedures for fundraising. It was not easy, but we trusted the Lord and banked on His help. It worked.

Interestingly, people took notice of what we were doing. For instance, on December 9, 1962, the US Sunday school publication *Adult Power* (Scripture Press Foundation, Wheaton, Illinois) featured our ministry in Germany under the title *He Has a Vision for German Youth* (with a subtitle *Once a Member of Hitler Youth, Werner Bürklin is now energetically recruiting for Christ*) written by Wayne Detzler, a missionary with Greater Europe Mission in Germany. I first met him in Gelsenkirchen when he, as a teenager, was an exchange student from the US to Germany. He had attended our evangelistic crusade meetings we held in the town where he lived. Finding out that he had helped out in YFC rallies in his home town Detroit, we invited him to play his trumpet at our open-air meetings. He virtually became part of our team. Just a teenager, but someone with a passion to serve his Lord! No wonder he later became a missionary!

Those were exciting years. Year after year we crisscrossed Germany holding evangelistic crusades in churches, neutral halls, and during the summer months in large tents. I also kept directing the monthly YFC rallies in Frankfurt and started others in Wiesbaden, Wetzlar, Marburg, and other cities.

One of the more memorable evangelistic crusades I conducted was in Berlin. Bill Yoder, a YFC worker, had started a ministry in West Berlin. Those were the days when Berlin was divided into four sections (American, British, French, and Soviet). Anyone could roam freely within the three western sections but it was difficult to visit the Soviet-controlled partition.

On August 13, 1961, it became even harder—the *Berliner Mauer* (Berlin Wall) was erected by the German Democratic Republic's government. From then on, only the youth from the western section were able to attend the YFC rallies.

It just so happened that the wall was beginning to be built just a couple of weeks before my crusade was scheduled. Martin Homan, a JFCD evangelist, was the MC. Each night young people made decisions for Christ. On one night a number of Mormon missionaries tried to mingle in with our counselors and we had to remove them from the counseling room.

For the final night we moved to the Kongresshalle, branded by the Berlin people *Schwangere Auster* (pregnant oyster). This beautiful and unique building, with its 2,000 seats, was built in 1956/57 and had been presented as a gift by the government of the United States to Berlin. Young people from across Berlin overflowed the hall and close to fifty of them accepted Christ that night. *Welt am Sonntag*, one of the largest newspapers in Germany, interviewed me and brought a full report of that event. All of us rejoiced what God had done during that crusade.

I shall never forget my visit to a portion of the wall near the Brandenburg Gate. I peered across the barbed wire and could not believe that human beings were capable of such destructive and hurtful behavior. Whole families were torn apart. I saw some relatives waving to their siblings across the barrier. A few tried to overcome the wall by tunneling under it, climbing over it, ballooning over it, crashing through it with trucks. Some made it and others were killed while trying to escape. Many of them would never see their loved ones again—they were too old to experience the collapse of the wall twenty-eight years later on November 9, 1989.

While I traveled extensively, Inge stayed home with our two boys, now three and two years old. She hosted many from all over the world for a meal or a bed. On October 29, 1961, God gave us another healthy *Sonntagsjunge* (sunny boy): Stephan. With his big blue eyes, blond curls, and easy disposition, he won everyone's heart. Now we had "three musketeers." We prayed persistently that they would grow up to become "men of God." They did.

I also was looking for other ways to reach the youth. *What about evangelistic films?* I thought. They are using them in the States? So to begin with, we synchronized the American film *Singapore Story*. Up to this time, no evangelistic films had been used in Germany. It turned out to be extremely successful and subsequently I asked Ken Anderson of Gospel Films to come over and produce a film "Made in Germany." He did and we were able to release the first German-made film *Aufruhr im Jugendheim*. This was widely used with great blessing all across German-speaking Europe.

In August of 1962 the Communists organized the Eighth World Youth Festival in Helsinki, Finland. Youth for Christ International asked me to attend it as an observer. I flew to Helsinki and to save money took a room with a Finnish family.

"What were you doing marching with Communists in their parade," Joe Weatherly, an evangelical minister and employee of Gospel Films asked me sheepishly after the spectacle. He had spotted me and could not believe what he saw. *How is it possible for a YFC worker marching along with Communists?* he must have pondered. "Well, as an observer I wanted to be as close as possible," I responded, "and in that way I at least was able to take close-up photos." It was fun walking with all those Communists from

145

around the world. As a Christian I had a total different world view from theirs but I enjoyed interacting with them—even while marching with them.

One day a young Communist from the Middle East sat at my table eating lunch. We, of course, had a lively discussion on Communist ideology. "Why do you always refer to the Iron Curtain," he asked me, "I don't believe there is one." "Churchill in a speech held in Fulton, Missouri, on March 5, 1946, had coined that phrase," I explained. "It separates two ideologies: Communism and capitalism. Then I explained the gospel to him. I shared with him what Jesus meant to me after having placed my trust in Him. "Once I was following Hitler like you are now following Marx," I explained, "but he let me down. Then I turned my life over to Christ and decided to follow Him and His teaching, and not once did He let me down. Furthermore, what do you think of the statement Martin Niemöller made in his speech the other day?" I asked.

Pastor Martin Niemöller (1892-1984), former German sailor and a U-boat commander in the Great War (1914-18), had become a pacifist after his incarceration in two Nazi concentration camps (Sachsenhausen and Dachau) from 1937-45. At the beginning of Hitler's reign, he had trusted him because he had been told by Hitler personally that he would protect the rights of the church. Only after Hitler turned against the church did Niemöller become an opponent of Nazism. He also is famous for his saying:

> First they came for the communists and I didn't speak out because I wasn't a communist. Then they came for the trade unionists and I didn't speak out because I wasn't a trade unionist. Then they came for the Jews and I didn't speak out

because I wasn't a Jew. Then they came for me and there was no one left to speak out for me.

The Communists liked him because of being an anti-Nazi and for his anti-war stance during the Vietnam War. He was even given the Lenin Peace Prize in 1966.

However, in his Helsinki speech I heard him say the following:

> I could never become a Communist. I know what real freedom really is. As a prisoner in the concentration camps, I had a guard sitting outside my cell. I was free sitting inside the cell, whereas my guard was not. I was free because I voluntarily had done what my conscience and Christian beliefs impelled me to do. My guard was enslaved because he had to do involuntarily what his superiors told him to do. I was free and he was not.

To this my lunch partner had nothing to respond while absorbing the truth and the veracity of Niemöller's statement.

Later I met Martin Niemöller in his office in Wiesbaden, Germany. At that time he was the *Kirchenpräsident* (chief executive officer) of the Protestant Church in the State of Hessen-Nassau. He was interested in our YFC rallies in Frankfurt. He sent a delegation of his church office to explore what we were doing. They took their seats on the right-hand corner on the balcony. During my visit at his Wiesbaden office he said, "I was told what you are doing and I like it. On my visit to Australia, I once came across a team of Open Air Campaigners and was impressed with their commitment to evangelistic preaching on the street corners. Keep on doing what you are doing."

And so we did.

Take the city of Lünen in Germany's industrial area, also called *Ruhrgebiet*. On September 7, 1966, I wrote to our friends:

We have had a most profitable summer. During the month of July young people from over ten different countries of Europe converged on Lünen, a little city in northern Germany. For four weeks we turned the community upside-down for the Lord.

In the mornings we trained them. "How do I cope with members of sects?"; "How do I lead a person to Christ?"; "What do I do in my house-to-house ministry?" In the afternoons we sent them in small teams from door to door, selling evangelistic literature or passing out tracts. What a thrilling sight to see then move into different directions with the Word of God in their hands.

Others helped out in homes, hospitals, or on playgrounds; we visited all of the schools with sharp teams explaining why they believe in God and follow Christ. Then we had street meetings, held services in churches, shot a documentary film, and finally had large evangelistic crusade meetings in the evenings.

The doors are still wide open in our country although it gets more difficult as the years go by. Materialism has gripped the hearts of the people and just a few care for the things of God. Please continue to pray for us.

In the same letter I wrote:

And now a little soprano voice is singing in our male trio—for on Sunday morning, September 4, 1966, the Lord gave us a healthy sweet little girl, Linda Jeanette, thus fulfilling ours and our boys' greatest desire. Our hearts are overjoyed as we consider again God's handiwork of creation and life. To our boys this has been a real experience in God answering their very definite and earnest prayers for a healthy sister.

I shall never forget walking from the public telephone booth that morning after having talked to Inge about the newborn. I was walking on air! I never knew what it is like to walk on air, but that morning I experienced it. Our three boys were still in bed when I walked into their bedroom, expectantly awaiting the news I would bring—a boy or a girl. For weeks they had been praying fervently for a girl. All three were covered with their blankets up to their noses. Only their eyes were sticking out. I exclaimed, "It is a girl." With one jerk they threw their blankets in the air, and with screams of joy they jumped into my arms. God had answered their and our prayers!

CHAPTER 10

JAMAICA, HERE WE COME

NOW I WAS in my mid-thirties. Life was wonderful, yet it became more hectic from year to year. In the midst of my YFC ministries, I was also drawn into the orbit of Billy Graham's organization. He asked me to become a member of his board in Germany. On one occasion while meeting with him in London, he asked me to direct his ministry in the German-speaking parts of Europe. "I plan to reduce my overseas offices," he said, "however, only if you are willing to run the German affairs, I will keep the German office open." I accepted that challenge. In fact, later I moved his office from Frankfurt and combined it with my Europe YFC office in Langen, close to Egelsbach where we then lived.

What drew me to Billy Graham? His integrity, his evangelistic zeal, and his commitment to Christ. He was a loving and gracious man; however, he did not mince any words when sharing his convictions. Here is just an example of what I mean, taken from

a sermon he preached at the famous military academy of West
Point in 1959:

> To a large extent, the American church has become merged
> with the world. It has accepted so many of the world's ideals
> and standards that it has lost the ability to stem the tide of
> crime, deception and immorality that is sweeping the nation.
> For millions of church members there is no deep commit-
> ment to the cause of Christ, no regularity of attendance at
> public worship, no sacrificial giving, no personal religious
> discipline.
>
> The Christian should stand out like a sparkling diamond
> against a rough background. He should be more wholesome
> than anyone else. He should be poised, cultured, courteous,
> gracious, but firm in the things he does or does not do. He
> should laugh and be radiant; but he should refuse to allow
> the world to pull him down to its level.

He was a great evangelist, but it also became clear to me that
he was a great defender of the Christian faith.

Billy Graham was the first employee of Youth for Christ.
Torrey Johnson, founding president of Youth for Christ
International and pastor of a prominent church in the Chicago
area, saw in Billy Graham a budding evangelist. After graduating
from Wheaton College, Billy pastored a basement church in
Western Springs, Illinois, and was then challenged by Torrey to
help him fill the multitude of requests for evangelistic meetings.

Billy Graham became the renowned evangelist ministering
around the world many of us now know. One day he invited
me along with several European evangelists to meet with him

in Paris, France. There he impressed upon us the importance of evangelism. "Theological seminaries today lack teaching the intricacies of evangelism," he told us, "but to reach the world for Christ, aggressive evangelism is needed."

In October of 1966 he held his first Congress on Evangelism in Berlin, Germany. Close to 1,000 evangelists from some one hundred countries convened in the famous *Kongresshalle*. For the first time I had the opportunity to rub shoulders with my counterparts from many different countries, and it became another turning point in my life. Billy Graham challenged us all to step up our evangelistic efforts. Many of us rededicated our lives to this endeavor.

But at that time I was still deeply involved with YFC.

I had been elected as treasurer for Youth for Christ International. While attending a board meeting in Seattle, Washington, I was asked by Neville Whittier, director of Jamaica Youth for Christ, whether I would be willing to prepare and direct a World Congress of YFCI that had been scheduled in his Caribbean country. This would have made it necessary for my entire family to move to the West Indies. "No," I answered, "I am willing but I cannot. I am too busy with running my program in Germany."

Traveling home, the phrase I had uttered, "I am willing but I cannot," kept coming back to me again and again. *Was God calling me to a new challenge after all?* I reflected. I had to talk this over with Inge and when I did, she was aghast. By then we had four children. Linda, our youngest, was only a few months old at that time. *Who will pay for this?*

One thing we knew. So far, we ourselves had to raise all the money we needed. We lived on faith.

Finally, both Inge and I surrendered to what was to come. *"Mitgefangen, mitgehangen,"* Inge one day said to me. This is a German saying, meaning "once caught together results in being hanged together." In other words, she was willing to go with me whatever the cost. This, of course, was a great release for me. I shall ever be thankful for an understanding and cooperative wife. She was a real trooper—more than that, she willingly shared with me wherever the Lord would lead us. The Lord was all in all in her life.

The day came when we had so say good-bye to our beloved staff in Germany. In June 1967, ten years after our wedding, we arrived in the United States to do fundraising for our new assignment. For two months we crisscrossed America ministering in churches, YFC rallies, and Bible clubs. Once we had to split up our kids and hand them over to friends who took them in. Erik and Stephan (nine and five years old respectively) flew by themselves from Chicago to Detroit to stay with Ford's leading designer in his lovely lakeside home. Wes Dahlberg with his wife, Dagmar, had lived near Köln (Cologne) as the head designer for Germany's Ford company. They had invited me then to preach at their international church in Bad Godesberg, and we became close friends.

Following that service I received a call from the embassy of Ethiopia: "The ambassador is inviting you to meet with him in Bonn." *When an ambassador calls, you better go*, I thought. So I did. I shared with him the gospel and later I met with him again when he was transferred to Geneva, Switzerland.

But now we had to mind the welfare of our children in the States. Erik and Stephan flew to Detroit. The other two children, Heiko and Linda, stayed in Wheaton with Wendy Collins' family, the home of the overseas director for YFCI. Inge and I left for the West Coast.

What a thrill to meet again my old GI buddy from Shanghai, Rick Zapata, now living in Fresno, California. He was one of the Christian GI's that had befriended us when we were teenagers. They represented the victorious Americans and us the beaten Germans. But they showed no animosity or hate. Rick often visited our children's home in the Great Western Road. He also attended our Ambassadors for Christ youth meetings at our church whenever he was off duty. As a Mennonite he was not willing to take up arms, so as a conscientious objector he had signed up as a medical assistant (*Sanitäter*) in the US army. He became the closest buddy I had in Shanghai. Now I saw him again.

Fresno is a very fascinating place. Sort of the fruit capital of the States. I was amazed at the size of the fruit orchards. I had never seen anything like it. Vast fields of peaches, apricots, or oranges. "Watch out," Rick cautioned, "don't slip." We were walking on peaches—literally; peaches that were thrown on the ground to dampen the dry pulverized dirt. Growers would simply cover the dusty paths between rows of fruit with peaches—thousands, or hundred thousands, of them! *How many hungry people could have been fed with all that decomposing fruit?* I rationalized. But, of course, those were vain and futile contemplations.

On our ultimate trip to Jamaica, we picked up our kids and traveled to Miami. When we checked in at the airport we were told that without a visa or a Jamaican work permit we would have to purchase a round trip ticket for the entire family, just in case the border officials in Jamaica would not let us in. "How much money do we have in our pockets?" I asked my sweetheart. We scraped together all we had and just made the amount needed.

Walking into Jamaica's oven, we were held back at the passport control. "How long do you plan to vacation in Jamaica?" the official asked. "Well, we really want to stay a year or so, because we have been invited by Jamaican Christians to help direct a youth congress," I answered. "Then you need a work permit," he politely advised. "If you do not have one, then we will have to send you back."

We were exasperated. It was hot, really hot. Sweat covered our bodies and we were tired—especially our four kids. I tried to reason with him until we were the only ones left standing at the barrier. I was about to give up when I saw a black gentleman in the distance waving a big brown manila-size envelope. "Why don't you check out what he wants," I encouraged the official.

It was the work permit!

"I just picked up the work permit at the Labor Department a couple of hours before you landed," Cleve Grant said as he led us to greet other members of the welcoming committee. I was somewhat annoyed, because months ago I had asked them to work on the work permit. *Why did they wait to the very last moment?* I asked myself. Later I understood that things are done a little more casually in Jamaican style. This was one thing I had to learn in this beautiful botanical land. Things are done much more slowly here.

In fact, the first couple of weeks I got so annoyed with a number of things. For instance, lack of punctuality was one of them. Germans are known to be punctual—overly so. Here in the hot climate they went by what they called "Jamaican time." This could mean anything. It drove me crazy. Sitting and waiting for an appointment for half an hour, or one hour, or sometimes more drove me batty. It became a real problem for me, so much so, that one day I had to ask the Lord for forgiveness and had to surrender myself to the way things were done here—and that without resentment.

What a release! From then on I prided myself in always coming late and to my amazement, I was always on time! People usually showed up at the same time. It worked!

Our family was packed into a Mercedes Benz. Wow, I did not know that Jamaicans were that advanced, driving German cars! Even Mercedes! We were driven to a lovely house with a huge garden. Palm trees, orange, lemon, ackee, breadfruit, mango trees, and banana plants filled our grounds. Amazing! It was dry, however, and the grass brown. It had not rained for weeks. In fact, only a hurricane passing by Jamaica several weeks later brought some relief. It rained cats and dogs for a few days.

But I was more concerned about the money I had paid for our tickets in Miami. "Could you please give me a refund for the unused return tickets," I asked the Pan American agent. "No problem," he responded. After tabulating the amount he handed me several hundred dollars, much more than I had expected. "This is more than I originally paid," I said. He recalculated but came up with the same amount. "No," I said, "I cannot accept that. You are making a mistake." He started to argue with me. "I will talk this over with my manager when he comes in. Why don't you come back later?"

I took a stroll through town and then re-appeared a couple of hours later. The manager handed me the same amount previously offered. "I cannot accept this," I explained. "There is nothing I can do," he countered. "You either leave it or take it. It is up to you." I knew these were his last words.

So I took it.

And I thanked the Lord for this special and unique gift.

To live and work in Jamaica without a car was almost impossible. The money we had raised for our Jamaica assignment would not cover the purchase of one. But then another miracle happened. Let me share what we wrote our parents on October 30, 1967:

> You asked about our car. It is a new English Vauxhall which we were able to purchase with the help of a bank. It is absolutely essential to have a car here. We got one for a special price, but it still was very excessive compared to our income. However, the Lord again put us to shame—we were folks with so little faith. A businessman in Atlanta, who had heard me only once giving a ten-minute report in his Sunday school class, had heard about this need. He felt led to pay off the entire loan we owed the bank—$1,185 (DM 4,740)! We could not believe it! Now the car is paid for, it belongs to us, and the debt is gone. The Lord is so good to us, and this is another indication of God's leading in our lives. We see in it that the Lord has confirmed His path [our move to Jamaica].

Our three sons began school at Hilltop Christian School. This was not easy for our two older ones, since they had to switch from German to English. Stephan started his education in English, which for him was a real advantage. But it was amazing how fast these kids adjusted. They made friends quickly, enjoying the kids from different races and nationalities. The real benefit for them was that all of our kids grew up bilingual, and in the future it paid off.

The minute we arrived in Jamaica the preparations for the world congress began. We had only eight full months to get ready. However, I was supported by exceptionally talented and qualified committee members. We worked hand-in-glove. It was a real joy interacting with them, and we quickly loved living and working in Jamaica. Only one of them gave us some headache. He was the treasurer. He held the purse strings and thus was a very important member. The chairman, however, was not only extremely intelligent but also very effective as a shepherd and a friend. As a true shepherd pastor he had learned to deal with problematic issues. His consistent and patient counsel was a big encouragement.

One day the treasurer came into our office while I was absent. "So wonderful to see a Bible sit so prominently on Werner's desk," he told my secretary. As a successful businessman he probably was not used to seeing Bibles on desks of other executives. From then on he was much more congenial. He stuck it out until the end and became an integral part of our endeavor. God again had given us unity we greatly needed.

I was constantly on the go all over the island. One late evening I was traveling back from Port Antonio on the northeastern coast of Jamaica to Kingston. Earlier I had been warned not to enter some areas in Kingston, Jamaica's capital. The murder rate was one of the highest in the world. "There is much illegal drug usage," I had been alerted by the chairman, "and crime, especially towards foreigners, is rampant there." This had made me more sensitive to people who looked suspicious to me. That night on the desolate road, I was alone in the car and suddenly saw a vehicle pull up behind me. Two young men were following me. The faster I went, the swifter they followed. It took me more than thirty minutes to outpace them. Finally I was alone again. I sighed with relief and thanked the Lord for bringing me home safely.

All of the windows in our home had iron bars to protect us from burglars. "Don't be so sure about safety, however," one of our Jamaican friends had counseled Inge, "because burglars are clever. They may squeeze little children through the bars and instruct them to unlock the doors from the inside." Often when I was gone, she felt uneasy with fear. However, for the entire stay in Jamaica we never had any intruders. No kids ever crawled through our barred windows! God had protected us. The windows had to stay open day and night because we had only one air-conditioning unit, in our bedroom. We were constantly visited by mosquitos, lizards, and cockroaches—even mice! It took some time to get adjusted to that.

One of the first events was a pastors' breakfast at which the governor general, the representative of England's queen, gave an encouraging address. The German ambassador with his wife also attended and took pride in the fact that the director of the congress hailed from Germany. Furthermore, the mayor of Kingston, and the bishops of all major denominations graced the tables. Even the prime minister, Hugh Shearer, encouraged me, when I visited him in his office. It was very apparent that the leadership of the Jamaican government rallied behind our efforts. Also the minister of education emphasized the importance of the coming event.

The day of YFC's world congress (February 6-11, 1968) finally arrived. The main evening meetings were held in the National Arena seating 5,000 people, and the final rally was held in Kingston's stadium. Every one stood when the limousine with the governor general came through the gates and drove around the tracks. Between 16,000 and 17,000 attendees sang the national anthem before he sat down in the president's box.

Shortly after the meeting began, a few drops of rain came down. In Jamaica this spells disaster, and immediately some got off from their seats to leave. I quickly made my way to the microphone but was restrained by David Burnham, the main speaker, who said to me, "Let me handle this." He took the microphone and boldly declared, "Please do not leave, the rain will stop," then prayed and sat down. To everybody's amazement the rain did stop and we finished the closing rally with several hundred (exactly 562 recorded) making decisions for Christ. It was an amazing evening.

Throughout the week of the congress we literally covered the entire island with teams ministering in one hundred fifty schools reaching some 66,000 students. We also conducted seminars every day for over four hundred pastors, youth leaders, Sunday school teachers, and other interested parties in Kingston. It was a busy and blessed week.

We also had evangelistic meetings in the larger cities across the nation. In Montego Bay they started with a march of 2,000 young people through the town, and 3,500 attended the meetings each night. One evening the electricity went out—not too unusual for Jamaica—so the evangelist kept preaching in darkness. Also in Mandeville, Port Antonio, Highgate, Brown's Town, and Lucea the venues overflowed with young people. In some places crowds outside were as large as inside! Even the archbishop of the Catholic Church endorsed the meetings. We could not grasp the magnitude of the events we experienced.

On February 21 I wrote my parents:

Please continue to pray for us. We now have the great responsibility to oversee the follow-up and the consolidation of the entire YFC ministry in the Caribbean Sea. We are overjoyed to serve our Lord. The Lord has blessed beyond expectation. Many, many thanks for your prayers.

God truly had done a great work! But I wanted to put the ministry on sound footing. For that I needed a godly and capable young man. Inge and I continually prayed for the right person. Then I remembered an encounter I had had with a handsome Jamaican on the first Sunday after arriving in Jamaica.

We attended a Baptist church close to our house. As we entered the church I saw a white Mercedes drive up. A young and tall man in his late twenties or early thirties alighted. I was impressed. *For someone to drive a German Mercedes Benz shows a streak of exceptionalism,* I cogitated. Very seldom you are struck with someone, but something set him apart. As the service began this same man stepped up and led the service. He was good-looking, sharp, and extremely articulate. He was not the pastor but I immediately recognized in him a unique and extremely gifted person.

Following the service I approached him. "Sir, I am from Germany to direct the Youth for Christ congress and need members for our board. Would you be interested?"

"No," he answered, "and I tell you why. I am extremely busy in my job and then use all my free time to serve my church."

I had never received such a decisive rebuff in all of my life. He was not rude, just very resolute. I did understand why and what he was saying.

"For such an important assignment you need people who can live up to it," he concluded. "I would not be able to give my best. I am too busy."

Nice try, I thought. *Too bad, but God certainly has others that can help me in my venture for the congress.*

I never saw him again during all the months we lived in Jamaica. We attended a different church and our paths never crossed. While praying for the right man to direct the YFC ministry, this strange yet reasonable encounter reentered my mind.

So I invited him for lunch. Knowing how quick he made known his decision, I did not give him a chance to reveal his thinking. I must have talked for twenty minutes nonstop before I gave him a chance to answer. I had told him how much we needed a competent man. "We have had an amazing congress," I explained, "now Jamaica needs someone to take up the torch to bring the youth of this nation to Christ."

Pensively he looked at me and then stated, "If I now go home and tell my wife, Sonia, of this offer, she would say, 'See, Gerry, I have told you for some time that you should go into the ministry.'"

I knew then that half of my battle was won.

"Werner," he went on, "give me two months to think and pray about it and to counsel with some of my spiritual mentors. I will let you know by the end of October."

We continued to build a financial base for Jamaica Youth for Christ. Again I crisscrossed the island to challenge Christian leaders and churches to rally behind the ministry. We prayed and believed that the best days for the ministry lay ahead.

Weeks went by without hearing from Gerry. Finally October 31 arrived. Going to bed that night I mentioned to Inge, "Well, he has not called, so God must have some other person in mind."

At 11 o'clock that night the phone rang, and Gerry was on the line. "Werner, I promised to call you by the end of October. I only have one hour to go. Well, I feel led to accept your challenge

163

and am willing to begin taking over as YFC director for Jamaica at the first of next year. I will have to talk this over with my boss."

We were in high heaven! When I informed some of my Jamaican friends about this development, I was met with disbelief. "Are you talking about Gerry with the surname of Gallimore?" they asked. "Do you know who he really is? He is one of the most gifted preachers, a solid lay leader in his denomination. He is one of the top businessmen on the island. His father was a renowned member of parliament, and his brother Neville succeeded him in this position."

I was amazed that the Lord had led me to this valuable man.

Later Gerry told me about the meeting with his boss. "He was stunned," Gerry said, "'how can you do this to me?' my boss expressed. 'We groomed you to become the president of our business. Tell me what salary you want and we will give it to you.'"

Of course it had nothing to do with money. Gerry knew without a shadow of a doubt that God had called him into the ministry.

Interestingly, the boss had a farewell party for him in his gorgeous home. Before they sat down for dinner he addressed those in attendance, many of them representing his executive staff:

When Gerry came into my office to hand in his resignation, I was dumbfounded. I could not believe what I heard. That evening I sat down to eat, but I could not. I stepped out into the garden to wrestle with the reality of Gerry leaving us. I do not believe in a God, but I looked up into the starry sky and said, "God, you know that I do not believe in you. However, if you are there, I am now willing to let Gerry go to work for you. You have chosen the best from our organization."

"Hardly an eye was dry after this speech," Gerry mused.

On November 26 we said good-bye to the many friends who saw us off at the airport, knowing that we were leaving the ministry in good hands. Inge had written the following to our friends:

> After the usual hectic days of preparation, we said *Auf Wiedersehen* to the many YFC workers and friends who had gathered at Palisadoes Airport in Kingston. In fact, the good-byes took so long in real Jamaican style that the Bürklins were the last ones running to the plane and boarding just before the doors closed. That last minute rush spared us some of the pain of leaving, for Jamaica had really become home to us.

It had been a good and blessed fourteen months.

CHAPTER 11

THE TOUGHEST DAYS
OF OUR LIFE

WOLFGANG LEO WELCOMED us at the Frankfurt airport with a new car that he had helped purchase for us. Years ago I had hired him to head up our YFC's film department. He was one of the actors in the movie I had made with Ken Anderson from the US. *Aufruhr im Jugendheim (The Accuser)* was the first evangelistic movie in Germany and later was synchronized into English for US consumption.

How much had changed! When we started in the ministry many years ago, Inge and I often had to pray for the next meal. Sometimes we did not even have enough cash to buy streetcar tickets. Now we were able to order a new car after we had sold our car in Jamaica, and it was paid for.

We settled into a Christian retreat center in the hills near Frankfurt. It was cold, bitter cold. The deep snow on the ground delighted our kids and they could not get enough sledding down a hill. Before we had left for Jamaica in 1967, we had seen modern row houses being constructed in our village of

167

Egelsbach. They were quite unique with split level floors, and very attractively built with beige bricks and external wood paneling. We liked the looks of those homes and wondered whether some of them were still for sale.

All of them had been sold. However, one buyer backed out just at the moment we went to Egelsbach to find out. Within a few days we closed the deal and were able to move in. Before leaving for Jamaica, we had sold all previously owned furniture. But again the Lord supplied enough money to get going and within a few months we had a beautiful and cozy home with the help of both of our parents. All our four children spent their childhood years within those walls and loved it.

"What is the best memory having lived during those years," Inge once asked Linda when she had her own family and home. "Coming home from school, smelling something was cooking, and knowing that you were there," she answered. What a wonderful testimony!

While I travelled the world, Inge stayed behind "by the stuff" (1 Sam. 25:13b) taking care of our four growing kids, hosting many visitors, working as my secretary, translating numerous books for Christian publishers, and writing many articles for Christian magazines, thus helping a bit with our always meager income. She was a "stay at home mom" and felt this was her calling.

Comparing Germany to Jamaica was quite sobering to us. Spiritually speaking, Jamaica now seemed far superior to Germany to us. The response to the gospel there was so much clearer and ardent. Liberal theology had destroyed the church life across Germany so much that church attendance was at its lowest, and people in general were uninterested in spiritual things.

We were abhorred reading an article in Germany's prominent periodical *Der Spiegel*:

> They convened in rubber boots and slippers, had Mao's red bibles in their pockets and Lenin pins on their sweaters. They donned full beards and shoulder-length hair. They sang "*The Internationale*" and bellowed "Jesus lead us on" while they drank beer and smoked pipes. Their discussion was spiced with foul language.
>
> The place: Bochum, West Germany.
>
> The scene: a four-day conference of 200 theologians and theological students, some of them in their last semester.
>
> Their objective: the destruction of capitalism and the shattering of the church as a desirable second aim.
>
> Said their leader, a young pastor from Bremen, "We will establish an anti-church with a council system" while his listeners shouted, "Mao Zedong" with raised fists.

We were stunned to read this. Upon arrival from Jamaica, we were appalled not only by the spiritual darkness of our homeland, but by the seeming bleakness of its future. Imagine, those young men will in the future fill the pulpits of our churches! However, we were determined not to give up.

Soon thereafter we were encouraged when we experienced God's power in the town of Ebingen in southern Germany. A very small church with fifteen active young people had invited us for an evangelistic crusade. I took with me a musical team of three and experienced an amazing development. Although just a handful, they had rented the biggest hall in town with a seating capacity of 1,000. To our amazement, over 500 showed up the first night and hundreds of them were kids with no church affiliation. Night after night they came, and night after night young people came to Christ.

God was at work, and He was answering our prayers.

An added responsibility was placed upon my shoulders when I was elected chairman of Europe Youth for Christ, which post I then held for several years.

The year 1969 was the toughest of my life.

On September 5, one day after the birthday of our three-year-old Linda, Inge and I were working all day in our garden. It was the last day of my vacation. Late in the afternoon I decided to see my doctor. After a thorough examination, he told me to see a specialist, a surgeon, right away. It was already after 5 p.m., the hour when most offices close. Driving away from his office, I decided to go straight to the surgeon's office even though it was after office hours. I rang the bell at the locked door. "I am sorry, but our office is closed," his secretary said opening the door. "My primary doctor told me to see the surgeon as soon as possible," I advised her, "and today is Friday, the last day of a working week." When she saw the diagnosis sheet and had taken it in to the specialist's office, he decided to examine me right away.

"Mr. Bürklin, I need to admit you to the hospital at once and operate on you immediately," the doctor said, "come to the hospital first thing Monday morning."

I hesitated. "I am going to leave next week with a team on a mission trip to Yugoslavia." "Mr. Bürklin," he answered somberly, "if I were you, I would forget about everything you have planned and go to the hospital."

Being curious why he made it so urgent, I asked, "Is radiation necessary after surgery?" I knew from experience that doctors are usually apprehensive to abruptly come out with the truth. He knew what I was thinking and pensively answered, "Yes, it might be possible." I knew then that he was suspecting cancer.

Driving home while it was getting dark, I thought the world would come crashing down. I could not believe what was happening. *"Cancer! Cancer is striking my body,"* I said aloud. *"How is that possible?"* To me it was the worst kind of illness. I just could not grasp the severity of this fact. *Why me, oh Lord. I am still young with four little children.*

The next day, that fateful Saturday, I was lying on my bed, resting. Before that, Inge and I had visited a friend of ours, a medical doctor, whose two daughters had come to Christ in our Frankfurt YFC rallies. He openly shared with us that the tumor in my right testicle could be benign or cancerous. If benign, then the entire matter would be over within two or three days. If cancerous, then it was a serious and grave matter. "Seminoma is one of the most vicious and fast-growing cancers, especially for young men," he said.

My little daughter was next to me sleeping. Again and again I looked at her pretty face, and then the thought struck me that I might not see her grow up and have the thrill of leading her down the aisle to meet her groom on her wedding day. *A sweet little daughter looks so pretty when asleep,* I thought to myself.

This was too much for me to bear. Just at that moment Inge entered the room, and seeing tears coming down my cheeks she asked, "What's wrong, honey?"

"Sweetheart," I responded, "I have reached the point where nobody can help me; no wife, no children, no parents, no pastor, no friend—nobody, but God alone. Later that evening I left the house to pray and went into the fields behind our little village. There under the stars I knelt on the dusty path and poured out

171

my heart to God. I did not want to die. Not so early in life! The peace I had known ever since becoming a believing Christian so many years ago had vanished. Finally, in despair, I lay prostrate and prayed, "Okay, Lord, now I am not asking for deliverance. I will accept whatever you have in store for me. Life or death, I will accept your will. All I am now asking for is your peace. The peace I had known before!" The peace that passes all understanding.

Once I surrendered to His will, the peace of God flooded back into my life. Instantly! It was amazing. I was able to rise, and with a song in my heart and a renewed spring in my step, I returned home. Taking my love into my arms I said, "It is all right. Everything is fine. God has met me out there on the fields. I accept His will, no matter what. His will be done."

The next day, on a lovely Sunday afternoon, we took our kids into the nearby woods for a picnic. We wanted them to have a memory of a blessed family time in case the Lord would take me home. We romped around, laughed a lot, and simply had a good time.

The following weeks were rough. After surgery I was told that I did have cancer. In those days chemotherapy was in its infant development, but radiation was the in thing.

We called our pastor and some brothers in Christ, including my father and brother, to anoint me with oil and pray over me according to James chapter 5. It was a sacred and momentous moment as I humbled myself and confessed some of the worst sins I had committed in the past. Often the confession part is overlooked in that passage by folks who claim it, but I was willing to go all the way. But other roadblocks seemed to be thrown at me.

Should I go through with the prescribed radiation treatment was the next struggle I now had to overcome. *After all, if I have faith to be healed, do I need treatments?* The answer I received came during my quiet time the next day. My policy for years had been to read through the Bible once a year. That morning I came to the passage in the Gospel of Matthew, chapter 4, where the devil tempted the Lord three times. This spoke to me very clearly. The final tempting took place on the pinnacle of the Temple in Jerusalem. "If you are the Son of God, throw yourself down from here," Satan challenged. "It has been said, 'You shall not tempt the Lord your God,'" Jesus answered and walked down as He had walked up. *This is what I am going to do,* I decided.

I took this as a confirmation to go ahead with the treatments the doctors had prescribed. I would take the natural course. Again I had total peace about this situation and moved ahead.

A few days after I was to have the first cobalt treatment I had a circulatory collapse. Inge described this in an article she later wrote for a Christian magazine entitled "My Darkest Hour:"

> He was still in bed that morning while I was getting breakfast ready. I was wondering why he did not get up, for we did not have much time left to get to the clinic in Frankfurt. Finally I ran upstairs—and stopped short.
>
> Pale as a sheet, Werner was perspiring profusely and had a very strange expression on his face. With closed eyes, he looked more dead than alive.
>
> "I am so dizzy and weak. Call the doctor," he whispered with difficulty.

173

With flying hands I dialed the doctor's number. "Jesus, Jesus," I groaned. *He is going to die,* I thought. "Lord, are you taking him now?"

The doctor did not sound reassuring. "Call an ambulance and bring him immediately back to the hospital! I'll call the hospital to get everything ready for him."

I cannot put into words what I felt as I followed the ambulance to the hospital. I don't think I prayed. I was too numb, too stunned, too bewildered. Werner told me later that in between spells of unconsciousness, a deep peace flooded his entire being in the ambulance, and he was completely without fear.

The next morning he was operated on the second time.

Then came October 4, the darkest day in my Christian life! When I called the hospital to ask about Werner, the doctor said, "Mrs. Bürklin, I have to talk to you frankly. I know how you stand." (He was referring to our Christian faith to which we had both testified). "I am very much concerned about the bad cough. Also the terrible dizzy spells are alarming. I must tell you, if the cancer has reached his lungs and brain, then there is absolutely nothing we can do for him."

Why didn't the world come to an end? Why did I not faint or scream? What I had just heard was my beloved's death verdict! Slowly I put the receiver down. I stood there for a long time. There was just a great blank within me.

I did not die. God had something else in mind. Fascinatingly, the peace that had engulfed me on the dusty path that momentous night was still with me. In fact, it had grown even deeper as days had gone by. But my sweetheart was struggling with her own feelings in a womanly way. She had borne our four children and was faced with widowhood. How would she cope with raising them all by herself? In her article she continued:

> As I tucked the children in that evening, we sat together on one of their beds, and I told them that Daddy was really very ill and that God might want him to come to heaven very soon. I told them that the doctors could possibly still help Daddy, but that only God could really heal him, if it was His will, because His will is always best. Together we wept and prayed for a long time.

The prayer our second son Heiko uttered that evening blew me away when Inge mentioned it to me much later. He prayed, "Lord, we love our daddy very much, but if you want to call him to heaven, then it is okay."

In her article she continued:

> Then, with my duties all done and with the house quiet, I faced all alone what I call "the darkest hour of my life." I just broke down and despaired. On my knees, with my Bible open to Psalm 91, which we had read and claimed as a family before Werner went to the hospital, I wept as I have never wept before.

> Where was God? He seemed so far away! This was my hour of trial—the point where nobody but God could help and comfort me. I pleaded, "Give me your peace, God—the peace that passes all understanding, that you have promised in all circumstances to those that love you. Take all the fear and give me the assurance that all will be well according to your will!"

Amazingly and wonderfully so, at the end she did not despair. As a committed Christian she was determined to trust the Lord. In her Bible studies with other women she always had taught that Christ is all-sufficient, even in periods of confusion, disasters, or doubts. Now the time had come to prove that what she believed was not only rational but above all valid. This is what she experienced:

While I was on my knees, the Holy Spirit brought to my memory a message about Abraham and Isaac that I had read several days previously—a familiar passage but with new aspects this time. I did not have to think hard to find out who my Isaac was; the dearest and closest person God had given me on this earth. Abraham put Isaac on the altar as commanded by God, raised his knife, and—how long does it take for a raised knife to come down? Just a fraction of a second! Why did God go so far with Abraham? Because God loved him, and He wanted His very best for him. God himself wanted to be first in Abraham's life.

I prayed, "Are you first in my life, God? Really first? I know you love me and want the very best for me—even if this best does not look best humanly speaking. Blessed God, give me the strength to leave my Isaac on the altar, as long as you see fit—even if there is no ram ready for the sacrifice." I knew God could intervene, if this was His will.

Slowly the peace of God began to flood my heart—an experience that is almost impossible to describe, but so real, so very real. I had not prayed for Werner's healing during my darkest hour and did not dare to ask God to keep him alive. I had just desperately wanted peace of heart and mind that lifts the Christian above normal human despair—and God had answered the cry of my heart.

Looking back, I now thank God that He had dealt with both of us individually and both of us had surrendered our will to the Lord. And that is exactly what followers of Jesus need to do. Once experienced, this will always be a good reminder in times when catastrophes strike. God will forever be real.

God not only gave her the peace she coveted but He also furnished the "ram."

The next morning, thinking I was half-dead, she found me sitting in my hospital bed, greeting her, "Hi sweetheart, how are you doing?" The time of recovery had started. For the next five weeks I was treated with the cobalt bomb at the medical clinic of the University of Frankfurt. Those were long five weeks. The doctors were amazed with the way I was reacting so positively to the treatments that they decided to add one more week.

Finally I was released from hospital, and it took me a few months to regain my total strength. I took short walks in the nearby forest, and then prolonged them day by day. Then I started to jog short distances, then longer ones. I did this for several months. Finally I took short sprints and then extended those until I felt fit to travel again.

The first long travel took me to Cyprus to attend the leadership conference of Youth for Christ International. Fifteen directors representing world areas from the Pacific (Australia, New Zealand), South East Asia, Asia, North America, South America, Europe, and the Middle East wrestled with the challenges of youth evangelism across the globe.

One morning I had been asked to give devotions. I recounted my struggles and victory. I looked at the circle of men and said, "I was told that one out of four will die of cancer. I don't want to scare you." Then I pointed to one and started to count, "One, two, three, four," aiming at the fourth. Again I continued, "One, two, three, four," pointing once more to the fourth. I continued counting and after having covered everyone in the circle I said, "So not to scare the ones I had pointed to, let me start with someone else. Again I started, this time with a different person, "One, two, three, four." Well, they understood what I was getting at. No one is exempt and all of us need to be ready when calamity strikes. It is good to know then that God is the all-loving and all-sufficient One who helps us through those challenging phases. "Remember," I concluded, "all we need to do is to surrender to His will."

On February 7, 1970, I wrote my parents from Atlanta, Georgia, where I had stopped over to see my sister. "Tomorrow, exactly five months ago, I entered the hospital. Repeatedly I thank the Lord for having brought me through. Everything went well. Above all, I am thankful that I now can make this trip—for me personally a proof that I have conquered the illness."

But then, one year later, my father came down with cancer. I had a flashback, remembering my father visiting me at my hospital bed soon after my surgery. Leaning over me with an embrace he said, "I wish I could take your cancer upon me. I have lived my life and you are in the midst of yours." Later one of my nieces pondered, "Perhaps the Lord did fulfill his wish."

I sent him a letter in which I tried to console and encourage him in his battle with cancer.

Again and again I think of you and then pray for you. Do you have any headaches? Radiation sometimes causes severe headaches. Or nausea is another symptom. However, take it easy, those side effects can in time disappear again. Just be aware that those things are common, and then it will be easier to handle them.

By the way, on November 14 last year I received my last and final radiation treatment; in other words, exactly one year has gone by since my release from the hospital.

To me this was a real milestone. Once every month I had to see the doctor for x-rays. Those monthly visits were phases of anxieties for me and Inge, always wondering if the cancer had come back. Therefore, one year of clearance was a moment of immense psychological release.

However, on December 21, 1970, my father passed away into God's presence. Even while in hospital, he did what he had done all of his life—passing out tracts. When I once visited him, I discovered him standing in his morning gown in front of the hospital gate passing out tracts to those who came to visit their relatives and friends. Once a missionary, always a missionary! My father was a true hero of the Cross! Now he was in heaven worshiping the Lord he had served all of his life. No tracts were needed there.

The Lord gave me new strength to carry out the ministry He had set before me. Inge later told me, "The most fruitful days have been after your bout with cancer." Looking back I agree with her assessment.

I remember once traveling with Sam Wolgemuth behind the Iron Curtain. YFC did not have any outreach into that part of the world. So we traveled to Yugoslavia and Hungary to meet with Christian leaders to see whether it was viable to establish a youth ministry in Communist-controlled countries. In Budapest we had tea with a pastor of a small Baptist church. Besides being pastors, many of them also held secular jobs to augment their meager income.

"Are you a painter?" Sam asked.

"How do you know?" the pastor responded. "Oh, now I understand. You probably noticed the white paint under my nails."

Whenever I now see ladies in the US with the latest fad to have the tip of their fingernails painted white, I am always reminded of that Hungarian pastor. It didn't look nice.

Hugh Shearer, prime minster of Jamaica with Rev. Cleve Grant,
chairman of the world congress of Youth for Christ International in 1968

As chairman of Eurofest in 1975

Geração 79 with Billy Graham, Leo Janz, and Luis Palau in 1979

My friend Henry dating back to 1948 after imprisonment
for over twenty years in China's gulag

Bishop K. H. Ting who helped us to get our ministry established in China

Our first China Partner teaching team in Nanjing, 1981

Farmer in the province of Jiangxi in 1995

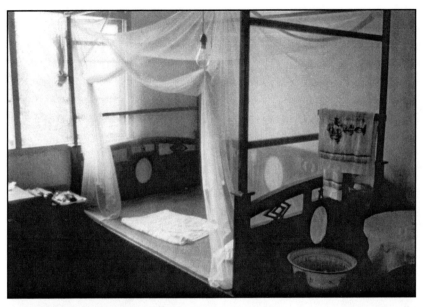

Linchuan "Hilton" in 1984

Meeting with congregants after the church service in Hefei, China, in 2001

Lu Chuan Fan of the China Christian Council, my confidant in China, in 1984

Groundbreaking service of the new church in Ningdu with Rev. Lin Feng

Teaching with our interpreter Dr. Daniel Hsu

CHAPTER 12

NEW HORIZONS AND FRESH CHALLENGES

ONE OF THE ministries I had started was a new approach to evangelism. I had hired a young man, a nineteen-year-old "whiz kid" in music. Klaus Heizmann hailed from the Ruhrgebiet and was extremely talented. I sent him to Fort Wayne College (later part of Taylor University) in the United States for further musical training, especially in regards to evangelism. He developed the well-known *Jugend für Christus Chor* that traveled all across Germany, Switzerland, and Austria and even performed in the world famous *Notre Dame* cathedral in Paris, France.

In the fall of 1969, during the time of my severe illness, I originally had been scheduled to travel with the choir on a tour through the United States. Martin Homann, whom I had employed just after his graduation from the German Bible Institute, and who had become an outstanding preacher and evangelist, had to fill in.

The next few months following my convalescence, I picked up my evangelistic preaching again and had many meetings in

Germany, Switzerland, and The Netherlands. The additional
responsibility as European Director for Youth for Christ took
its toll. Finally, on March 10, 1971, I flew to Malaga in Spain
and checked into the Marbella Hilton Hotel. In a letter to my
parents, my sweetheart wrote:

> Yesterday, after demanding days of continuous work, Werner
> left for southern Spain to begin his needed vacation. Only I
> know of his whereabouts because no one should be able to
> reach him. Otherwise people would go after him even while
> being in a foreign country.

> Even though it was very, very hard for me to let him go,
> I know that he desperately needs those two weeks of total
> repose and relaxation. Since his critical illness, I have never
> seen him so exhausted and drained. We had to make the
> decision: NOW he has to take a vacation! I am so thankful
> that financially we were able to swing it due to the additional
> income from his European ministry.

The next major overseas assignment for me was to travel with
a Teen Team I had formed to South Africa. Klaus Heizmann had
trained five musically gifted teenagers to form an evangelistic
musical team. They were scheduled to travel for three months all
across that land and also the country then known as Rhodesia,
now Zimbabwe, holding evangelistic meetings. On April 13,
1971, our team of seven boarded a Lufthansa plane in Frankfurt
and headed for Johannesburg. The plane was not too full, so all
of us were able to stretch out on this fourteen-hour-long flight.
We arrived rested and right away were thrown full force into the
battle. Every night we were holding meetings. During the day

we ministered in high schools and colleges. It never seemed to stop—a relentless blitz of meetings.

Once I stayed in a home of a well-to-do businessman. He loved hunting. I took up his challenge to go hunting with him. He threw me out of the bed at 4 o'clock in the morning. Off we went in two Jeeps—he, his friend, and I in one Jeep and three servants with several dogs in the other one. It was a long trip and finally we arrived in the veldt, a vast portion of land belonging to him. He ordered us to get out of the cars and start marching with guns on our shoulders. He hoped to run into kudus. So we did in a file.

Suddenly I heard a bang. "I shot a kudu," he bellowed. Excitedly he said to me, "You stay and I will find the kudu I shot."

He and the others took off. I looked for a rock and sat down with the gun between my legs. It was quiet and somewhat surreal, not knowing what to do.

Unexpectedly I heard and then saw a bunch of animals stampede by. Not knowing what they were and in quick succession I fired three times and then they were gone. Minutes later my host reappeared and shouted, "What happened?"

"Well, I don't know. I just saw a bunch of animals rush by and I shot," I said.

Some hundred meters away we found two wounded animals and a blood trail leading to another one hiding in the bush. I had to give the *coup de grace* to all of them.

"Amazing," my host mumbled. "In the last few months I have not seen let alone killed one kudu. You come along and dispatch three within a few minutes." As a souvenir I took along a hide with me when I returned to Germany. The one he apparently had seen and shot at was a hoax. He never found it.

But we also had some amazing meetings. After six weeks of intensive ministry, I left the team in Durban and traveled to Johannesburg to catch my flight back to Frankfurt while the rest of the team traveled on for another six weeks. A gentleman joining the flight in Durban happened to be an elder of the Baptist church where I had preached the night before. "Would you consider taking over our pastorate in Durban?" he asked me. "We are looking for a shepherd and our board feels you are the right man for us." I had to decline, because I felt led to continue with the ministry God had given me in Europe.

South Africa was not to be, but later I began traveling worldwide as an evangelist for Youth for Christ International.

Meanwhile back at home, we had to counsel with my distraught mother. The death of my father had left a huge hole in her life. Inge tried to encourage her as best she could. In a letter to her she wrote:

> I understand your feeling so well, struggling with homesickness. The wound and emptiness you now face I understand so well, thinking back to Werner's illness when we did not know whether he would live. I am now much more appreciative to let Werner go to serve the Lord, even though I have to cope with acute homesickness. Nevertheless, I do not want to say anything nor complain, since he will again return! But at times it is tough to bear.

> I learned anew that God is sovereign. He permits someone to die and the other to get well again because his time is not up as yet and He still wants to use him to serve Him. The other one He takes to Himself because his work on earth has been done. There was nothing I could have done to hold on

to my beloved Werner if God had chosen otherwise. HE is great. And in this way we have to understand the home going of our father. Otherwise we would always return to the question WHY.

Inge felt the pain of my mother. Even after consoling and encouraging her, Inge was still hurting herself when the next separation came around. But she was a real trooper. "If the Lord called you to minister anywhere in the world," she told me over and over again, "I let you go."

We were encouraged by people all over the world who prayed for us. Dave Foster, a YFC coworker of ours from England, told me, "Recently I was preaching in Eire (Ireland) and during the service they had a special prayer for Werner Bürklin. I did not know how they had heard about your illness!" But they did as multitudes in different parts of the world. Even our mailman shook his head in bewilderment as he delivered countless letters and cards. Puzzled he would ask, "Do you have to answer all those?"

In a newsletter to our friends we wrote:

If you could see what your prayers have accomplished, your hearts would surely rejoice. Werner looks and feels as good as new. What a changeover from just a few months past! What a testimony to God's miracle working today! Different doctors have told him that only the early recognition and operation saved his life since he had one of the most dangerous and fast-spreading types of malignancy. We have truly experienced that the God of old is still the same today, and we love Him even more through this trial.

Werner felt so well that his doctor permitted—in fact recommended—that he travel to take part in YFCI's Midwinter Convention in the US. He was to abide by some rules: travel only in the warm South, work only half days, rest often, and take no preaching assignments. This he complied with gladly. Psychologically this trip meant more to him than any previous one. To Werner this was the outward sign of the triumph over his illness. No wonder he looks and feels so good!

Besides being Chairman of Youth for Christ Europe, I had become its Executive Director in January 1971. I remained the national director of Germany YFC, but the extension of my ministry was very demanding. I knew I could only handle this for one year or so.

A few days after returning from my trip to the US, I was off to another European conference. Trips after trips followed and I enjoyed every moment of it, covering Scandinavia in the north to Spain and Portugal in the south.

In Portugal I gave the Bible lessons in a YFC youth camp on the shores of the Atlantic Ocean. We met on the site of a rustic retreat center. Forty young Portuguese kids had a terrific time of serious Bible studies combined with hilarious fun time. Once playing basketball on a cement court, I broke my large toe. It stuck out to the side and hurt terribly. Since there was no doctor available and the nearest hospital was a long way off, I decided to wait until I would get home. The next day we celebrated farewell with some skits and some fun games. I was hardly able to attend. The broken toe hurt like hell. But I did attend; after all, it was the last night. Six of those kids had accepted Christ and several others had recommitted their lives to the Lord.

"Werner," the camp director said, "our kids have chosen you to be the center of our final event. You will have to stand in the center of the room, a funnel will be placed behind your belt holding up your trousers, and then we will place a ping pong ball on the top of your forehead and you must slowly let the ball roll down your face and have it drop into the funnel."

"Easy," I said, "no problem." Balancing the ball on my forehead and concentrating on having it hit the target, those rascals poured water down the funnel. With the strange sensation of having my pants wetted, I jumped sky high. I screamed with pain. My broken toe took the full force. I hobbled to the next available chair. Taking off my tennis shoe, I noticed that my big toe was back where it belonged—next in line with the other toes!

Later my doctor at home in Frankfurt asked, "What in the world did you do?" "Is it broken?" I asked. "Broken?" he shouted, "It is shattered."

However, the ping pong encounter at least had one advantage. It put the toe back in line with the others. I inquired what can be done about it. "Nothing," the doctor said, "It only needs to heal." And heal it did.

As a member of the German board of the Billy Graham Evangelistic Association (BGEA), Inge and I participated in the Billy Graham Crusade from April 5-12, 1970, in the famous *Westfalenhalle* in Dortmund, Germany. From there the meetings were relayed into thirty-four halls all across Europe, from Norway to Yugoslavia! 800,000 people attended the meetings and 15,000 of them responded to follow Christ. We from YFC were heavily involved in those meetings as was our music director, Klaus Heizmann, assisting Cliff Barrows directing the massive crusade choir.

YFCI's President Sam Wolgemuth felt burdened to help me raise the additional funds needed to carry out the ever-escalating ministry. He wrote to our supporters:

> In addition to their excellent work in Germany, we will never forget the year and a half which they spent in Jamaica. This stands as one of the most significant short-term missionary projects in the history of our organization. As a result of their efforts, we have today a strong indigenous program of youth evangelism in that country. His present goal is to move full time into the Europe-wide responsibility, leaving behind in Germany one of the finest national staffs we have anywhere.

It was an enormous challenge. But what a thrill to expand our outreach into so many European countries! The German board asked me to remain as chairman of the German YFC board but the heavy lifting was going to be done across Europe.

Finally, I had to relinquish my responsibilities with Germany YFC. My feeling is best expressed in the following:

> The decision to leave Germany YFC did not come easy. There is plenty of excitement ahead for Germany in 1972-73 with its 25th anniversary, expansion of the center [headquarters] to include a new office building, use of the old house as a training center, the many camps, campaigns, musical tours, etc. We would have liked to remain right in the middle of all this, but there is excitement on the European front as well. There is some hard work and prodding to be sure—but also enormous possibilities.

CHAPTER 13

PRESIDENT NIXON GOES TO CHURCH AND OPENS THE DOOR TO CHINA

O N TOP OF my new responsibilities, I was asked by the world leadership to help out in other continents as well. For three months I returned to the Caribbean to teach at YFC Leadership Training Schools. Since we had left that area, the YFC work under the leadership of Gerry Gallimore in Barbados and Jamaica had increased tremendously. Now it seemed that the world had become my parish.

In Barbados I went deep-sea fishing for the first time in my life. Jim Groen and I rented a yacht and went far out to where our pilot said would be the best fishing grounds. That may be so, but the waves got bigger and bigger, and both of us never saw one fish. We were flat on our backs fighting sea sickness and feeding fish. One hour later we were back on shore. Fishing is not for me, at least not the deep-sea fishing type in troubled waters!

But the teaching was exhilarating. To see young people drink in the principles of biblical leadership was heartwarming. I shall never forget those wonderful hours. At the end of the seminars one of the young students handed me his violin. "I want you to have this. Your teaching meant so much to me." Wow, what a privilege to be involved in this kind of ministry!

Sadly, on leaving Barbados, I put the violin in the rack above my seat and then forgot to retrieve it when deplaning. It was lost forever and I hope that someone else used it for his and others' delight. I flew off to Miami, where Inge joined me for several weeks of friend- and fundraising.

At the Key Biscayne Presbyterian Church I was asked to give a report of our ministry. John Huffman, with his lovely wife Anne, was the senior pastor. I had a standard story with which I usually tried to break the ice. I began:

"When I first traveled through the United States I was always asked the all-American question, 'Where do you come from?'"

'I am from Germany.'

'Where did you learn your English; you hardly have an accent?' always was the next question.

'In China.' This invariably stunned the questioners and made them laugh.

'In China? Give me a break!'"

On this particular morning, it just so happened that President Nixon strolled in with his wife Pat and their children Julie and Tricia and their husbands David Eisenhower and Edward Cox. His summer home was in Key Biscayne right on the ocean. They sat in the first row. I had never seen President Nixon laugh so much after he heard my introduction. He was rolling in his chair! On TV he always looked so grim. But not this morning.

PRESIDENT NIXON GOES TO CHURCH
AND OPENS THE DOOR TO CHINA

President Nixon had just returned from his history making China trip. The world was surprised to see this notorious Communist hater and basher make that trip. But it was only someone like him who could get away with this. In fact, he opened China to the western world. Ever since then, China returned to the fold of the world family. Their isolationism collapsed.

Over lunch John quipped, "Werner, very few people have had the President's undivided attention for eight minutes. Remember, he is the President of the United States."

Later that afternoon, John and I took a walk and saw David and Julie Eisenhower in the garden of the Nixon home. There was no fence and the house was in full view. "Let's go and meet them," John said. But that was not so easy. Out of the bushes a Secret Service guy appeared and asked, "What do you want?" "I am the local pastor and know them," John answered. Sure enough, that worked and we had a nice chat with the Eisenhowers. Just normal people, when you get close. The media always makes people like them so special—celebrities—which they are not. Just normal people!

During the summer 1976 I took our third son, Stephan, to the Olympics in München (Munich). We wanted to see the 100 meter dash. We remembered Armin Hary, a German, won the gold medal in the 100 meter dash at the previous Olympic Games in Rome. He was the first athlete ever to reach the 10.0 second mark, thereby breaking the world record. This time the gold medal went to the Russian, Bozov. Amazing, how fast these guys can go! Usually the Americans won this event.

A few days later, at 4:30 a.m. on September 5, eight Palestinians, also known as Fedayeen, invaded the Olympic

Village and took eleven Israeli athletes hostage. Hans Dietrich Genscher, Minister for the Interior of Germany, beseeched the terrorists of the *Black September* movement to free the captives, but to no avail. All of the terrorists and living hostages (two of them had been killed during the assault) were taken in helicopters to the nearby airport at Fürstenfeldbruck, a NATO airbase, to be flown out to an Arab country. Sharpshooters tried to kill the terrorists, but due to insufficient lighting, it ended with disaster. All of the hostages were murdered by the terrorists inside the helicopters. The planned transfer to a Boeing 727 jet, which should have taken them to an Arab country, was thus thwarted.

In the process of the shootouts on the tarmac, Issa, the leader of the terrorists, was killed along with four of his compatriots. The other three were imprisoned and held for trial until on October 29, when hijackers of a Lufthansa passenger jet demanded their release. They were welcomed back home as great heroes.

"Let me have a word of prayer with you," Ian Paisley said as he got out from the chair behind his desk during my visit to Northern Ireland. He was the controversial politician from Belfast. Some called him a militant Protestant leader, fighting for the Irish to stay as part of Great Britain. A born-again pastor of a Presbyterian church, he was much admired by some and held a Parliament seat in the House of Commons. I liked him and was thankful for his prayer.

It was December and about time to celebrate the Advent season, which is the period where most Germans commemorate the coming of our Lord. Before going home, though, I stopped in Paris, France, to meet with our *Jugend für Christus Chor* (Youth for Christ chorale) on their concert tour. The Catholic hierarchy had invited us to give a concert in the historic and picturesque *Notre Dame de Paris*. This must have been a first for a Protestant choir.

In a newsletter to our friends I wrote, "Many of you prayed and were concerned for my annual physical check-up. With overflowing hearts we can report that all the tests were okay. Free and released for another year to serve! We are praising God for His goodness."

The year 1973 began with a bang. I had to attend YFCI's Executive Council meeting in Hong Kong from January 15-19. On the way I met with Leonard Rogers in Karachi, Pakistan, to teach at a YFCI leadership school. He was YFC's area director for the Middle East and helped out Victor Manogoram who was in charge of Asia.

We met in a lovely retreat center operated by Presbyterian missionaries. missionary activity there was extremely difficult but we felt by training young Pakistanis, youth could be reached.

Food was something that we had a little difficulty with. Late after our last session Len said, "Why don't we have a meal in a western restaurant?" But we encountered a locked fence gate. No problem. I wonder what the Pakistani guests thought when they saw us climb over the fence. Returning later we had to do it one more time, but we were more skilled the next time.

In Hong Kong some of us were on the way to a fancy restaurant. "Listen, fellas," I said, "we really ought to try out some genuine local food, and not the westernized stuff we are used to in the hotel. But to my horror, when we turned a corner and approached the restaurant in deep "China town," I saw a guy spitting into the container of hot water in which he was washing dishes.

"No way; let's get out of here," I spluttered. In no time we were back in a sophisticated eating place.

But the highbrow meetings of our YC leaders went well.

While the other leaders went on to South Korea for more leadership training, I took a quick trip to Australia and New Zealand. I did not at first realize that it is a long haul from Hong Kong to Sydney—twelve hours in those days.

In Sydney I had an experience that threw me for a loop. I never had such an encounter before and never since. I was settled in well at my hotel, bone tired, and delighted with the hours of sleep I finally had. It must have been around 3 a.m. in the morning when someone knocked at my door. Sleepily and grudgingly I opened the door. A lady stood there and in a disappointed voice she muttered, "Sorry, the wrong man."

I banged the door hard in her face.

Back home in Germany, I quickly had to get ready for my next assignment. Our first European YFC staff conference came up from February 13-17. We met in a brand new conference center in Dorfweil, a little town in the Taunus Mountains northwest of Frankfurt. What a gorgeous center; with indoor swimming pool and all!

Each YFC country is autonomous, so it is easy to get involved only in the national program at the expense of caring for the other countries of Europe. Realizing this, I had prayed that the Holy Spirit would use the conference to bind us together.

The conference was a great spiritual success. For the first time, many of the staff felt they belonged to a greater YFC family.

We talked, listened, ate, fellowshipped, learned, and prayed together. It was a wonderful and new experience!

Together we pursued the idea of helping one specific country in Europe. We targeted Denmark. We sat aside one entire evening to pray particularly for this nation. The prayer meeting went on and on and finally ended at midnight. The spirit of unity touched us all. Our delegates demonstrated the willingness to work together for a common goal.

As a result of this conference a trilingual (English, French, and German) news bulletin was begun. Finally, the European coworkers found each other, shared with, and prayed for each other.

CHAPTER 14

TERRORISTS IN LEBANON, BUT BILLY GRAHAM'S AMAZING OFFER

IN JULY, A period when the Middle East was sitting on a powder keg once more, Len Rodgers, YFC's area director for the Middle East, pointed to button two as he was taking me up in an elevator in one of Beirut's building and cautioned me, "That entire floor is one of the strongholds of the Palestinian commandos—you are going to stay on Floor eight."

This sent shivers down my spine.

Never before had I felt so close to the Middle East problem. Of course, the awful scenes of the Munich massacre flashed through my mind. This capital city of Lebanon, less than 300 miles north of Tel Aviv, was full of dedicated Palestinian freedom fighters. That night I was sleeping a few floors above some of those threatening terrorists!

YFCI had asked me to teach at a leadership training school in Lebanon. The political situation was very touchy. Weeks before, five of our students who had planned to attend were on a Russian plane that had crashed in Jordan. None of them were seriously injured. However, since only one weekly flight was operating between Jordan and Lebanon in those days and the borders between those two countries were closed due to the political situation, they were not able to attend.

We had a thriving YFC ministry in Lebanon, but we wanted to expand into other Arab countries. Missionaries from the outside were not appreciated, so we wanted to train Arab youth to begin YFC ministries in their respective countries.

The attendees came from Egypt, Lebanon, Syria, and the African nation of Kenya. They included two medical doctors, a law student, several teachers, and an air force pilot. An outstanding group of men! I wrote my friends:

> Tomorrow the school begins. Here I sit on the eighth floor looking out over this beautiful city of Beirut. I can make out the lights of a few fishing boats out on the ocean. My heart goes out to the many Arab youth, many of whom have never yet heard the story of love through Jesus. Many of them only know hate, because all they have experienced so far is a world of malice, strife, and war. How I wish to become like those fishing boats out there—catching "fish" for our Lord.

Things changed rapidly in our lives. In the middle of a two-week vacation I received a call from the wife of our YFC director in Portugal. "Please come down to Portugal and speak at our YFC camp! My husband was supposed to be the featured speaker, but he fell off a ladder, broke a vertebra, and is in a Lisbon hospital."

Three days later I was on a plane heading for Portugal. I met an enthusiastic crowd of young people right on the coast of

Southern Portugal, and for one week I saw the Lord do a work in the hearts of many of them.

But I did not dare to play basketball! My big toe was not willing to take another whack.

In 1974 a big day for us arrived. *Jugend für Christus in Deutschland* celebrated its twenty-fifth anniversary. More than 3,000 packed into a hall in Gießen that seated only 2,200 for this celebration. Our national chorale with seventy members performed, which was at that time ministering with great effect all over Germany. At one performance they had an audience of 20,000! It seemed that we were in the midst of something special that God was doing through the ministry we were involved with.

It was during this busy time when Billy Graham asked me to meet with him in London. "We want to close down some of our overseas offices, and Germany is one of them," he told me.

"You cannot do that," I responded, being a member of his organization. "Your ministry is extremely vital in our land. We need you!"

"Well, if this is the way you feel about it, I must ask you to take over our office there. Only then will I will be willing to keep it open."

Now I was stuck. I told him about my full-time responsibilities with Youth for Christ. After much prayer I then accepted his challenge. And what a blessing it turned out to be! I moved his office from downtown Frankfurt to Langen, only two miles away from our home in Egelsbach. I combined the two offices of Europe YFC and BGEA, and for the next few years this became the hub of my activities.

In a newsletter to our friends I wrote:

Some of you may have heard by now that I was asked to take over the work of the Billy Graham Evangelistic Association (BGEA) in Germany on a part-time basis. I already served on their board for a number of years. After much heart-searching and prayer I decided to give part of my time to this work, plus continuing on with Youth for Christ in Europe. Now, with the new situation, the new link has proven to be a positive element in many ways.

Again I can only praise the Lord how things fell into place. It was so rewarding.

Malta is a tiny speck in the Mediterranean Sea. Three hundred and twenty thousand people lived on that island when Inge and I vacationed there in June of 1974. However, it was big enough to be a member of the European Union. Early Phoenicians settled there and ever since then it has been rich with history. Napoleon conquered it, and in 1830, or thereabouts, the British took over. During the Second World War it was a much fought over and heroically defended place. In 1963 the Maltese received their independence, and ever since then they have been trying to lure tourists to their shores.

We were two of them. We traveled with Air Malta; its services had just started a few weeks before on April 1—and that with only two planes. To our amazement, the prime minister of Malta traveled with us.

We found the island uniquely beautiful but spiritually dead. On Easter Sunday we visited the small Brethren Assembly—the only evangelical church on the island—and worshipped with a handful of English, Irish, and two Maltese Christians. You could count all Maltese Christians on two hands.

The year before a few foreigners wanted to pass out tracts and were stoned off the island—literally—the people picked up stones and drove them back onto the ship. The Catholic Church had a firm grip on the people and suspicion was rampant and unbridled.

Time and again, as we walked through the densely populated little towns and saw the many young people cluster around everywhere, our hearts went out to them. "We must do something for them," I wrote to our friends. "No doubt, Malta is one of the darkest and most difficult places to reach for Christ in all of Europe."

Right after the First International Conference on Evangelism held in Lausanne from July 16-25, 1974, sponsored by BGEA, Youth for Christ International invited a little over one hundred of its world leaders to Les Diablerets in the Swiss mountains. Those were terrific days. The highlight was when Billy and Ruth Graham showed up. Both of them shared, and Inge was especially moved by Ruth's comments. Ruth had been her distant mentor and now she had the thrill to meet her in person.

Other Christian world leaders who ministered to us were Bob Pierce, founder of World Vision; Francis Schaeffer of L'Abri Fellowship; Paul Little of Inter-Varsity Christian Fellowship, who soon after was killed in a tragic auto accident; and Ted Engstrom, President of World Vision; among others.

Following those mountain-top experiences I wrote:

> With all of this exciting development I am more aware than
> ever that we, as YFC, are only playing a small part in achieving
> this goal [world evangelization]. Together with other outstand-

ing organizations we want to see our world evangelized. However, this "small part" is God's part cut out for us. My heart's desire is to be found faithful in God's vineyard.

In Germany we started a new type of evangelistic ministry. We bought an old English double-decker bus, the ones you see in London, and transformed it into a traveling coffee house. We called it *Teemobil* (Teamobil). Coffee houses had become en vogue at that time, but instead of being stationary we drove the bus from city to city, parking it in the city center or near a high school and inviting young people in for some coffee and a chat. Multitude of youth who never went to church were thus reached. The bus was staffed with eight YFC workers, and they had the time of their lives inviting their counterparts to decide for Christ.

From a little town in northern Germany I heard the amazing news, that twenty-eight young people had committed their lives to Christ and that another twenty-five were counseled. In southern Germany a young man on his way to a bridge to commit suicide saw the bus. He entered and found the Lord. Miracle after miracle took place in the rolling coffee house!

Suicide at Eurofest 75

Billy Graham again invited me to join with twenty-five other European church leaders from many denominations to meet with him in Paris to study the feasibility of inviting 15,000 young people to a Bible teaching and evangelistic event. We chose Brussels, Belgium, for the occasion. I was asked to become chairman of the executive committee. With so many other responsibilities already at hand, I was now thrown into another one. I accepted the challenge with fear and trembling.

We rented several hundred thousand square yards of available camping space for youth and ten exposition buildings for meetings. These were located on the famous Brussels Fair Grounds (built for the 1958 World's Fair) with the famed Atomium in its center. This phenomenal structure with its nine spectacular spheres is now the most popular tourist attraction and the symbol of Europe's capital. One of the spheres houses a restaurant high above the ground.

Eurofest 75 took place from July 24 – August 2, 1975.

It turned out to be an exciting event. Thousands of youth from all across Europe overran the city. Every morning for the first Bible hour I woke up the crowd by challenging them to clap each time when I would cross my hands. I warned them only to clap when my hands actually crossed. I started slowly crossing them. Cautiously they would clap. I went faster, so they did. Then I would feign doing it, but before crossing my hands I would stop. Thousands of claps thundered through the hall with screeches of laughter. We started all over again. Cautiously at first they would clap, then faster and faster until I stopped crossing my hands again. Again they misread the cue and thousands of claps resounded through the hall with hilarity. It was fun and everyone was wide awake, ready to study the Scriptures.

After the Bible hour, seminars on specific subjects were given and then the participants split up in mini-groups of ten. That's where the greatest impact was achieved. In these groups they got to know each other personally and were able to have in-depth discussions and dialogues, which resulted in in-depth commitments. We had set up a special room called Oasis, where hundreds of them were counseled by a team of select counselors. They did not come to accept Christ—most of them were Christians—but they came to have their problems solved and to have their deep spiritual needs met.

In the afternoons further optional seminars were given. Thousands went out into the streets to witness.

I was standing in the midst of some young people one morning, when unexpectedly one of our leaders approached me saying, "Something terrible has happened." He pulled me aside. "City authorities informed me that one of our young participants has committed suicide."

Stunned, I went to find out. "This morning we found him hanging from a tree in the park nearby," a policeman soberly told me. "We identified him as one of yours by his name badge."

How is this possible? These kids came to study the Bible and now this! They led me to the morgue where they pulled the cover off his face. A young man, still in his late teens, had for some reason decided to end his life.

He had been part of a small group from Steyr, Austria. I called his pastor and made arrangements to have his body taken back to his home. Then I assembled his close friends, about seven, in my office and shared with them this terrible news. Some of them broke down and wept. "Why did he do this?" they asked. I had no answer. But again I realized how important it is to help young people through challenges and troubles they have deep inside. This was the first and only time in my life when I had to deal with suicide.

CHAPTER 15

OUTREACH
INTO THE WORLD

BACK AT HOME, Inge was busy with our kids. In a letter to our friends we wrote:

> We are starting a different approach to tell neighbors and friends that Christ is the answer. We do not want to forget our next door neighbors while we try to reach Europe! We started a YFC club in our home. This way we hope to reach their parents, not just mothers. Our three teenagers are assisting us eagerly in this new venture. Erik is president, Heiko is vice president, and Stephan is treasurer. One week we gear our program to non-Christian kids with lots of games, singing, a short Bible talk, and of course refreshments and the other week for Christians with Bible study and prayer. We started with fourteen kids.

The daughter of one of our neighbors in Egelsbach (Steffi Bernatzki) found the Lord and later married a young man (Gerd Hutschenreuter), who also became a believer through our effort.

In fact, our daughter Linda, still a child at that time, had led her to the Lord. Steffi later became a medical doctor and he an engineer. They now live near Hannover in northern Germany and are members of a thriving church and supporters of China Partner. What a blessing they have been over the years. But it all started at Frankfurter Strasse 18 in Egelsbach—our home.

When Erik and Heiko left for the States to attend Houghton Academy in the State of New York, we had our final get-together. Thirty-five teenagers crowded into our small living room on that occasion. It was thrilling to see kids so open to receive the Word of God! Even more thrilling to see it happen in our own home. The lives of our children have been an inspiration for many, and we as parents thank the Lord from the depth of our hearts for having kept them close to Him. Today Erik is president of China Partner, Heiko senior pastor of Neely's Creek Presbyterian Church in Rock Hill, SC. Stephan is a senior executive of a financial company in Boca Raton and is sometimes wondering whether to change to get involved in spiritual ministry fulltime, besides being involved in his church. Linda fell in love with China and is contemplating to work for China Partner.

My love for our own children was so strong that I often wrote about them in my journal. For instance, on March 2, 1988, I wrote:

Great time with the Lord, how wonderful to be in this ministry, even though I am lonely; my sweetheart so far away! This draws me closer to her and our children. Quality prayer time for them, prayed for by name, as I always do, but petitioned for their individual needs.

On September 1, 1989, I wrote this:

Stephan and Barbara came over for pizza dinner—how wonderful to have them with us! While playing tennis with our kids, I had a deep, deep satisfaction and joy—it almost "hurt" in my breast—to have such kids! They mean so much to me. God gave us so much in them!

In May 1975 I was in Vienna, the beautiful Austrian capital. The head of the YMCA had invited me for a six-day crusade. "Don't expect anything big!" he had warned. "If eighty young people show up in the evening meetings, we are doing all right. One hundred fifty is the absolute maximum." Austria was known as a stronghold of Catholicism.

No wonder for such a gloomy forecast, if you consider all of Vienna with a population of 1.5 million and not more than 1,500 born-again Christians. That is one tenth of one percent!

Well, it turned out altogether differently. On the first night we had one hundred kids. It steadily increased, so that by the last night some three hundred youth overcrowded the YMCA hall. They even had to install a closed-circuit TV system to broadcast the service to a downstairs hall. One Christian leader marveled, "Not since 1937 have I seen so many kids come to this hall! This is absolutely amazing." Best of all, each evening young people found Christ.

Portugal is another country with very few followers of Jesus. Youth for Christ in that country had started a new type of ministry by forming a YFC Ping-Pong team. When they started this new phase of their outreach to kids that otherwise would never enter a church, little did they realize what an unusual impact on sports-oriented kids this would make. They won every contest in the Lisbon area except one against the national champions. When receiving their trophies, they would always give a testimony of their faith in Christ.

I was down there and watched them win the finals of one of their tournaments. The newspaper wrote them up as "a team who is not only out to win, but also uses their talents to gain interest in their ideology." Their ideology of course was Christ. In the beginning the opposing teams mocked them for their strange name. *How can you call a ping pong team "Youth for Christ,"* they ridiculed. Then they changed their mind and respectfully feared them. God was working in hearts of Portuguese young people.

One added blessing of serving on the European BGEA board and directing Billy Graham's ministry in German-speaking Europe was to be invited to his team meetings. Travel and accommodation were paid for and therefore we were able to accompany Erik and Heiko when they moved to and settled in Houghton. It was bitter cold early in January of 1976, and I can still see them staggering through deep snow, coming from the dorm to say farewell. The director of the academy drove us and our boys to the airport in Buffalo, NY, where we huddled one more time as family to pray together. Then came a heart-wrenching good-bye for God knows how long. On the plane Inge was weeping all the way to New York, where we transferred to reach Orlando for the team meeting. She was heart-broken and understandably so. Our nest began to empty at that time.

The presence of the Lord was always evident in those meetings. Generally, all of his associate evangelists spoke, but when Billy was on, something exceptional was in the air. God's anointing was clearly on that man. The longer I knew him, the more I was impressed. I do not know of any other person who so noticeably walked with the Lord. I often thought of Enoch "who walked with God: and he was not; for God took him" (Genesis 5:24). In another version it says: "He [Enoch] enjoyed a close relationship with God throughout his life. Then suddenly, he disappeared because God took him."

Sometimes I wondered why the Lord did not do the same with Billy. I should have asked his wife, Ruth, why He did not. She knew him better than anyone else and no doubt she saw his weaknesses that we did not. But Billy Graham is an exceptional man.

During the summer of 1976, youth organizations across Germany hosted another large youth training event called Christival. It was so refreshing to band together for the common cause of evangelism and discipleship training. A new generation in love with Christ was emerging. Evangelical seminaries and Bible schools were bulging while liberal training centers in universities were declining. In the early '80s, universities once filled with liberal students had to make way to dedicated born-again evangelical students. A noted liberal theologian stated, "I fear a complete takeover by evangelical students."

Jamaica is a beautiful country. During the time we had ministered there in the years from 1967-68, we had developed close friendships with many wonderful Christians. In the summer of 1976 Walter Hart, with his wife Joni, a well-to-do businessman in Kingston, offered his vacation home on the north coast to us—and that free of charge. Erik and Heiko traveled by Greyhound bus many hours from Houghton all the way to Miami, and together from there we hopped over to Jamaica.

The sunny and warm climate was just the right thing for us Germans. Lying on the beach soaking up the sun and snorkeling in the pristine turquoise waters was absolutely gorgeous. Our four children have never forgotten those two weeks; neither did their parents. A Jamaican lady working for the Harts cooked and cleaned house for us. It probably was the best vacation we have ever had!

When we said farewell to the Harts in Kingston, he handed us a pile of Jamaican money. We couldn't believe it! It took care of all the groceries for the entire two weeks. Wow. God was so good to us.

To top it all off, the final evening we attended a Youth for Christ rally in Kingston. 4,000 young people filled the auditorium and more than one hundred were counseled at the close of the meeting. The Lord had mightily used Gerry Gallimore to propel the ministry forward like never before. This Jamaican firebrand was overseeing twelve weekly rallies across the island. Evangelistic thrusts were carried out by special teams all the time. He had overseen the purchase of a centrally located youth center. YFC was reaching tens of thousands of youth in every major city of Jamaica.

Brazil and Geração 79

In February 1977 I wrote:

With mixed emotions I am winding down my ministry with Europe YFC. Initially I had pledged to give five years of my life to the task of directing our YFC ministries across Europe. However, our national directors asked me to stay on for one more year, until a new director can take over. I am on my last stretch now—four months to go! Joy and satisfaction flood my heart when I think of God's choosing and appointment of the new man. He is the man I have prayed for over a period of three years. In June he is ready to take over the helm.

The Lord is leading me into a new phase of ministry. My first assignment as Director of Outreach Ministries for our world program is a huge training and evangelistic event scheduled for Brazil—just like Eurofest. This coming Friday I am leaving for Brazil to put into place some initial groundwork. It will be a five-week-long trip. With new horizons, new responsibilities emerge. Please help us shoulder them.

As I look back over those years, I am made acutely aware that only with the prayers and financial support of many friends we were able to do what we did. I shall be ever grateful for committed people who made this possible.

For the upcoming event in Brazil named Geração79, I had to raise $500,000. Half of this amount would come in from fees of the participants, but the other half I had to shoulder. When I mentioned this to Billy Graham on one of his trips to Europe, he said, "I think we can help." I had asked him to be the keynote speaker for this event. A few weeks later I was on a fundraising tour through the States. Waiting at the airport of Cleveland, Ohio, I heard my name on the loudspeaker system: "Werner Bürklin, please call the airport facilities." I did and was told that the office of BGEA tried to reach me.

One of Billy Graham's secretaries informed me that the board of BGEA had approved $50,000 for Geração 79. This was a phenomenal start. Later they sent an additional $50,000.

Before moving to Brazil, I was on the road constantly. I don't think I have ever done as much traveling as in the months prior to Brazil. It was a great thrill to see so many friends and to make new ones. But it is also quite a chore. I never knew traveling could be so taxing. Often I felt lonely. However, the love for Christ and the love for young people kept me going. During those tempestuous times I learned that the grace of God is all-sufficient. Rereading my journal years later, I found this entry written on July 1, 1989, during a sleepless night in China:

> Back to bed at 4 a.m.—still couldn't sleep, prayed and thought much about my life. Feel so lonely on trips like these; sometimes question whether it is all worth it. Others can stay home, have a regular job, enjoy recreation, go to church, and do all those things that make life so important to millions of people. But then I realize what privilege I have traveling in the name of Christ, representing several hundred friends who pray and give towards my ministry. Above all I am an ambassador for Christ and then a representative or "spokesman" for countless Christians.

Inge at home had bought study books and tapes to learn Portuguese. "You will be in committee meetings where English is spoken," she told me. "But I have to go shopping in the market-place." She was right.

Then in July of 1978 we were off to Brazil with Stephan and Linda in tow. We were amazed how wonderfully God had gone before step by step in the weeks that preceded our move. And in so many details! It was not easy to uproot a family, especially at our age with children who were still going to school. But I was especially yearning for a spiritual venture. I wrote to our supporting friends:

My prayer is that God may give us a deeply committed teaching staff. We need a staff "who walk the talk" and [teachers at the congress] who will really live [out] what they teach. And then I pray for thousands of young people who will come expectantly and openly, and who are willing to drink in what will be offered to them. May God revolutionize thousands of Brazilian youth! May this be another turning point in Brazil's history!

Confident and in good spirits, we boarded the train in Frankfurt on July 10 which took us across France to Cherbourg, where we went aboard the beautiful new *Queen Elizabeth II* to make a memorable and most enjoyable Atlantic crossing to New York. Five days later, after a smooth and relaxing voyage, we arrived amid dark clouds, lightening, and heavy rains at six o'clock in the morning.

Despite two hours waiting in line at customs, we did not have to open one single piece of our eighteen pieces of luggage. Three pieces were shipped directly to Miami, where we wanted to pick them up after two weeks of fundraising in America.

But they got lost. We had to leave without them on July 30, and only after four weeks of desperate searching, friends in Miami located them and shipped them on. What a relief to finally receive and unpack the precious items in Brazil.

The staff in São Paulo to prepare for Geração79 had grown to ten committed people. The first night there, we settled into the Novotel on the outskirts of that metropolis. This large city with a population of 18 million was founded in 1532. It was the first permanent Portuguese colony in the New World. The streets were clogged with some 8 million cars when we arrived.

221

The traffic was horrific. No one cared about traffic lights. The joke of the town was this:

A tourist was stunned and scared when his taxi went through red lights with incredible speed but stopped when they turned green. "Stop doing this," the tourist shouted. The taxi driver replied, "Do you think I am crazy? Going through on green lights would be suicide being hit by all those cars coming from the other side!

Amazingly, the next day looking for an apartment, we found one on the eighteenth floor of a skyscraper only twenty minutes' drive from the center of town, where our office was located. It was the perfect fit for us and we moved in the following day.

Brazil as a nation deeply intrigued me. The people in general seemed to be "forward looking." This reminded me of Israel, a nation with tremendous pride and expectation for the future. The first time I visited Israel, I was struck with its people being courageous, hardworking, innovative, and pioneering. Out of a desert they built an amazing infrastructure. Brazil to me appeared similar. I also sensed it in the churches I visited across Brazil. They were full of life and enthusiasm. Young people appeared to be everywhere. I was told that 70 percent of the population is twenty-five years old and younger.

From our eighteenth floor four-room apartment we often looked over the many skyscrapers of this immense city with its millions of people, and felt so lost and insignificant and powerless and so overwhelmed by the task ahead of us. "Stand with us!" we wrote to our friends, "Uphold us! Strengthen our hands and hearts!"

And they did.

When I spoke at a youth camp in Belo Horizonte, scores of kids surrendered their lives to Christ.

One of the girl attendees was Miss Brazil '75. She had come to Christ through YFC. She was born in Blumenau in southern Brazil, a gorgeous town with a large portion of its population of German descent. "I want to go to Bible school," she told me, "and then work for Youth for Christ."

We rented the Anhembi Exhibition Center with its 23,000 square meters of covered space. Initially the city authorities were reluctant renting it to us when we told them about our plans to house thousands of young people in that locale. We had done it at Eurofest in Brussels! So they relented. We had to install showers, kitchen facilities, and spaces for training. We planned to house, feed, and train up to 15,000 young people all under one roof. It was a massive undertaking.

The rent alone was $53,000.

A week before the congress a receptionist at Anhembi came running up to me exclaiming, "I will attend the congress!" Two days before I had witnessed to her about the Lord. She had been so interested in what we were trying to do with thousands of young people. She was amazed that so many would come for one week of studying the Bible. She then admitted that she was searching. I asked two of our staff to go see and talk to her at her home. She was a Jewish girl. Her parents entered into the conversation, which lasted until 1 o'clock in the morning. At that time she and her parents accepted Christ!

This was just the beginning of what was going to be a phenomenal congress.

The rhythmic congress song "Unidos no Corpo de Cristo" (United in the body of Christ) that was sung with enthusiasm by thousands of South American youth was something to hear and behold. It had been composed by a Brazilian congressman. Holding hands and with smiles on their faces, those young people sang it day after day.

They had come mostly from Brazil, but thirteen other countries were represented. Let me just share one amazing incident.

A girl from Manaus in northern Brazil was heartbroken. She had arrived in pouring rain after having been on the bus for five days. The person who had promised to pay her registration fee did not follow through. Shivering in the unusual cold, she sat alone until 5 p.m. and then started to weep. She did not know what to do. Someone noticed her, took her to the registration booth, and through some available scholarships she soon joined the throng of smiling and happy young participants.

Another girl had all of her money stolen at a bus station on the way to the congress. A group of young people put their money together and paid her registration fee.

Anhembi became an anthill of young people with sleeping bags, mattresses, guitars, and Bibles. Seventy-five toilets and three hundred showers had been built under the guidance of a few competent volunteer engineers. The gigantic hall had been portioned off by zigzag wooden walls into girls' and boys' dorms. A huge area remained for meetings and other activities.

The Bible was the center of everything. First the Epistle to the Colossians was taught by one of Brazil's foremost Bible teachers. Then groups of three hundred were instructed by competent pastors and group leaders. Finally clusters of ten were formed for discussions and then they prayed by twos or threes. Throughout the morning those young people sat on the floor, literally at the feet of their teachers.

At the closing meeting more than one-fourth streamed forward, some with tears running down their cheeks, dedicating their entire lives to the Lord.

60,000 people attended the final evangelistic rally in the huge stadium. Billy Graham preached and hundreds walked forward to accept Christ. A Brazilian news commentator reported after the rally, "Many large events took place this afternoon. The Formula 1 Grand Prix attracted 35,000 people, at the horse race the largest number ever were present. A soccer game at the Pacambu Stadium attracted thousands, but Billy Graham topped them all with 100,000 coming out to hear him at the Morumbi Stadium."

Well, he somewhat got carried away! However, Billy did attract more than all other events. The bottom line: The final rally was a fitting and gratifying conclusion for this remarkable congress.

After Brazil, Stephan, our third son, moved into the home of Stephan and Gigi Tchividjian in Coral Springs, Florida. Stephan and Gigi had been very good friends since their wedding in Montreux, Switzerland. His father Ara and her father Billy Graham had encouraged me as a young evangelist. Now this godly couple accepted our son as their "seventh child" into their lovely home. They had a son Stephan's age, whose name also was Stephan. They roomed together and went to the same high school, the Westminster Academy in Ft. Lauderdale. Now they had three Stephans in that home!

With all the blessings coming our way, we sometimes had to struggle in our ministry but it seemed it mostly had to do with finances. We depended upon the Lord for our income. True, we received a salary set by Youth for Christ International, but we had to raise it and keep our accounts administered by YFCI

in the black. In December 1979 I had to inform our friends of
the new reality facing us:

> Before I say anything else, I want to share a burden we have.
> Over the last couple of years, our missionary account has
> replenished itself month by month, so that it was consistently
> in the black. But last month it went into the red for the first
> time in a long while.

> We asked ourselves why? Do people think that having finished
> our assignment in Brazil, financial support is not as necessary?
> Or do they think that having moved up to direct worldwide
> projects, our salary is now guaranteed? What is it?

> We look back and see how beautifully the Lord has led us.
> From my conversion and then consecration to full-time
> Christian service in Shanghai, China, as a teenager, I was
> led into Youth for Christ to evangelize and disciple young
> people for Christ. Our ministry first started as a local YFC
> director in Frankfurt, then it expanded to all of Germany,
> and then to Europe. For the last two years or so, our call and
> assignment was to the world.
>
> Have we slackened our thrust? Or is there disobedience?
> We can sincerely say "no." Our love for the Lord and His
> calling and ministry is deepening and maturing. Our desire
> to walk with the Lord and to stay in His will is as fervent as
> ever. Our constant cry is to stay pure and pliable for Him. Is
> financial support no longer necessary? Is the salary automati-
> cally guaranteed? Again "no." We still depend on friends who
> so faithfully have stood behind us all these years. Our salary,
> fixed and paid by YFC, can only be given as long as enough
> money is in our missionary account kept in trust by YFC.

We know we cannot do it alone. Deep down we know that God is with us. And you are our co-workers, you have been a part of our "team" and we thank you for all you have done to make our ministry possible.

A couple of months later I was able to report, "…we want to thank so many of you for having responded to meet our financial need." Again and again we were amazed how the Lord supplied. And He did this year after year!

We were not only involved in large endeavors. In February 1980 I received a call from Ruth Graham. "Would you be able to help a young soldier in Germany?" she asked. "I met his young wife who told me of her husband, who is lonely and homesick living in a foreign country, being separated from his wife and surrounded by people that speak a strange language."

I traveled to Kaster-Putz, a little town near Köln (Cologne) with 7,000 inhabitants, a few stores, and a village church. I entered the US facilities nearby and found that thirty GIs led by a first lieutenant were stationed there. I met and counseled with the nineteen-year old in the cafeteria. He told me that as a Christian he did not have any Christian fellowship and had no spiritual help. A chaplain visited that outpost only occasionally.

"Do you read your Bible," I asked. "No, I do not and I don't know of any other Christian in my unit," he complained.

I then asked to see his superior. I told him that David, above anything else, needed spiritual help. "I am also a believer," the lieutenant admitted.

Two secret Christians lived side by side and did not know of their beliefs. No wonder they needed help.

Right there, while many of the other soldiers sat around the tables eating and watching, we had a time of prayer. The one a foot soldier and the other an officer—and both were believing Christians! None of the others knew, but then they knew. Here were two Christians who now could show the other soldiers what Christ is all about.

Meanwhile Inge spent many hours in counseling. She translated books on the Christian family into German. This and her counseling made us realize that something should be done in helping wives and mothers with their many diverse problems affecting the home and the family. The needs in Germany relating to home, family, and marriage are just as grave as everywhere, possibly even more so because of our culture and our political system. There is hardly a Christian home that we knew of that did not have enormous problems with their children or in their marriage. Why? Liberalism and secular socialism had challenged biblical truths and morals. This had left devastating marks on the Christian home life.

Both Inge and I were deeply concerned, however we felt so overtaxed with the many other responsibilities we shouldered that we were not able to do some of the things we wanted to do. Nevertheless, in a small way we tried to confront this with our home Bible sessions and translations of suitable books.

Walled city in Hong Kong—phenomenal church growth in Korea and China

Have you ever been inside the notorious "walled city" in Hong Kong? Hong Kong is such a glittering city, with its gorgeous skyscrapers, glitzy stores, scrumptious restaurants, and opulent country clubs, that most visitors miss the deficiencies of that megacity. In June of 1980 I visited it for the first time. The YFC director, David Chu, led me into this frightful place. This was the only area under the jurisdiction of Communist China, while the rest was governed by the British. It was said that it is one of the most dangerous places in the world to walk through. Foreigners are scared to enter it. We were advised not to go, however David knew a Christian lady who was helping the neediest there. I was appalled with what I saw! Hard to believe that people can subsist in such squalor! And that in the middle of one of the richest cities of the world! David Chu was considering what YFC could do for its young people.

South Korea is another amazing story. After the disastrous Korean War, that country had made a phenomenal economic recovery, just as Germany did after the Second World War. But what interested me most was the spiritual development. Contrary to Germany, South Korea experienced revival seldom seen in the history of the world. I was told that 35 percent of Korea's capital city Seoul's population goes to church! In Germany only 3 percent do, perhaps even less. When I first entered the city driving by night, I saw red crosses everywhere! Every cross represented an evangelical church. I was told there were two-thousand or more of them. Unbelievable but true.

Billy Kim, one of the most prominent Korean pastors and its YFC area director, interpreted for me speaking in churches and several high schools across the nation. 2,100 students and in another school even 4,200 students attended and hundreds of young people accepted Christ. When we visited the mayor of Seoul, he pledged his support. Amazing! While traveling through Korea, I was reminded of President Kennedy's remark after his tumultuous reception in Berlin many years ago: "When I conclude my presidency, I will leave a note in my presidential desk stating, 'If ever you get discouraged, go visit Germany.'" That's how I felt about my visit in South Korea.

Singapore is another beautiful and fast-moving country. The airport alone at that time was worth seeing. I attended a church where the average age of its members was twenty-three years. I faced hundreds of eager young faces. The oldest elder was twenty-seven years, and the pastor was twenty-five years old. Youth for Christ had a significant influence on the church life in Singapore, particularly in this one.

Ever since my departure from China in 1949 I had a deep desire that one day I would be able to return. It seemed impossible. We had heard disturbing stories of how Christians had been imprisoned or even executed for their faith in Christ. Thousands of mainland Chinese escaped to Hong Kong. All of that did not sound good. Truly, the bamboo curtain had descended.

Then Mao Zedong died in 1976. With new leadership some of the stringent policies were overturned. Finally Deng Xiao Ping proclaimed an open-door policy. "I don't care," he said, "whether the cat is white or black as long as she catches mice." In other words, Communism is not the ultimate answer to the needs of the people. He threw the doors wide open to other choices. Capitalism was one of them.

This is my chance, I thought. Toward the end of 1980 I began making plans to visit China. I called the Chinese embassy in Bonn but was rebuffed. "You may go but you have to join a tourist group," I was told.

I thought they can do better than that! I knew that no tourist group would travel to those places I was interested in. I got my car out of the garage and drove straight to Bonn, the capital city of West Germany at that time. The Chinese embassy had just been built by workers flown in from China. They did not trust the German workers; *they could have installed listening devices to*

230

spy on the activities, they must have reasoned. Not an unusual assumption! Such things had been done numerous times in other embassies.

A petite, attractive, and well-groomed lady from Beijing met with me. She was the head of the cultural department. I had come to apply for a visa. After a few pleasantries she asked, "What is a church?"

I was stunned for I had not expected a Communist lady to come out with such a straightforward question. No doubt, she must have done her homework. How else would she know that I had something to do with religion? Perhaps before meeting with me, she had delved into the archives of missionary activities of the past and found out that I had lived in China. Anyway, she seemed to be well informed about my past.

Interestingly, a couple of years later, on another visit to China with our son Stephan, he was stopped by the border police and asked to enter an interrogation room. "You are Stephan Bürklin," the official said. "What is your Chinese name?" "I have none," he answered. The official handed him a book filled with names. As Stephan leafed through the pages, he was amazed to spot the name Bürklin. "You see," the official said, "You do have a Chinese name: Lin." With that he let him go.

To us this was a confirmation that the authorities knew exactly which foreigners and where they had lived in China. Stephan was the grandson of missionaries, and the authorities knew it.

Now back to Bonn.

"I come from Beijing," she continued. "I have been here for two months. While exploring the countryside, I noticed big buildings with steeples. Are those churches?"

"Yes, those are churches. But the real church is made up of people who follow Jesus Christ," I replied.

"Who is Jesus Christ?" she probed.

No doubt this intelligent lady had heard about Jesus. Officials who work in an embassy are well versed in the culture of the land in which they serve. I sensed she wanted to know more about Him besides what she had learned during her university studies.

I wanted to be sure that she would really understand why people worship in those buildings. "Real churches are not just buildings but are made up of people who worship Jesus, the Son of God."

"Do you think the church can change man?" was her next question.

Wow, what a question!

"No, the church cannot, but Jesus can," I replied. Immediately I thought of Mao Zedong whose goal had been to change man. In the process he enslaved an entire nation, but people did not change for the better. In fact, they got worse. He raised a nation of hypocrites. No wonder she was intrigued by Jesus, who not only changed man but also altered history. She wanted to find the truth.

Finally, in March 1981 I left for China.

Let me quote what I wrote about that first trip back to China:

It was March 1949. A small ship [SS Rena], formerly used to ferry people across the English Channel, floated down the Huangpu River from Shanghai on its first leg to Europe. I was on that ship to return to my home in Germany. Many, many years later an even smaller boat took me back to China. It was a three-hour trip from Hong Kong to Canton [Guangzhou]. What an exhilarating experience to touch Chinese soil after thirty-two years!

However, to continue from there it was not as easy as I thought. In my book *Jesus Never Left China* I had given a vivid description of my encounter with Chinese authorities:

A young Chinese met me at the pier. Claiming to be a tourist guide, he offered to show me Guangzhou. I wondered whether the authorities had sent him to keep an eye on me. During those years few foreigners ventured into China, and the authorities were suspicious of them. But I did not care. I wanted to go home.

"Please take me to the immigration office," I requested.
"Why?"
"A telex is waiting for me there."

This nice young man accommodated my wishes and did not argue. Once we arrived, the officials promptly informed me that I had come in vain.

"There is no telex for you. We don't even have telex machines in our offices."
"I am going to go back to Hong Kong," I told my new friend as I retrieved my passport.
"Oh, no!" he exclaimed. "You have come to see China!"

Yes, I had, but the China I wanted to see was not on any tourist trip. But I changed my mind.

From Guangzhou I proceeded by train to Shanghai. I knew I would be traveling through Jiangxi, the province I was interested in. It was a thirty-hour-long journey. As I woke up at 7 a.m., I saw the name of the station, Changshu. That was the place where my brother Friedel had been born and so I knew that I was close to where I wanted to go.

"I wonder whether I can just get off at one of these stations," I asked a businessman from Hong Kong, who was sitting in my compartment.

"You are crazy," he responded. "In the middle of China? No doubt you will run into difficulties. You cannot trust those Communists!"

But I did not care. I was going to take a chance. At the next stop I got off. Some of the train conductors followed me but had to jump back on when the train started to move again. I stayed put. I waved at them and they waved back.

There I was in the middle of China not knowing what to do. The station manager made a phone call and motioned me to wait. I sat down on my suitcase and read my Bible. That was my habit each morning. I also prayed and said, "Lord, give me courage to do the unusual and sensitivity to know when to stop."

After a few hours a car drove up. A younger man walked up to me and asked in good English, "What in the world are you doing here?"

He drove me to the police station in Nanchang, the capital city of Jiangxi.

The head of the police sat behind a table. He was dressed like Mao. All Chinese at that time were dressed alike. He lectured me on what I could and could not do in China. One forbidden thing was getting off a train in the middle of China without permission. Several policemen watched as I tried to explain why I had jumped off the train.

"I wanted to go home," I replied. This startled him.
"What do you mean, 'go home'?"
"I used to live here."
"How come?"
"My parents lived here," I replied.

At that point I felt a little uneasy. Perspiration dampened my collar.

I had heard that Communists were tough, but my interrogator was surprisingly courteous. I guess he kind of liked me for having done what I did. *Not too many foreigners would jump off a train in the middle of China,* he must have mused. *This guy is weird.* He wanted to know more about me, and his questions were relentless.

"So your parents lived here," the uniformed commander ventured. "What in the world did they do here?"
"My parents were missionaries."

Then I placed the identity card that had been issued when we lived in Jiangxi on his table. He examined it closely. It contained Chinese characters with my Chinese name and the address where I had lived. He smiled as he studied the photo of a sixteen-year-old. Many years had passed since it was taken. He showed it around, then getting up from his desk, the police chief walked toward me. While shaking my hand, he said, "Welcome home." Within three hours I had a special permit to visit every town and village I wanted to see.

I was back home.

I was given a car, a driver, and an interpreter and headed off into the countryside. Although I went to places where foreigners had not been for over thirty years, I sensed no hostility whatsoever. I was wined and dined at every stop. Usually the mayor of town threw a banquet. I really lived it up. I was taken to the remotest areas, walked through towns and villages, visited homes and farms. I was allowed to see the former mission compounds and "Jesus halls." I saw the churches where once my father had preached. I walked through the dining rooms and bedrooms where I formerly had lived. It was an amazing experience I shall never forget.

Another thing I learned through this experience. As I said above, I had been beholden to prevalent opinion that Communists are dangerous, cruel, unforgiving, callous, inconsiderate, and hard to deal with. This may have been true during the early days of their régime, but things had changed. Henry Kissinger in his book *Henry Kissinger on China* expressed a different view:

> Chinese diplomacy has learned from millennia of experience that, in international issues, each apparent solution is generally an admission ticket to a new set of related problems. Hence Chinese diplomats consider continuity of relationships an important task and perhaps more important than formal documents.
>
> By comparison, American diplomacy tends to segment issues into self-contained units to be dealt with on their own merits. In this task, American diplomats also prize good personal relations. The difference is that Chinese leaders relate the

"friendship" less to personal qualities and more to long-term cultured, national, or historic ties; Americans stress the individual qualities of their counterparts. Chinese protestations of friendship seek durability for long-term relationships through the cultivation of intangibles; Americans equivalents attempt to facilitate ongoing activities by emphasis on social contact. And Chinese leaders will pay some (though not unlimited) price for the reputation of standing by their friends.

In all of my visits starting with the first one I found this to be true. The Chinese, whether Communists or not, are generally courteous and genteel. I quickly fell in love with them.

CHAPTER 16

GOOD-BYE TO EGELSBACH— IMMIGRATION TO THE US— CHINA IS BECKONING

HAVING LIVED IN Egelsbach for several years, we were burdened for the many residents who did not know Christ. Egelsbach at that time had a population of nine thousand. When we moved there in 1964 we only knew of one other Christian believer—a woman.

Over the years we used our home for youth Bible clubs, ladies' Bible classes, prayer meetings, and women' seminars. This had been our way to reach out to our neighbors and community. We had been involved all over the world, yet we also wanted our home to be used at least in some small way as an evangelistic base for our home town. But we wanted even more. We wanted the entire town to have a chance to hear the gospel.

So we asked Wolfgang Leo, YFC's film evangelist, to show evangelistic films for an entire week. As far as we know, this was the first evangelistic thrust in Egelsbach. What a wonderful experience to see unbelievers come out. Not large crowds, but attentive ones. They filled the little town hall and stayed on for

239

questions, sharing, and discussion. Many of them were young people, and on some nights sixty percent of them had no clue what Christianity was all about. We did not have a great harvest but we saw individuals make commitments—some publicly and others quietly.

A start had been made and God had worked. This was the last endeavor we made before leaving Egelsbach for good. In late 1982 we became resident aliens of the United States. We sold our house for DM 410,000 (we had bought it for DM 100,000 in 1969) and bought a condo in Boca West, Boca Raton, Florida.

The reason for our move? All our four children wanted to attend Christian colleges in the US. We reasoned that they would probably find their mates there and then settle in the States. They did. We wanted to be close to them and later our grandchildren. It was a wise decision and move!

While preparing and directing the International Conference of Itinerant Evangelists (ICIE), also called Amsterdam '83, I spent most of my time living in the Apollo Hotel in Amsterdam. Inge established our home in Boca Raton, Florida, because our Linda was attending high school at the Boca Raton Christian School. Erik had joined YFC Ft. Lauderdale, and Heiko took up studies at Gordon-Conwell Seminary in Boston following Amsterdam '83. Stephan transferred from Taylor University to Florida Atlantic University in Boca Raton for one year.

Directing Amsterdam '83 took me around the world. Never before have I traveled so much. We were looking for worthy evangelists. 5,100 registered participants crowded into the huge, blue-draped, and nicely decorated Southhall of the enormous and internationally known RAI Exhibition Center.

70 percent of them came from the Third World, and most had never attended a major conference at any time before. A large number had never traveled outside of their own countries. The average age was forty-one.

For ten days the evangelists met for inspiration, exhortation, encouragement, and motivation. We conducted more than one hundred seminars and workshops on top of plenary sessions in the mornings and evenings. The plenary sessions were simultaneously translated into nine official languages. We had many highlights and climaxes, but the last evening reached its absolute peak, when all participants made a solemn affirmation of their calling to preach Jesus Christ. When 5,000 voices sang the closing hymn, all of us felt something of what it must be like in heaven. For Inge and me it was a fresh commitment to serve our precious Lord with renewed vision, strength, and love.

Three years later I was directing the second of such conferences. A number of amazing events took place before that.

January 6, 1984, was a big day for us. Our eldest son, Erik, married Tammy Rediger—a Boca girl. It was quite an event and a first for Inge and me. I am glad that we did not have to pay for it. Imagine, 560 guests showed up and all of them had to be fed! Inge joined other ladies to roll 2,000 meatballs! It took days to get everything done in time. But we were proud to see our eldest get married to such a fine girl.

I always had wanted to show China to my Inge. My first few trips there, starting in early 1981, had been fact-finding tours. The time had come to engage in real ministry. I wanted to continue the ministry my parents had to abandon after Mao's takeover. So in May of 1984 we made the long trek through China, mostly through Jiangxi, the province where my parents had labored.

The trip deep into that province was a severe challenge to her. We had rented a car with driver—driving in China was not permitted for foreigners in those days—and followed the same dusty roads my parents had traveled on. They were still unpaved, and hundreds of workers were scraping dirt and gravel into potholes the old-fashioned way. No machines! The scenery was beautiful; however the villages and small towns were grubby and polluted. Just like in the old days, undesirable food was thrown under the table in restaurants. The guesthouses and inns were crude.

It was hot, very hot, those July days. Linchuan had one of the most rudimentary inns we ever stayed in. It had no showers and bathrooms. The outhouse was even worse. Indescribable! There were no air-conditioning units. The bed had no mattress, only a mat woven with bamboo strands. It was so hot during the night that sweat poured down our bodies. We had stripped off all clothes, using hand-carried fans to cool down our faces and hoped the night would end soon. *How were my parents able to cope with such heat and live under such conditions for all those years,* we thought. Inge sat down later and authored a book in honor of my parents and all missionaries who had faithfully served the Lord in China: *Auf ungebahntem Weg* (On un-trodden roads in China).

We also visited the sights in Beijing and the Great Wall. Over a period of some 2,000 years this wall had been built by farmers, soldiers, and slaves (476 BC to 1644 AD). It stretches for 5,500 miles from Hushan in the province of Liaoning in the east to the Jiayuguan Pass in the province of Gansu in the west. It is often compared to a huge dragon winding up and down in the mountains, grassland, and deserts. Once you have visited and seen the Great Wall, nothing else in the world can compare to it in its vastness, grandeur, and impressiveness.

One of my close friends from Shanghai days had been exiled to Baoding south of Beijing. Henry Lee had attended our Ambassadors for Christ youth group at the Free Christian Church in Shanghai. Born in Hawaii, his Chinese parents had moved back to China after the Second World War and took their son with him. He had studied medicine and became a surgeon. When all foreigners had to leave China after Mao's takeover, he stayed.

He was caught listening to BBC and Voice of America, which to the Communist government was a crime. For twenty-two years, from 1958-80, he languished in prisons and labor camps. His parents had died during the Cultural Revolution.

Miraculously we were able to find out about his whereabouts from friends in Hong Kong. I had written him from Germany and encouraged him to meet us in Shanghai. He had no money to travel so we decided to take the train from Beijing to Baoding. From the train station in Beijing I had called him and asked him to meet us at the train station in Baoding. Stepping off the train we didn't know how to spot him among hundreds of people milling around. Inge and I just stood there waiting. Finally a man stepped out from the crowd, covered with a big straw hat and with quivering lips he asked, "Are you Werner?"

From the moment I saw Henry, I sensed that here is a broken man. For twenty-two years he had been denied the basic rights. Everything had been taken away from him—his profession as a surgeon, his family, his friends, his freedom, and his Bible. However, they were not able to take away his faith, and yet they left a man broken in spirit.

243

We found a quiet place in the station; in fact, one of the station managers opened a private room for us. As foreigners at that time we were celebrities. What a blessing to sit down with him to share and pray together. His hands trembled as he reached out for the Bible we were able to leave with him. He had not seen one in all of those miserable years. We also gave him the latest *TIME* magazine.

Henry Lee represented thousands, possibly hundreds of thousands, who had suffered for being followers of Christ during that time.

So much has been written about revolutions, such as the American Revolution (1775-83), French Revolution, (1789-99), German Revolution (1848), Russian/Bolshevik Revolution (1917), Chinese Revolution (1949), Cultural Revolution (1966-76), and Velvet Revolution (1989). For years the French Revolution has been stuck in my mind as a good revolution, because when I studied and lived in France for three years, the Bastille Day, also known as *La Fête Nationale*, was celebrated every year on July 14. I went along with all the festivities; however, later I had second thoughts about the rationality of it, when I was made aware of the carnage the French Revolution had caused to the masses of French people. Ann Coulter in her extremely well-researched book *Demonic* gives a factual yet gruesome account of what actually had taken place:

> ... the most chilling murder of the September massacres was that of Princess Lamballe. This wealthy young widow had been Marie Antoinette's best friend and superintendent of the queen's household. ... The mob accused the prudish and sensitive princess of all sorts of monstrous depredations, including a lesbian affair with the queen.

GOOD-BYE TO EGELSBACH—IMMIGRATION
TO THE US—CHINA IS BECKONING

After the mob attacked the Tuileries in August 1792, Lamballe had been moved to *La Force* prison, away from the royal family.... On September 3, 1792, Princess Lamballe was dragged from her prison cell and brought before a revolutionary tribunal presided over by the brute Jacques Hébert. Hébert had nothing but admiration for the "sacrilegious excesses" of the revolution, cheerfully announcing that the universe would soon contain "nothing but a regenerated and enlightened family of atheists and republicans."

He demanded that the princess swear "devotion to liberty and to the nation, and hatred to the king and queen," threatening her with death if she refused. Lamballe replied that she would take the first oath but never the second, because "it is not in my heart. The king and queen I have ever loved and honored.

Have you ever heard of what is illustrated below? I haven't. I was shocked when I found out. The bestial conduct of the French mob is inconceivable, yet true!

In the next instant, she was thrown to the howling mob, gang-raped, and sliced to pieces. Her head, breasts, and genitalia were chopped off by the sansculottes multitude and her mutilated corpse was put on public display for the crowd to jeer at and further defile.

Thus began the "Reign of Terror," purging all "enemies of the revolution." The enforcers, Robespierre and his allies, demanded death to traitors, spies, moderates, and anyone who disagreed with Robespierre.... There were up to fifty executions a day, by guillotine set up next to the statue of Liberty in

245

the *"Place de la Revolution,"* formerly *"Place Louis XV."* More than three thousand aristocrats were sent to the guillotine, with huge crowds on hand to cheer the carnage.... With the Jacobins in control, the "de-Christianization" campaign kicked into high gear in 1793. Inspired by Rousseau's idea of the *religion civile,* the revolution sought to completely destroy Christianity and replace it with a religion of the state. To honor "reason" and fulfill the promise of the Declaration of the Rights of Man and the Citizen that "no one may be questioned about his opinions, including his religious views," Catholic priests were forced to stand before revolutionary clubs and take oaths to France's new humanocentric religion, the Cult of Reason.

Other revolutions like the Russian in 1917 or the Chinese in 1949 and later the Cultural Revolution starting in 1966 were also inhuman to say the least, but nothing like the one described above. Better yet, the Velvet Revolution in Czechoslovakia in 1989 can be compared to the one in Berlin in the same year. They were done peacefully and no blood was spilled.

CHAPTER 17
AMSTERDAM '86

THEN AMSTERDAM '86 loomed before us. From the time Billy Graham had asked me to direct that conference I knew it would be a challenging task. Inge and I were moving to Amsterdam again. I wrote to my friends:

> We need your prayers more than ever, as no doubt Satan will attack us from all sides. He certainly does not want thousands of evangelists to unite in an all-out effort to win the world for Christ. His attacks can be made so much easier from a place like Amsterdam, a city which is known as Europe's largest drug scene, the cradle of child pornography, the center of devil worship, and a city rampant with crime, homosexuality, and prostitution.

In between we had celebrated two weddings. On May 11, 1985, our second son, Heiko, married a beautiful girl from Boston, Kay Nanfelt. They had met at Gordon Conwell

Seminary. And on December 27 our third son, Stephan, married Barbara Rediger, another beautiful girl and the younger sister of Tammy, who was married to our Erik.

I had to travel all over the world to form screening committees to pick the right and worthy evangelists. Early in March I had the unique experience to speak at the National Presbyterian Conference in Nagaland in the mountains of northeastern India. Some 70,000 people sat in the open air scattered across the rolling hills—a majestic sight. These were tribal people, whose forefathers had been headhunters only some ninety years before! As I addressed this huge throng, my heart was moved to see what the power of the gospel can do to people. A number of evangelists representing these unsung heroes attended Amsterdam '86.

In preparation of both Amsterdam conferences ('83 and '86) I traveled to more than 120 countries. In South Africa I met with a former black terrorist. As a non-Christian he had been heavily involved in undermining the apartheid government. In the process he lost one of his legs. His brother served a twenty-year prison term. Then he became a believing Christian. This changed his entire outlook on political issues. "Only through a regenerated heart can the political situation be altered," he told me. "Billy Graham is the one who started the process of reconciliation in our land."

This goes back many years to 1973. For years Billy Graham had been invited to evangelize in South Africa. Only after the authorities had agreed to integrated crusade meetings—where all races could sit together in the stadium wherever they wanted—did he consent to come. This took years! However, it happened because all concerned Christians worked together.

"This is where it began," my black South African friend said, "and God will continue to bring healing through the cross."

Living in Amsterdam was a great challenge. I wrote:

Up to now I have not mentioned the darker side of living in Amsterdam because we did not want to overdramatize situations. However, now I feel I should mention the need for intensive prayer for Inge and me and our staff. Amsterdam is a dangerous city in which to live. Several of our staff apartments have been broken into. Cars have been smashed open, staff members molested on the street, and one of our staff was robbed at knife point.

Last night it touched our own lives. Our 1976 Ford Grenada was stolen right off the parking space in front of our apartment. Twenty-five cars are stolen each night in Amsterdam.

We were without a car for nine weeks. Drug addicts steal cars; drive them around and when they run out of gasoline, they simply abandon them. We had given up hope of ever seeing it again. Then the police called. "We found your car. Come pick it up."

Several hours after Inge and I had retrieved the car, I was on a plane to another overseas assignment. The following morning at 5:30, halfway around the world, my assistant from Amsterdam called.

"Are you sitting down?" she asked.
Oh no, I thought, *not again!*

Well, it did happen again. In Amsterdam everything is possible. This time the car had been in our possession for less than twenty-four hours!

Once we almost panicked. The police arrested three IRA (Irish Republican Army) terrorists in our neighborhood. With it they uncovered a cache of firearms, including machine guns and bombs. All three of them were overpowered in a swift police raid. Those terrorists had been our neighbors for six months! We had to take prodigious cautionary measures to protect our staff.

In a staff meeting I said:

You may be living within immediate danger without being aware of it. We must be vigilant and act responsibly, but as Christians we should never doubt God's protection. We may truly rest in the arms of Jesus.

I concluded:

I believe that God has called us to Amsterdam. He called us for a purpose, and therefore we are in the center of God's will. Nothing will happen to us that is not foreordained by Him.

Everyone relaxed. So did I.

Amsterdam '86 came and went. According to a United Nations official, Amsterdam '86 was the most representative conference ever held in the history of mankind—religious or secular. For me it was a foretaste of heaven.

On the opening night I greeted thousands, welcoming them all to the conference and then opened it with this prayer:

At the beginning of our conference and during this beautiful celebration we first of all want to acknowledge you, our Lord, as our Heavenly Father, who cares for us and loves us. You love us so much that you have sent your Son—your only Son—into our world to die for us on the cross. Father, we thank you for this and we shall be ever grateful to you. And out of this gratefulness comes our desire to serve you.

We also want to thank you for each one assembled here this evening. We are children who need a new touch from you as we move into one of the most significant events ever to take place on the face of this earth.

We come to you, because we recognize our sinfulness and weakness. In the glory of your presence we are but filthy rags. And yet you have called us to a royal mandate and we are the bearers of Good News. Help us to serve you in humility, with love, and with total commitment to you and to one another.

And now, we want to dedicate this service and this conference to you. Speak to our hearts, we ask in the name of Jesus Christ. Amen.

10,105 participants from 174 countries and territories attended.

We hosted 300 accredited media people from twenty-eight countries, printed 18,000 photos, created 550 news releases in eighteen languages, and produced 410 radio programs in twenty-one languages. Worldwide there were more than 12,000 airings of Amsterdam '86 programs. "Virtually everyone in the world was within earshot of Amsterdam '86," reported our communications director Ed Plowman. 700 stewards cared for the evangelists' needs, and over 185,000 meals were served.

In spite of the enormity of the conference's food service, it is sometimes the small things that are appreciated most. One evangelist from a small village in India wept when he saw hundreds of bottles of water in the dining area. "It's so clean," he said with a broken voice. "In my village we have nothing like this."

Following the conference I took to heart what I had experienced while traveling the world for Amsterdam '86. I saw indescribable needs, yet was confronted with unprecedented challenges and potentials.

In Damascus, Syria, for instance, I had met with the Patriarch of the Syrian Orthodox Church, who showed an interest in evangelism for which I had not been prepared. This was generated through reading books by Billy Graham. He showed me the latest book he authored, and in it one whole chapter is devoted to the teachings of the new birth. Squeezing my hand as we parted, he said, "You people form the West look at us in the East with our robes and mitres and think those things belong in a museum. You may be right," he continued, "but you must know that I love Jesus very much in my heart."

As Billy Graham reflected on the International Conference for Itinerant Evangelists at Amsterdam '86 he said, "We have heard the groans of the world." He could not have said more clearly what I had sensed all along as I travelled into seventy-six countries in preparation for that conference.

Therefore, I decided under God to go back into evangelistic preaching. As I traveled the world and as I faced thousands of evangelists in Amsterdam, God tugged at my heart to go back to what I had been doing in the early years of my ministry, some thirty-four years past. My desire was to join the countless evangelists across the world in the front trenches "doing the work of an evangelist" (2 Timothy 2:4). With a heart full of conviction,

I addressed the 10,000 participants at the opening ceremony in my remarks of welcome: "Now I can truly say—welcome fellow itinerant evangelists!"

This is what I had said in full:

I greet you in the name of our Lord Jesus Christ. We have prayed for each one of you for many months. Of course we did not know you personally, but God did. We could not call you up by name, but God could. Therefore we were so dependent on the Holy Spirit to translate our prayers in such a way that God understood we meant you and you and you each individually. Thus you are someone special to us. In today's world with all the latest equipment and machines and computers which we did have to use to make this conference possible, we may have come across very methodical and perhaps sometimes a little cold. In fact, because of these machines and computers, we gave each one of you a number which you bear on your badge.

Today someone asked us what this number is for. Well, that is the reason why we had to do it. But let me tell you, you are not a number to us! You are a living person with a God-given personality and as such we see you and treat you and respect you and love you. And with that in mind we have done everything in our power to make your trip as efficient and pleasant and to make your stay here as comfortable and enjoyable as possible.

I don't think I have ever worked with a more dedicated, committed, and very hard-working staff in all of my life, coming from twenty-one countries. They came from Brazil and China, South Africa and Australia, Japan and Cost Rica,

253

Taiwan and Canada, France and India, Egypt and Holland, United States and Jamaica, Argentina and Germany, and others.

And by the way for those World Cup soccer fans, I am German and we had some Argentinians, and it was a little tough for me, that after we lost the game, to work with my Argentinian brothers, but we made it after all.

Isn't it wonderful that such a diverse group coming from so many different backgrounds, educationally and culturally, representing different races and nationalities, speaking different languages, isn't it wonderful that such a group has banded together and committed themselves to each other and to the Lord, and worked in such a way that everything that you now see here, and hear around you, was made possible.

By the way, as a young man I started out as an itinerant evangelist in Germany. As years went by, step by step I was given other responsibilities, helping here and there administrating and serving the Lord mainly from behind the desk. But then I started to work for Amsterdam '83 and then again for Amsterdam '86, this time traveling to sixty-seven countries within a year or so. I met evangelists all over the world, sharing and praying with them, and seeing what God is doing and then sensing again the need for world evangelism firsthand. The Lord tugged at my heart and I heard a quiet, still voice saying, "I want you back in evangelistic preaching." Therefore I can declare to the world and to you tonight: I have decided under God to again start preaching the message of the cross as an itinerant evangelist! And therefore, I can truly say: Welcome, fellow itinerant evangelists!

In front of my parents' last mission station in Ningdu,
Jiangxi, in 2009 with Linda, Jerusha, Erik, and Tilon

"Welcome, fellow itinerant evangelists," at Amsterdam '86

With Billy Graham at Amsterdam '86

Preaching to college students in Korea

Rafting in Jamaica in 1968

I loved playing tennis, here in Kaohsiung, Taiwan, in 1991

My love as a young mother

Inge at Uluru/Ayers Rock in central Australia

With Inge at Ephesus in 2006

Almost soccer World Cup champion in 2008 with Erik,
Heiko, and Stephan in Berlin

Our four kids, Heiko, Linda, Stephan, and Erik in 1970

Our family in 2008—generations of blessing

CHAPTER 18

RENEWED THRUST THROUGH EVANGELISTIC PREACHING

IN THE CLOSING days of 1986 I was back in Germany ministering at Germany's YFC Tween Congress (Tween stood for teens and twenties). We met in Nürnberg, the city where Hitler used to address thousands of young people in a specially built stadium. Now young people met to be trained in evangelism. Scores of them made commitments for Christ! We met in the famous castle overlooking the city, at that time used as a youth hostel.

Ever since we ministered in Jamaica in the late '60s, our hearts responded quickly to the call from the Caribbean. Trans World Radio has one of its broadcasting centers in Bonaire, a little island in the Dutch Antilles and one of the three ABC islands (Aruba, Bonaire, and Curacao). Besides the local language of Papiamentu, they also speak Dutch and English. Inge and I enjoyed this lovely island with gorgeous beaches surrounded by clear turquoise waters, when I spoke at a Caribbean leadership conference. There we heard again of the political unrest across the Caribbean area, which was so apparent even at the time we lived in Jamaica. Someone said:

> Politically the Caribbean is now the only area in the Third World where politics based on free elections, multiple parties, and liberal democratic freedoms are still predominant. However, despite the relative stability, one factor which has affected the witness of the church, and is still a potential threat to Caribbean democracy, is political violence.

During one of Jamaica's election cycles, over 800 persons had been killed.

After Bonaire we had a blessed crusade in Kingston. The week was one of the most spiritually refreshing weeks in years. I spent hours each day in prayer, study, and sermon preparation. Having been involved in administrative responsibility for so long, it was a thrill to be on the front lines of evangelism again. I also learned that besides evangelizing, we must also be ministering to the church—the body of Christ—to help enlarge its vision for evangelism. Furthermore, before evangelistic thrusts, Christians must be trained for evangelistic outreaches.

We also noticed afresh that the Caribbean has a matriarchal society. This is especially apparent in the church. Men as a whole do not shoulder their part of responsibilities. A Jamaican national said, "There has been a conspicuous absence of men in the Caribbean church. Religions call for commitment and many men do not appear to respond to the call for a strong commitment."

Therefore we were especially glad that many of those that had committed their lives to Christ during our crusade were men.

RENEWED THRUST THROUGH
EVANGELISTIC PREACHING

Peru was our next stop. Manco Capac founded the Inca Empire, which had its center in what is now known as Peru. Peru was ruled by the Incas from 1080-1535 AD. In 1535 an illiterate adventurer from Spain, Francisco Pizarro, with some one hundred followers, conquered Cusco, the capital city of the Incas. That was the end of the Inca Empire.

I had been invited to hold a crusade in one of Lima's churches. A new church had been started in 1982 in one of the *Ciudades Jovenes* (young cities) on the outskirts of Lima. People from rural areas flocked into these suburban communities! They were extremely poor with hardly any sanitation. Seldom had I seen so much misery, filth, pollution, and frustration.

However, even there the church is making an impact. I wrote to my friends:

> Today the above mentioned church is touching thousands of people. Several hundred have been converted and many have joined the church. Now they called us to help with another evangelistic thrust. They aimed right at the heart of Satan's dominion.

What a thrill to see people walk the aisle night after night! Often they started walking forward as a sign of commitment even before the invitation hymn was begun. Seldom had I seen such a hunger for salvation.

It was hot, very hot! South Korea has extreme cold winters; however the summers are extremely hot. Billy Kim, area director for YFCI and pastor of a Baptist church in Suwon, had invited

265

me to hold evangelistic meetings all across the country, and that during early summer. He is an amazing person, and without his help and blessing we would not have been able to accomplish what we did.

"Today alone our office received close to four hundred decision cards by mail," Billy said at FEBC (Far Eastern Broadcasting Company) headquarters in Seoul. He had asked me to speak at a farewell chapel service after three weeks of ministry. "…and this has been going on for several days now."

The first year of renewed and total evangelistic preaching in 1987 was incredible! We ministered in thirteen foreign countries and territories on three continents (Germany, United States, Bonaire, Jamaica, Peru, South Korea, China, Hong Kong, St. Vincent, Barbados, Philippines, Dominican Republic, and Brazil).

106,000 people had attended our meetings and 6,433 inquirers were recorded.

When I publicly announced at Amsterdam '86 that I would go back to evangelistic preaching, I did not know what to expect! But I did know that God would walk before. And He did.

It was a year of faith, and it was a year during which God's faithfulness came through in an amazing way. For the previous thirty years of ministry, I had to travel and work without having Inge along. This last year was different. On almost all travels she accompanied me—what a blessing and what a thrill. Often she had a ministry of her own. God had truly done more than we had ever expected.

The other miracle was that we ended the year in the black. I had to raise all of the money myself. It turned out to be true what God had promised in Malachi 3:10:

RENEWED THRUST THROUGH
EVANGELISTIC PREACHING

Bring ye all the tithes into the storehouse, that there may be meat in mine house, and prove me now herewith, says the Lord of hosts, if I will not open you the windows of heaven, and pour out a blessing, that there shall not be room enough to receive it.

Often my mind would go back to Shanghai as a twelve-year-old, when I learned the art of tithing. I started tithing then. When Inge and I got married we started to give 25 percent of our income to the Lord's work. And we always had enough. Our kids learned to understand a slogan we designed for our immediate family: "*Kein Geld, aber alles machen*" (No money, but being able to do everything).

I was surprised when I received a letter from Dr. Gleason Archer, Professor of Old Testament and Semitics at Trinity Evangelical Divinity School (T.E.D.S.). It was strange because it looked like the devil wanted me to get sidetracked.

A week or two ago I contacted Dr. Robert Coleman of our missions faculty at T.E.D.S. and put a question to him. I said, "Do you know of any seasoned missionary with real evangelistic gifts and a heart for the European mission field and an extensive experience in serving there—and one with organizational and managerial skills? That is the kind of man we need as president of GEM (Greater Europe Mission)." He promised to think and pray about it, and then within half an hour he phoned me back and said, "The only man I can think of is Werner Bürklin, who did such an outstanding job at the recent Billy Graham Evangelists' Conference. I think he is at a transition point in his career at present, and is thinking of an evangelistic conference ministry under independent leadership. It may be that he is God's man for GEM.

If you think that protracted prayer and earnest consideration do not lead you to a positive attitude towards this open door, please tell me who on earth you know besides yourself who possesses the qualifications, the gifts, and the experience you do—that we may turn to him.

Previously, at the end of 1986, I already had been called by GEM's search committee to meet with its leadership in Wheaton. I will never forget returning to my hotel that extremely cold night. It was so cold that I thought my behind would actually freeze to the leather seat in the car. Really! I was shivering all the way. I got out of the car and literally ran to the warmth of the motel. I had declined their offer of becoming president of GEM. Was it because I knew that I would have to move to cold Wheaton if I would accept? But now they had approached me again.

"Presently I just don't feel I can accept your gracious offer," I wrote back. "I feel that I am too old, not competent for the task, and my strong conviction to pursue my calling for evangelistic preaching leads me to this decision."

I was preaching in Bangalore, India. At the same time Bishop K.H. Ting with an entourage of thirteen Chinese Christian leaders was there also. Bishop Ting was the head of the Protestant Church in China. God, as so often in my life, arranged a get-together at the airport when I was waiting for my flight departure. Han Wenzhou, the General Secretary of the China Christian Council, led me to the bishop. "He is tired," Han cautioned, "but I think he would like to meet you."

So we did. When he heard that I was born in China to missionary parents he said, "Please come and see me the next time you are in Nanjing." I flew off back to Europe and he to

China. This was the beginning of a long and wonderfully blessed relationship with this titan of a Christian leader in China. He was the president of the Three Self Patriotic Movement (TSPM) and chairman of China Christian Council (CCC). He was the one who had opened the door to my ministry in China. God saw to it that with this one encounter, I was propelled to the top of the Chinese church.

I soon found out that to many evangelicals in the West, Bishop Ting was extremely controversial. They claimed that he was a lackey or crony of the Chinese Communist Party, that he even was a card-holder of the Party!

I found him to be a brother in Christ and *the* person who lifted the downtrodden church to a place of acceptance and honor in China's society. He was the product of Union Theological Seminary in New York, theologically a very liberal school. But he stuck to his biblical beliefs when challenged. In a letter on October 12, 1987, I asked:

> Recently I came across a bulletin—copy enclosed—in which it is stated that the TSPM (Three Self Patriotic Movement) "has restricted pastors from preaching on the return of Christ, suffering for Christ, separation from the world, casting out demons, and healing the sick." Would you please clarify this, so that I can rectify this misunderstanding at the Consultation [this consultation was scheduled to be held at the Billy Graham Center in Wheaton, Illinois].

He answered:

> Other friends have also asked us about the restrictions the 3-S Movement has supposedly imposed on preachers in

China. There simply have not been these restrictions, or any of them We want the state to practice fully the principle of religious freedom. It is only right that we should put [this] into practice ourselves. And Chinese preachers are not as docile and unmindful of their obedience to the Biblical revelation as to be told and accept what human authorities dictate to them as to what they should preach and should not preach.

For years I had to live with the criticism leveled at churches of the China Christian Council (CCC) in general and its leadership in particular. More than ever I was convinced that if all of the unregistered churches would register according to the law with the government, church leaders would not be prosecuted for engaging in illegal activities. Of course, I do not agree with some of the restrictions the Chinese government places on its citizens, but I praise God for the relative freedom they now experience. The constant criticism some of the Christian groups in the West direct at the Chinese government is counterproductive. Also for them to encourage house church leaders to resist the policies of the government only increases the hardships for those people. So much false information is constantly put forth by the media, even the evangelical media! To set things straight I published the following:

- It is not true that members of registered churches have to pay allegiance first to the government and then to Christ
- It is not true that sermons on the Second Coming of Christ are not allowed to be preached in registered churches (It may be conceivable that churches with a liberal drift may not preach on that subject just like what

270

happens in liberal churches in the US). However, I have
never come across such churches

- It is not true that pastors of registered churches receive
  their salaries from the government [as done in Germany],
  and thus are subservient to the government
- It is true that in some areas the government makes land
  available free of charge to registered churches so that
  they can construct church buildings
- It is not true that manuscripts of sermons have to be
  submitted to the government before delivery
- It is not true that a list of newly baptized members have
  to be submitted to the government as it was done during
  the Cultural Revolution
- It is true, however, that registered churches give annual
  reports related to finances, number of baptisms, plans
  for new church buildings, and other activities to
  government agencies as done in the US where audited
  financial reports have to be released to its government
  departments
- It is not true that "the Chinese government continues to
  control the financial, leadership, and doctrinal decisions
  of all registered religious groups..." as reported by the
  US Commission on International Religious Freedom
- It is not true that children under the age of eighteen are
  not permitted to attend church services. Many churches
  hold Sunday school classes for children

India has something in common with China—its population
growth. In 1988 India had a population of close to 800 million
but specialists predict that at its current rate of growth, India

will almost double in size by 2030 to 1.53 billion, overtaking China, which will peak at 1.46 billion.

With India's six main religions (Hinduism, Islam, Sikhism, Buddhism, Jainism, and Christianity) and fourteen major languages, she has a fascinating yet puzzling society. I had been invited to preach in five major cities; in three of those to hold crusades (Pune, Madurai, and Visakhapatnam). Although the crowds were not as large as anticipated, the response was the greatest I had experienced in a long time. Several times between nine and eleven percent of the attendants responded openly to the invitation to receive Christ.

"What's the matter with you?" A lady in her 60s elegantly dressed and with a West German passport in hand scrutinized me carefully. We had been patiently standing in line at the border patrol of East Berlin's airport for twenty-two minutes, and the line did not move. I was the culprit, for the border guard was giving my passport a very thorough examination. He probably had never seen a passport with so many entry stamps from around the world. His face was young and not unpleasant to look at—but he was slow.

It was the first time ever that I was about to enter Communist East Germany. Several times over the years I had been refused a visa to preach in East Germany. This time I had the proper visa but I had run into a bureaucratic "worry-worm." He wanted to be sure that everything was in order—one hundred percent! Finally he handed the passport back to me and let me in. The lady behind me heaved a big sigh of relief as she faced the guy. "Finally," she murmured.

I had flown in from Cyprus. My destination was Woltersdorf, near Berlin.

After a four-week separation I fell into the arms of my sweetheart. Together we experienced one of the most unforgettable weeks. Nearly one hundred evangelists with their spouses had met for their annual evangelists' conference. I was one of the speakers and delighted to meet many East German evangelists. The hunger for a change of heart and the search for new life are as strong in a Communist-run country as in other places around the world. And people were finding Christ.

To live as a believing Christian in East Germany had its cost. Young people who chose to follow Christ understood that they would also choose to forfeit their right for higher education. All of the Christian young people we met were earning their livelihood through manual labor. This was a choice they had to make, and they made it gladly.

Even Communist China did not have such harsh stipulations.

We observed their simple and strong faith. What we saw was genuine. They did not put up a front. Their lives had been tested as by fire, and they still had a true and visible desire to share Christ within a Communist-run society.

One morning at breakfast I saw one lit candle in front of the placemat of one of the evangelists. Wrapped in birthday paper, I noticed a cucumber with the two ends sticking out. *What kind of a gag is this?* I thought to myself. "This is not a joke," someone corrected me. "This is his birthday, and the cucumber is a precious gift."

The East Germans had not seen cucumbers or bananas or oranges in months! An indication of how badly the system worked. But the evangelists didn't mind. They worked. They prayed and they evangelized.

Damascus, Syria, taught me to see evangelism differently. Christians were not allowed to minister openly. At the time I visited the city, Syria had beefed up their troops in neighboring Lebanon. But not so in its own country, at least I did not notice it—no military buildup! Rather, I was impressed with a seemingly stable society. Of course I knew that dictatorships could make this possible using draconian methods.

Not being able to hold public evangelistic meetings, Christians meet mainly in homes similar to what Christians in China experienced during the Cultural Revolution. I was asked to hold a meeting in a private home. Over thirty people crowded into a small living room. Some were Syrians; others were foreigners representing different nationalities. After sharing from the Bible and explaining the gospel, eleven responded to the invitation. A local pastor offered to meet with them privately and lead them further in biblical truths.

Whereas the meeting in Damascus was small, it was different in Peru. When I flew into the heart of the jungle in the Amazon Basin, I was surprised to find such a bustling city. Iquitos had exploded on the banks of the Amazon, especially during the rubber and later the oil boom. However, never before had a united evangelistic crusade been carried out by the existing evangelical churches.

For several nights I was privileged to preach to thousands in the city square. Churches had set up their chairs and pews, and hundreds who could not find a seat crowded around. People eagerly responded after each invitation was given. Besides the crusade, I held a leadership seminar for up to two hundred fifty pastors and Christian leaders of the local churches. They were so receptive!

The highlight of the year 1988 took place during the summer. Since 1981 I had traveled to China seven times, but this time I had been asked to preach in China for the first time. The church leadership had been reluctant to open their pulpits to foreigners. The three self-principles (self-support, self-government, self-propagation) were deeply ingrained in their thinking. The government had encouraged them to stand on their own feet and refrain from becoming dependent on outside help. But now this had changed.

Erik and Heiko accompanied me on this trip. In Hefei, the capital city of Anhui province, we met with the church leadership. "Come, preach at our main church," one of the pastors encouraged me. This was especially intriguing to me. After all, Anhui was the province where I was born. So with great anticipation I entered the pulpit and preached my first sermon in China that Sunday. The church was packed.

My mind flashed back to the Free Christian Church in Shanghai. In it I had surrendered my life to full time Christian service. Thereafter sitting in one of its pews I wondered, *Will you ever preach from that pulpit?* It reflected a deep desire I had to one day come back to Shanghai to proclaim God's Word from that pulpit as others had done ministering to me as a young teenager. However, Hefei was first, but later I preached numerous times at the church of my youth. I had come full circle.

We were hosted by the mayor of Hefei to a sumptuous banquet. He welcomed us to the city and thanked us for

275

supporting the churches of his city. *Amazing, how leaders holding the reins of political offices have a positive interest in church life,* I mused. This was in total contradiction to what I had heard from western critics.

At the Amity Printing Company in Nanjing we visited its leadership who told us that during 1988 it had already printed 300,000 copies of the Bible and they were in the process of printing another 100,000. The United Bible Societies had donated the presses and the paper. (By September of 2011, close to 90 million had been printed). Even though Bibles were being printed in China in now the world's largest Bible printing press, still some western people pride themselves in smuggling Bibles into China. Why that? Is that really necessary? It is so much more efficient to print them there. Some people with their archaic views are strange.

While in Nanjing, I met Dr. Qi, a medical doctor and devout Christian. He had had no contact with other Christians in his city, and that for years. "I worship in my family church," he told me. His family church was made up of members of his immediate family, nobody else. I encouraged him to get in touch with an elderly lady I also had met while there. "You need to have fellowship with other believers," I counseled.

A few weeks later back home, I received a letter from that elderly lady.

> I want to tell you that the Lord really did a miracle for us. It was through you that the Lord brought Dr. Qi and me to know each other. Now we are great friends and fellow workers … Both he and his wife come to one of my meetings and his son James is an important member of my Bible

class.... You will be delighted to know that I am the first Christian that Dr. Qi has contact with after many long years.

What a shame that the church in China is so fragmented. Because of hardships and persecutions they had to endure for so many years, many of them had become suspicious of each other. Some of them had become extremely exclusive. Therefore, one of my goals for China was to build bridges. Christians had to learn to accept each other no matter to which camp they belonged.

CHAPTER 19

GREAT IS
THY FAITHFULNESS

THE SONG "GREAT is Thy faithfulness" had become my favorite hymn:

> *Great is Thy faithfulness! Great is Thy faithfulness!*
> *Morning by morning new mercies I see;*
> *All I have needed Thy hand has provided:*
> *Great is Thy faithfulness, Lord, unto me!*

On April 8, 1989, I was asked to represent the alumni of all the schools Robert Evans had founded in Europe at a banquet given in their honor. With it I was privileged to pay special tribute to them. Billy Graham gave the major address. Some 3,000 people attended the event in Chicago and it was transmitted to two other cities where similar banquets were held.

I also reminisced about the train ride I had taken from Paris to Germany thirty-three years earlier. I was about to begin my evangelistic ministry with Youth for Christ. I was young, inexperienced, and scared. I thought back to my graduation service at which our school director David Barnes had sung the beautiful and meaningful hymn above.

As I reflected on those early years, the beginnings of the ministry for our Lord, and the many experiences along the way, my heart warmed with deep gratitude. The Lord had upheld me and my family step by step and morning by morning. His faithfulness never ceased.

Our son Heiko had called me from Canada one day, as we were preparing for Amsterdam '86. "Dad, you need to invite Ravi Zacharias to be one of your main speakers at Amsterdam '86. He is terrific!"

I never had heard about the man, neither had Billy Graham nor Leighton Ford, my program director. Knowing Heiko, though, I discerned that he must be someone special to consider. So we invited him and were astounded. He was terrific—a godly and brilliant apologist! That conference propelled him into a world-wide ministry.

We were planning a conference for intellectuals in China. *Ravi is the perfect choice for such an undertaking,* I believed. I invited him to travel with me to China, a first for him. We did; however, the conference for intellectuals never materialized. The authorities were not ready.

However, I did introduce him to Wang Mingdao. He was the pastor/evangelist who had denied the Lord in prison. When he was released he walked the streets of Beijing weeping, "I am Peter, I am Peter. I have denied my Lord." He heroically returned to the authorities, rescinded his denial, and was thrown back into prison for "twenty-three years minus two months," as he had told me.

He looked chipper and greeted us jokingly. "I am half deaf and half blind!" This reminds me now of what Ted Engstrom, president of World Vision, had told me later: "Other than being half blind, half deaf, and half lame, I am doing quite all right." However, Wang Mingdao looked worse than the last time I had seen him. His wife, totally blind, sat next to him and interpreted when he could not understand right away.

To the question, "What is the hope for China?" he replied, "The return of Christ." What sustained him during his years in prison? "Micah 7:7-9," he answered:

> Therefore I will look unto the Lord; I will wait for the God of my salvation; my God will hear me. Rejoice not against me, oh my enemy; when I fall, I shall arise; when I sit in darkness, the Lord shall be a light unto me. I will bear the indignation of the Lord because I have sinned against Him, until He plead my cause, and execute judgment for me; He will bring me forth to the light, and I shall behold His righteousness!

To the church in the West he quoted Revelation 2:10 "… Be thou faithful unto death, and I will give thee a crown of life!"

I saw his old worn-out Bible on the table. Leafing through it I found a quote by Dickens: "Have a heart that never hardens, a temper that never tires, and a touch that never hurts."

Wow, I thought, *what a man. A man of God and a man of the world who lives in the real world.*

"Zurück nach Polen!" The Russian border guard spoke broken German and was unhappy. "Back to Poland!" he demanded.

Inge and I had just come from a wonderful ministry in southern Poland. Close to six hundred young people had filled a century-old, unheated Lutheran church. Several of them had made decisions for Christ. And then we had the privilege to teach young Christian leaders the importance of spiritual commitment and the qualities of biblical leadership. What a thrill again to see those young Polish Christians in a Communist country so attentive and so willing to learn.

But now we wanted to move on to the Soviet Union. We had been invited by the Lutheran bishop in Lithuania to minister in his city. However, now the Russian border guard was holding us back.

"Wait in the parking lot," he said.

We sat and waited for three hours. He said he had to consult with senior officials. *I wonder if he wants a backshish,* I mused. I never give bribes. So we patiently waited. Finally he motioned us over and without further delay he let us in—without backshish!

Klaipeda in Lithuania is the city where Inge was born. At her birth the city was called Memel and belonged to Germany, but after the Second World War the city was given to Lithuania, a land that the Soviet Union had annexed. Before leaving Germany on this trip, Inge had bought a doll to give to a girl in Klaipeda. When she fled to the West during the war, she had to leave her favorite doll behind. Now she wanted to cheer up a needy girl with that doll.

Amazingly, when we rang the bell at the door of her former home, a ten-year-old girl opened the door. She was overjoyed when Inge presented her with the gift.

When we called the bishop, he said, "First some further steps have to be taken with the authorities. Let us pray that the next time you come you can minister in our midst." The Soviet Union was still run by an atheistic government, and church leaders had to abide by rules and regulations. We had to wait for another year to hold evangelistic meetings in Klaipeda.

On May 10, 1990, a government limousine picked us up at our hotel in Wiesbaden, Germany, and Inge and I were driven to the Governor's Mansion to have lunch with *Ministerpräsident* of the state of Hessen, Walter Wallmann. Inge had been a schoolmate of him in Uelzen. This was soon after the reunification of Germany. He was a staunch Conservative. In a letter to Inge he expressed this unambiguously:

> The world has changed during the last few months. Marxism and socialism collapsed. It is obvious that people had been misled and that the real questions to life cannot be satisfied with socialist utopia. There are still some people who try to save socialism. They explain that socialism in the eastern European countries was simply a perversion and was nothing but Stalinism. We have to intellectually fight against it.

It of course was a distinct honor to be guests in the Governor's Mansion. We spent two hours together, discussing spiritual and political matters. How important to have men in government who are honorable and competent.

Meanwhile in China demonstrations erupted. Thousands of mostly young people demanded a democratic government. This went on for weeks until tanks made an end to the civil and mostly non-violent uprisings. One policeman was strung up by demonstrators hanging from a bridge. The demonstrations had begun on April 15, 1989, and Deng Xiaoping had waited until June 4 to step in. He ordered troops to bring back order. Several hundred were mowed down when they refused to clear the Tiananmen Square in central Beijing.

At the funeral of the Communist Party of China's (CPC) general secretary, Hu Yaobang, close to 100,000 mourners flooded Tiananmen Square in the center of Beijing. He had supported political liberalization and was therefore purged by the government. Students, intellectuals, and later even workers demonstrated to encourage economic and political reform.

The exact number of those killed is not known, but the estimate ranges from several hundred to 3,000 civilians. Four weeks later I traveled to Beijing to find out for myself. I took a taxi and asked the driver to take me to the square. "Please stop," I asked, got out of the car, and started to walk toward the center of the square. A machine-gun-carrying soldier stopped me and waved me back to the car. As we circled around the Mao Mausoleum I pointed to dark spots on the pavement and asked the driver what this was. It looked like burned stains. He just shrugged his shoulders, indicating that he did not want to talk about it. The next few hours I mingled with the people in the subway and overcrowded buses, and everything seemed to be calm and back to normal. It was an eerie calm.

However, I still found the people to be open to the gospel. In Shanghai I met a thirty-year-old medical doctor who worked as a masseur at the Hilton Hotel where I stayed.

"How come you work as a masseur?" I asked.

"I make so much more money this way," he answered.

While giving me a rub down, I told him about Christ. "I want to know more about Jesus," he insisted. So I invited him for dinner after his work in a simple Chinese restaurant. After carefully explaining the way of salvation, using my Bible all the way, I asked, "Would you like to believe in Him and accept Him as your Savior?" "Yes, I do."

Together we bowed our heads in that restaurant, and one more young Chinese opened his heart to our Lord.

"The book you read from must be very important in Christianity," he probed.

"You bet it is." He had never seen a Bible, so I gave him the one I had.

I truly was amazed how open and receptive the Chinese were to the gospel. How different from my home country Germany! I reflected on the experience I had on my previous trip in April. At that time, a fifty-year-old engineer had accepted Christ in my hotel room.

Again and again I was asked why the Chinese church is growing by leaps and bounds. The Chinese people were so disillusioned with Communism and what they had been taught that they had become "vulnerable" to the claims of Christ. In Christ they not only found the truth, but with it also peace of mind and the reality of God's existence. This is contagious!

Very few tourists traveled through China during those tumultuous times. The June 4 incident, also called the Tiananmen Massacre, frightened foreigners away. The hotel room cost only US $60—a steal! The Hilton was one of the first overseas hotels built in Shanghai. It had been constructed on the same site where the German Lutheran church once stood. Next to it was my former school, the *Kaiser Wilhelm Schule*. I relived some of my childhood experiences when I walked through the corridors and school rooms once more. A couple of years later, that building also had to give way to another hotel—Hotel Equatorial Shanghai.

Traveling through China was not easy, especially during the early days of my journeys. I often had to cut corners to get to my destinations. Often schedules were tight and I had to find ways to overcome barriers or obstructions. Here is one example:

I was caught in the newly built airport in Beijing, when hundreds of passengers were jammed in front of the train entrance between concourses. Something had gone wrong with the trains, and nothing moved while passengers were piling onto the masses already caught. I had to catch a plane to Nanchang only thirty minutes hence. *I would never make it*, I thought. But then I saw a group of airline attendants disappear down some stairs and I quickly followed them. At the bottom they jumped on an airline bus and I did too. No one said anything and I had analyzed the situation correctly. The bus took us to the concourse where I could catch my plane just in the nick of time. While hundreds of others were trapped, I was on my way.

Back in Germany I once encountered a major problem traveling that was particularly annoying and memorable. I had bought a German rail pass letting me travel on every train on any given day for the entire period while in Germany, and that with no extra cost. I was holding meetings in so many different places that this was the best mode of travel—until I hit a snag.

I had missed my train taking me south to my last meeting, scheduled for 9:15 a.m. the following day—a Sunday. *No problem*, I thought, *find another train, even if I have to go north or south just so that I can make connections somewhere to get me to Koblenz, a city on the Rhine.*

It worked; however, it was 1:15 in the morning when I arrived. *No problem, I will just get a hotel room and someone can pick me up at 8:00 a.m. to get to the meeting in time.*

Bad news! All hotels were filled up. Not a single room to be had! What to do now?

No problem, I thought, *get back on a train going anywhere, turn around, and take a train back to Koblenz. With my rail pass I would be able to save hotel costs.* The last train out that night left at 1:45 a.m. and I was on it—this time traveling to Heidelberg.

I was able to sleep some, because in German trains you can pull out the seats to make somewhat of a "bed." But I had to wake up before I would hit Heidelberg in order to catch a return train back to Koblenz.

Everything went according to plan—except the particular train I needed to take back to Koblenz did not run on Sundays! By then it was Sunday morning—5:00 a.m. to be exact! So there I stood on the platform in Heidelberg and there were no trains leaving that would get me to Koblenz by 8:00 a.m.

No problem, I thought, *"take a cab to Frankfurt, just an hour away on the fast Autobahn and catch a train from there!"* I did find a cab, and man, did he travel! Fast! There was no speed limit on that stretch of the Autobahn. I didn't mind though—I had to catch the 6:15 train if I ever wanted to get to Koblenz by 8:a.m. (however, I did blow my saved hotel cost).

Well, I did make it by 8:00 a.m.—7:55 a.m. to be exact. Smiling, with my eyes propped open by proverbial toothpicks, I staggered to my friend who was at the train station to pick me up. Sixty minutes later we arrived at the church, where the service started at 9:15 a.m. sharp.

No problem, I mused. *Made it!*

September 20, 1989: was a dark day for us—a very dark day. Our son Stephan with his wife, Barbara, had been told weeks before that their first child would be born without kidneys. Such a birth is very unusual, but they faced it courageously and prayerfully. The day came and their little boy Daniel, weighing less than four pounds, only lived three hours. My heart broke when I saw the little one before he was taken away to die. He never had a chance. The funeral two days later was a lovely and peaceful event. Both of his parents were strong as they put their trust in the Lord. I am looking forward with great anticipation to see him in heaven someday.

This devastating experience was replaced by a most festive occasion when our daughter, Linda, married her lover three months later. David Pervenecki came from a solid Catholic family. He was religious, but not a follower of Jesus. Linda had told him that she could and would not marry a non-believer. But both were in love.

Inge felt compelled to do something about this. One day, as he was visiting our home, she asked him whether he would mind talking privately with her. Both withdrew into Linda's room, and there he committed his life to Christ after Inge had explained the gospel to him. "Now it makes sense," he blurted out, and with that he started out with his new-found faith.

This also paved the way for a wonderfully blessed marriage.

On December 16 I led her down the aisle. My mind flashed back to the day some twenty years ago, when I lay on my bed with tears running down my cheeks imagining that I might not be able to have this joy because of my cancer. Now the day had come when I was celebrating the triumph over my illness by leading my sweet only daughter down the aisle to meet her groom. I performed the wedding.

In a letter to our friends we wrote:

Our last child and only daughter, Linda, was married to David Pervenecki of West Palm Beach. Our entire family was involved in the wedding and reception. Heiko, the freshly ordained minister [at First Presbyterian Church of Lake Wales, Florida], started out the ceremony and handed the proceedings over to his dad, who first had to give the bride away. Kay played the flute, Tammy sang a solo, Barbara played the piano, Erik and Stephan emceed the reception, and Inge sat proudly in the first row, watching everything unfold.

The ministry in China now took shape. Since 1981 I had visited China every year, in fact several times each year, meeting Christian leaders and building relationships—a must for those wanting to work in China. The Beijing Massacre threw us back two years, but finally in 1991 things started to move again. However, it took us one year to prepare for this new thrust. An entry in my diary on June 6, 1990, shows the agony and anguish I had about that horrific incident:

This morning in my "Quiet Time"—this is the one period of the day I never miss! This keeps me going day after day. Some days I don't receive spectacular revelations or inspirations—although there is always something that I take with me into the hustle and bustle of the day—and on other days I get tremendous "lifts." This morning was one of those!

I am reading in [the Gospel of] Mark these days. It just so happened that last year at the exact same day I read the same portion. It was right after the Beijing Massacre. I was stunned as I watched it on TV in disbelief—I could not handle what

I saw. I grieved for those who lost their lives, but I was more concerned about the future of the Chinese church. Will she be persecuted again? Will the ministry I started stop? What will happen to our China plans? Then the Lord used Mark 4:40 to encourage me: "Why are you so afraid? Do you still have no faith?" Today I happen to read the same verse! On the margin I noted, "Yes, I believe." I deeply believe that we are on the right track. We must persevere. God will give us a tremendous ministry—in China!

A very good friend of mine, Larry Rybka, and a member of our China Partner ministry board, felt the work in China to be so important that he wanted as many as possible to get acquainted with our plans. We sent out a brochure and a video, which he produced and financed.

But we did not sit idly by waiting for that momentous occasion. There was still a lot to do throughout the year of 1990.

In February of 1990, 4,000 young people converged on Brasilia in Brazil for a youth training congress called Geração 90 (Generation 90), a follow-up of Geração 79 that I had directed eleven years earlier. This time the congress was run totally by Brazilians. I was greatly impressed with those God had chosen to do His work in Brazil. It was a joy to meet those again that had served on my staff many years ago and who were Christian leaders in their own right.

Being on the go and busy all the time, I knew that only by staying close to the Lord I would succeed. On August 15, 1990, my journal revealed the following:

This morning I had once more read through the entire Bible within one year—throughout my life now 62 times! How wonderful and inspiring to have a book like the Bible, that has guided, prodded, convicted, blessed, inspired, taught, searched, lifted, consoled, enriched, strengthened, redirected my life. I shall never give up reading and living by it!

The world's population at that time had reached 5.3 billion. 1.7 billion of those were Christians—300 million of them evangelicals. 1.8 billion or 36 percent were "unreached." Every day 364,000 people were newly evangelized, and the world had 2.5 million churches or worship centers.

These statistics were published by the Lausanne Movement. They were very meaningful to me, having traveled the world for many years. I saw faces behind those numbers. Whenever people accepted the claims of Christ for the first time I was thrilled. As an example, I had just received a letter from Pune, India, where I had conducted an evangelistic crusade before the release of those statistics:

Remember when you were here in Pune conducting an open-air evangelistic crusade? Professor Tripath and his wife accepted Jesus Christ. They are from a Hindu family. We kept regular contact with them ... and you will be very happy to know that on the 25th of December, 1989, both of them were baptized in our church. Our hearts were full of joy seeing this fruit of your open-air crusade.

We will start a Bible study group in brother Tripath's home. They are so eager to bring their Hindu relatives to the throne of our Lord.

CHAPTER 20

FIDEL CASTRO'S REACH-OUT TO CUBAN PASTORS

A S I WAS standing in a long line again, this time at the airport in Havana, Cuba, I was wondering what would await me in this repressive country. It was my second trip to Cuba; the first one I had made in preparation for Amsterdam '86. Now I was going to preach!

It was April 7, 1990, Saturday afternoon. I had come to preach but also to assess the political and religious situation in Cuba in light of the dramatic changes in Eastern Europe. Communist countries had crumbled there, but how would Fidel Castro react. Also, should Youth for Christ restart an evangelistic program that had come to an abrupt halt after the Castro Revolution some thirty years earlier?

John Huffman Sr., formerly director of Boston YFC, had been a tremendous source of information before I went in. He had taken a YFC evangelistic team into Cuba in April of 1949. They had had a prosperous ministry with hundreds responding to the gospel. He also had started a Spanish-speaking radio broadcast in Havana, *Alas del Alba*.

Two years before my going, he and his son John, senior pastor of St. Andrews Presbyterian Church in New Port Beach, California, had again visited Cuba in 1988.

Things were changing in Cuba, but to what an extent?

On April 2, one week before I landed in Havana, Castro had met with Protestant and Evangelical leaders in his headquarters. This was the first time since he had taken power. Fifty-six denominations were represented. He interacted with them for five hours and hosted a sumptuous dinner.

I sat spellbound watching the mind-blowing event that was put on TV after I had arrived. Two of the only Cuban channels broadcast this on two consecutive nights at 9 p.m. prime time. This was done simultaneously so that the entire nation was able to hear the views of those Protestant leaders. Imagine, a Communist head of state sitting down with Christian leaders! Here are some excerpts of my journal:

> The encounter with Fidel Castro was open: everyone could express himself freely, criticize, and exhort at pleasure. On numerous times Fidel showed signs of being deeply moved. Unless he is a superb actor—which he very well might be—this could mean that he will take to heart some of the things expressed. He was very impressive, demanding, jovial, and spontaneously entered into discussions, frequently moving up and down the room, stroking his beard, gesticulating wildly, eloquent, evangelizing his cause. It was a give and take.

> When responding to the leaders' criticism that the church had been persecuted, misunderstood, and maligned, Fidel said,

294

"We have to rectify the situation concerning the Revolution's attitude toward the church. But bear with us. The early Christians had lived through centuries of persecution! So thirty years of persecution here is not too bad, is it?" Everyone laughed.

Some of the quotes of the Christian leaders are quite revealing:

"We do not need liberation theology; we already achieved liberation, we need revolution theology. You, Fidel, inspired all of us since the first day of revolution to work for that."

Another quote: "As Christ used the whip to cast out the money changers from the temple, so must we," referring to those who are not for the Revolution.

How about this? "In the work of the Revolution we have seen the work of justice; a biblical reality is to work for the poor. We understand the Revolution of the poor not only through the Bible, but also through the Revolution. Fidel, you have a true sense of justice. This stimulates us to stand behind the Revolution."

A Methodist minister said: "We love the Revolution, but we are apolitical, and we also come close to the ones who suffer in need. We think what you do is just, but there are things that need to change for us. We have requests. Why are we discriminated against, when we seek offices in governmental structures? We want to build new churches, but we cannot. We want the *Commandante* [Fidel Castro] to know that we wonder why the mass media is closed to us. Cuban Christians need to express their faith openly."

In closing Castro said, "I think the militants in my party will understand. Pray for me, and pray that the heavy responsibility that I carry will be removed from me. I was moved by your expression as I met each one of you at the door, such as 'God bless you' or 'I am praying for you.'"

Finally, the Christian leaders stood and sang a Christian song: "The right hand of God is moving in our land."

How the expressions of those pastors portray the realities of their experiences, I wondered. Cuba is run by a dictator. The people do not have real freedom!

Resulting from my contacts with some of the Cuban Christian leaders at Amsterdam '83 and '86, I was well received. Since there were no diplomatic relations between the United States and Cuba at the time, it was quite difficult for a US citizen to make a trip to Cuba. As a German living in the US I had to get the visa through the CSSR embassy in Washington. This had proved very time-consuming. It would have been so much easier to get the Cuban visa through the Cuban embassy in West Germany or another country such as Mexico or Jamaica.

I had to travel via Mexico City, changing in Merida. At the airport in Havana I was greeted by three Cubans who took me by car to the Riviera Hotel in downtown Havana. It was an old first-class hotel with services typical to those in socialist countries—bad! But it was cheap, only US$ 50 per night.

The following morning I was taken straight to the First Baptist Church to preach. A young nineteen-year-old student interpreted. He was terrific. That evening I preached at the Upper Room Baptist Church, and at both services several made commitments to Christ.

Rev. Raul Suarez, president of the Ecumenical Council of Cuba, sounded very much like liberal Christians I had met in China:

> The Cuban Revolution started a program of rectification. Overseas Cubans would like to bring about a change in Cuba by toppling the existing government. The Cuban church, however, would like to bring about a change from within by keeping the good developments of the Revolution, such as education which resulted in a leap forward in literacy from 56 percent to 98 percent. We want to eradicate the failures of the Revolution by evangelizing through a spirit of sacrifice and love.

> We would like to see a liturgical renewal, which means that we would like to be closer to our own Cuban culture in worship services. This could be expressed, for example, by hymns born in Cuba.

With this interesting information in mind I flew to Santiago de Cuba, 650 km east of Havana. Elmar Labastida Alfonso, pastor of the Second Baptist Church, with his wife, Gisela, was a tremendous host. He showed me the sights of the area and interpreted for me at two church services on Monday and Tuesday. One was a Baptist and the other a Methodist church.

The most interesting site for me to see was the former home of Frank Pais. As a Christian he had been a revolutionary in the early years of Castro's revolution. As a twenty-three-old, he was in charge of logistics all across the country to keep the revolution going while Fidel and Raul Castro were fighting in the hills near Santiago de Cuba. Frank and his brother were killed one month apart in 1957. Frank is now respected as a national hero. Evangelical Christians in Cuba are split in their opinion about this young man; some say he did the right thing as a young Christian to help the Revolution while others are totally opposed to that view. However, he is respected by Christians and non-Christians alike.

At that time many wondered why Cuba refused to go the route of their big brother the Soviet Union. Gorbachev was voted "the man of the decade" following his bold move to get away from dictatorship in his own country and to agree to the reunification of Germany. Two questions emerged during those months, and people wanted to hear from me as a German—or better yet as a European.

"What do you think about the extraordinary developments in Eastern Europe? Do you think Gorbachev is for real?"

Of course I was thrilled and challenged with the new situation in Europe. I thought that we might enter a period in which all formerly Communist-controlled countries would experience an unprecedented thrust in evangelism. And that actually happened.

Then there was another question I was asked by some—not by many, but by some:

"Will a united Germany be a threat to the world?"

This question was offensive to a German citizen. When a Christian leader made some insensitive remarks on this issue in a magazine, I sent him the following letter:

I am greatly disturbed with your assessment of the fear European countries have as they face the imminent emergence of a "unified German superpower."

We Germans are deeply sorry for what the Nazis did under an Austrian-born Hitler [only a couple of months before he became chancellor did he receive German citizenship]. We have paid for those crimes over and over again. We are prepared to live with this shame for generations to come, as other countries had to live with theirs. Others are still to admit to their crimes, such as the Soviet Union, Poland, China, Cambodia—just to name a few. At least we are trying to accept our blame.

But for you, as a Christian leader, to fall into the trap so many journalists fall into! You quoted the Polish prime minister: "I worry not about the unification of the two Germanys, but I do worry about the unification of the Reich." And then to write—and I quote you: "And who can blame him for such fear and concern."

This is plain insensitivity to our German people. There is no new "Reich" planned, and nobody has to fear the new Germany!

By the way, the "Third Reich" existed exactly twelve years! In those years inexcusable crimes were committed in the name of Germany. But what about the forty-five years since 1945! Germany has developed into one of the most democratic, peace- and freedom-loving countries of the world. We have opened our hearts and borders to all those that seek refuge from political oppression. We did this, because we know from experience how it feels to be oppressed. This period is four times as long as those infamous twelve years!

We have sent more aid around the world than some countries put together. We have given billions of marks to Israel and those that had suffered under our brutality. No money ever will pay for the crimes committed, but we are at least committed to do whatever we can to lighten the load of those that have suffered.

This, no other nation that I know of has ever done in history—not one!

Germany is a country with a great history. Martin Luther, Gutenberg, Beethoven, Bach, Roentgen, Einstein, Händel, and Georg Müller have all formed our nation and the world. You don't have to be afraid of Germany. One day you may thank the Lord for Germany and for what she might continue to give to the world.

Let us pray for Germany. Let us pray that she might again experience a reformation and revival. Let us stand beside her as she is being misunderstood and maligned again by politicians and journalists who maneuver themselves into positions in order to bring gain to them and their agendas. Let us forgive those that cannot forget, for they still have an unregenerate nature.

I pondered before I wrote, whether I should write this letter. I chose to do so, because you must know how Germans really feel when they are faced with another barrage of accusations—and that forty-five years after World War II. I am glad that most Germans can't read English magazines like yours and thus are spared. And even if they could, most of them would say nothing, but choose to suffer quietly because

of their guilt and shame. Therefore, I speak for them. Let us
be fair and let us love—with Christian love.

I never received a response.

Spain is a Catholic country. I was invited to hold evangelistic
meetings in the far northern part. Bilbao, Vitoria, and San
Sebastian are cities in the Basque region—a terrorist region at
that time. Two days before I ministered in one of those cities,
five city buses were set on fire. While ministering in Vitoria, the
evening TV news showed in gruesome detail the spilled blood
of yet another terrorist who was gunned down in a battle with
the police.

The Basque country is an autonomous, but not an independent region of Spain. 90 percent of its population want to
remain in Spain. The rest—a small minority—want to become
an independent country. They have been fighting for it with
terror for more than twenty years.

Two million live in that region. 80 percent of them are
Catholics, but only 35 percent are practicing their faith. The
Reformation that had swept across Europe in the sixteenth
century never had reached here. In other regions of Spain where
it did reach, the Counter Reformation was unleashed with full
force. The Inquisition with imprisonment, torture, and burning
at the stake extinguished the last flicker of evangelical life.

A converted monk, Casiodon de Reina, translated the Bible
into Spanish in 1569 but had to flee to northern Europe.

I was shocked to learn that only 1,500 Spanish and thirty
Basque evangelical believers live in this area. Their churches are
extremely small. Some don't have more than ten members.

Now God had led me to the Basque to minister among
them. One night I preached in a "packed" church. One hundred

had assembled. What a glorious sight after having preached to thirty-five people or less in other churches before! This church was started seventeen years before, and each member won to Christ had to be prayed for, talked to, labored over, preached at, and counseled with until finally a commitment was made. What a difference to Korea where I saw hundreds make decisions in one meeting alone!

Europe is different than Asia. As Billy Graham once stated, "Europe has been inoculated with Christianity." Europeans had been Christianized for centuries. Most of them claim to be Christians but they are not true followers of Jesus. To most Asians the gospel message is unique, different, fresh, and thus embraced. Therefore, those who accept Christ become true followers of Jesus.

In Germany very few follow the teachings of Christ. She is known as a Christian nation, as so many European countries are, but churches are empty and secular revelries go on all the time. This I expressed in my diary of October 7, 1990, and that with deep concern:

Oktoberfest—glorified and super Kirmes! Hundreds, if not thousands, sit in huge tents, eat, drink beer, and are being inundated with *Blasmusik*. Fascinating to watch. Sat down on a bench outside the happening and just watched and listened. They all seem to pursue happiness and seek their satisfaction as part of huge masses of people. What is there to life? People must seek deeper meaning for life, however, since they don't know where to look, or disillusioned with the church and its pastors, they do what everybody else does—"drink, eat, and be merry." But I do understand them. Life otherwise would be so boring. Yet, just before rising from the bench I saw a yellow, dying leaf glide down from a tree, taking its place among thousands that had fallen already. Soon it along with all the others will be swept away, burned, or used as fertilizer. It spoke of man, finally gliding and falling to nothingness. But how can we reach them with the inspiring and enriching life of Christ?! They seem to be so unreachable!

In November of that year I celebrated my sixtieth birthday with this entry in my journal:

In the past my birthdays didn't mean much—somehow this one is different. I am aware of it, it is meaningful; there is a new commitment to the Lord and His work. To have seen so much love and warmth [by my family]! To know that all of our kids and in-laws love the Lord and have experienced a deep love from my sweetheart throughout the many years of togetherness! It is so nice to be married, to have a family that sticks together! And to know that all of this is possible because of our Lord! He gave me a life so enriching, worth living, and a ministry so rewarding. Thrilling to look back and see how He has led us step by step through valleys of illness and to heights of service. And then He has always supplied all of our needs. And then to have seen countless people receive our Lord—in large and small meetings, crusades, and one-one-one [encounters]. For sixty years God has been so good. I thank Him for it and I love Him for His faithfulness! It is easy to walk with such a Lord!

Gerry Gallimore, then President of Youth for Christ International, wrote a stirring letter to our constituents:

Werner Bürklin, his wife Inge, and their four children are very special people to Sonia and me. We first met when Werner and

303

his family moved on short notice to Jamaica in 1967. It was during this period in Jamaica that the Lord used Werner as His instrument to call me into the ministry of YFC, as the first fulltime National Director for Jamaica YFC. Werner made a profound impact on my life by his zeal and commitment, and helped me cross the "faith line" of trusting God to provide for me and my family.

Few of us will pack so much into sixty years as Werner Bürklin has done. Born of German missionary parents in China, educated in France and the USA, Werner began his ministry as a young itinerant evangelist in Germany and, in time, he would take the gospel into 102 [actually 126] countries.

God has used his organizing skills over the years. These have resulted in thousands coming to Christ and in thousands of youth leaders and evangelists from around the world receiving fresh inspiration and practical training for world evangelization. Werner has continued to look for promising young leaders to call them into the Lord's service. Today many, like me, thank God for this man's discernment and courage in laying hands upon us for the Lord's work.

Besides preaching and teaching in churches and holding evangelistic crusades, I also love to talk to individuals. I was not exceptionally successful in leading people to Christ through personal witness like, for instance, Dawson Trotman was. But I had learned from him to grasp opportunities when presented.

On my previous visit to China, I had the joy of leading a lovely girl in her twenties to Christ. She did not have any contact with Christians before, yet she was inquisitive and eager to learn. I mailed her a Bible. I immediately sensed in her a desire to grow in her faith. She did not speak English very well, but I understood what she was trying to get across in a letter she wrote to me after her encounter with the Lord:

> I'm so glad to receive your Bible and letter.... I like to say it is a golden opportunity for me to have met you ... I took it as a first step—or say it is the turning point in my life to know our LORD GOD. I wish I can move closer to our LORD through the Bible and your help ... I read your gift-Bible carefully. I demand to make myself more and more close to God.

What an encouraging letter!

CHAPTER 21

AN AGGRESSIVE AGENDA—WORLD-WIDE MINISTRY AHEAD

A S WE WERE planning for the year 1991, I realized afresh how much we needed the prayers of our friends worldwide. I expressed this in a letter mailed out on January 3, 1991.

Our dear praying and supporting friends!

The New Year with all its challenges lies before us! We wish you a most blessed one, a year that you shall never forget.

For us it will include a major milestone. This will happen in May. In my next letter I will say more about it, but let me start giving you a rough schedule for 1991.

So I do hope you will pray for us. Pray that all the meetings planned will be well prepared. Pray that people will come to know Christ as Savior. Pray that God will give us safety in travels which will take us into different parts of the world. Pray that the fruits harvested will be well preserved.

January and February will take us to several churches for ministry— all of them in the USA. During this period we must lay the financial foundation for the entire year.

In **March** we will preach in numerous cities in Germany. We also will try to lay the burden of the China ministry upon the hearts of German Christians.

April will see us holding major crusades in Korea and Taiwan.

And during **May** our long-planned and prayed-for China Seminar will be launched in Nanjing, a city on the Yangtze River. Please pray for this as you have never prayed for anything else.

In **June and July** we will be back in Europe. One major event in which I was asked to participate will be the first interdenominational Eurofest-type youth conference held in the former part of East Germany in fifty-eight years!

August and September will be spent at home and behind the desk, after we have been away for more than three months in one stretch.

October will take us into South America. We have invitations from Uruguay and Argentina.

November is planned for meetings down-under. The president of New Zealand YFC has invited me for some strategic rallies. Since Australia is not too far away from there, we might extend meetings into that country as well.

So far **December** is planned for the family.

Wow, I did not realize the enormous amount of travel we were doing in those days!

The huge meetings in Korea stand out. We traveled from city to city and wherever we went, record-breaking crowds greeted us. Billy Kim, who had done a marvelous job arranging those meetings, and his son, Joey, interpreted. We ministered in high schools, colleges, on army bases, in churches, pastors' meetings, and open-air rallies.

In Taejon in central Korea, some six-thousand high school students sat outside, and some six hundred to seven hundred stood to receive Christ. On an army base with over three-thousand soldiers present, more than three hundred fifty made a profession of faith. Never before had I seen such a response.

In Seoul 20,000 attended a church service. During those weeks I often thought back to Germany—or Europe for that matter—and wondered what was the difference? Why did multitudes flock to evangelistic meetings in Asia and not in Europe?

The answer may be that the Holy Spirit is now working in Korea just as He had worked in certain areas of the world throughout the centuries in selected times. Just to mention a few; look at what happened.

In Germany!

The Holy Spirit used Count Nikolaus Ludwig von Zinzendorf (1700-60) to start the eighteenth century revival. Born in Dresden, Germany, into a family of nobility, he decided as a young man to leave the court and establish a model Christian community in Herrnhut. After initial bickering among the believers, they "learned to love one another," and this resulted in revival. The Holy Spirit came down, similar to what had happened at biblical Pentecost. As a result, hundreds of missionaries moved across the world, which is now known as the beginning of Protestant missions. The Holy Spirit moved powerfully during that period using the Moravian Church.

Then England.

John Wesley (1703-1791), born in England and a cleric, was later influenced by Moravian missionaries in the colony of Georgia, returned to England, studied at Herrnhut, and founded Methodism. Together with George Whitefield (1717-70), he brought spiritual revival to England by traveling on horseback 250,000 miles and delivering 40,000 sermons. It was a time when the Holy Spirit worked mightily in England.

The Great Awakening in the United States.

Three or four waves of religious revivals took place in the US between the early eighteenth and the late twentieth century. Several ministers and also exceptional prayer meetings nurtured and advanced religious revival dramatically. Again it was the Holy Spirit that brought about these spiritual manifestations known as Great Awakenings.

Indonesia.

After the Second World War, in the 1960s, spiritual revivals began in Soe on the island of Timor and spread across Indonesia. Church membership in Central Java jumped from 30,000 to over 100,000 in a short time. The same happened all across the other islands of that country. Someone said at that time, "What the Holy Spirit is doing in Indonesia today is more like another chapter added to the book of Acts." The Holy Spirit was at work.

South Korea.

The 1907 revival in Korea was born in pre-dawn prayer meetings. It rapidly spread across the nation and after the Korean War every evangelical church had such prayer meetings (in the winter at 6 a.m. and in the summer, 5 a.m.). Through the overwhelming work of the Holy Spirit the church in Korea grew by leaps and bounds.

These are just a few samples of how the Lord used the Holy Spirit to work in different countries at specific times. This can now be seen in China. When I ask Chinese Christians how come the church of Jesus Christ is exploding in their midst, I always get the same answer, "We don't know. All we can say is that the Holy Spirit is bringing this about."

From Korea I traveled to Taiwan. In Taipei 2,700 young people jammed into a gym to hear the gospel. God had opened the doors wide into schools all across the island. Ed Lyman, known as the singing Marine, accompanied me. In one of my letters I wrote:

> One girl was so rebellious, that the teachers did not know what to do with her. She was a terrible influence on the other students. The principal gave up on her. But a pastor took her in to live with his family. She accepted the Lord within a year and went back to school so changed, that the principal said, "If Christ can make such a difference, I want Youth for Christ to help us."

That's why we were invited to minister to those above-mentioned teenagers.

And then we traveled to the Peoples' Republic of China—a Communist country where Christians had been persecuted for their faith for thirty-two years. The time of truth had come. I remember so well the emotions I had as I entered China.

Forgotten Christian leaders in China

The preparations for our first teaching seminar in China had been tedious to say the least and slow in coming. Top Christian leaders there were rather hesitant to engage foreign tutors. Visits in Nanjing and numerous letters between Bishop Ting and me had been exchanged. On January 16, 1991, he finally wrote me:

> I am glad that the series of lectures from May 23 to 31 has been fixed. I hope everything will work out well.
>
> You probably know that, thus far, we in Nanjing Seminary have only had lecturers from abroad who give one or at most two lectures. This is going to be the first time we have a number of lecturers from abroad giving several lectures each day for several successive days. There are bound to be those who are skeptical of this plan. We want to go about it as carefully as we can so that the end result will vindicate not the harm but the desirability of what we do, and insure an openness to future cooperation.
>
> You have already got a good understanding of our situation. I say these things just for the sake of preparing your colleagues' mind so that they would not easily get frustrated. I am going to be here in Nanjing in May. I am looking forward to seeing you all then. Meanwhile, God's rich blessing on each and every one of you.

So we knew what lay ahead.

Erik and I were traveling aboard a river steamer on the Yangtze River from Jiujiang to Nanjing. Two days later we were scheduled to begin our leadership training seminar in the foremost theological seminary of China. In the evening I was standing at the railing staring at the muddy water below. A thick blanket of fog rested before us. Every minute or so the ship's horn sounded a warning across the river. I bowed my head and worshiped the Lord for having led us to China. Finally!

AN AGGRESSIVE AGENDA—
WORLD-WIDE MINISTRY AHEAD

The fog before me reminded me of the unknown. Will everything go well? Will we be scrutinized? Will we be allowed to go through to the end? Therefore, once again I lowered my head and lifted my heart to God in prayer. Not knowing what lay ahead, I entrusted the future into God's hands.

And then everything fell into place.

All of the study books we had ordered in Hong Kong had arrived—hundreds of them. "You cannot do that," I had been warned by Christian China watchers. "They will be confiscated by the authorities." But this did not happen. The overhead projector had made it through customs without a hitch. We only had to pay $139 for customs. Even the Chinese study material we had developed for this occasion had been printed in Shanghai. We were ready to proceed.

I had asked four friends of mine to make up the teaching team: Gerry Gallimore, Jamaica; Bill Weldon, USA; Wilbur Wright, New Zealand; Ed Lyman, USA; plus my son Erik. The Lord welded us together in an exceptional way.

Eighty seminar participants sat before us eagerly waiting to learn. They had come from ten different provinces and were chosen church leaders who wanted to know more about the Bible. They wanted to learn how to preach evangelistically. We taught them how to stay fresh spiritually, how to develop a strong devotional life, and many more such subjects.

They were eager to learn—very eager. They took copious notes on almost anything we taught. Every time we mentioned a Bible reference, the rustling of turned pages filled the room. They asked penetrating questions: How did you find Christ? How were you called into God's service? Have you had sufferings in life and how did they shape your life?

313

At the close of our ten-day seminar, I asked them to stand and then led them into a prayer of dedication. When I looked up again, I saw some of them weeping. Others wiped tears off their faces. God had been in our midst.

I was overwhelmed with what we had experienced! For months we had prepared and prayed. Truly God had gone before, step by step.

Bishop Ting gave us a farewell banquet. He said, "Thank you for coming. I have not heard one word of criticism about what you taught or did. Please do this in other cities as well."

This was the beginning of our teaching ministry in China.

Following the seminar, I visited the small village of Wang Pai, high up in the mountains near Nanfeng in Jiangxi, where my parents had been interned during the Second World War. When I was leaving on that trip early in the morning at 6:30 a.m., the mayor of the city showed up. "I will accompany you," he said. The excursion up was quite precarious, first using a car and later a Jeep rumbling up narrow, dusty paths. Finally we had to walk the final kilometers.

We were warmly welcomed by the inhabitants. They led us to a tea house and offered their home-grown tea. Some of the older ones mentioned that my parents had lived among them. One of the ladies related that she had helped out in our home, and another mentioned doing the laundry for us.

On our way back, a well-dressed old lady stood in the middle of the path holding out her arms trying to stop us. I jumped out of the car to greet her. She grabbed my hand and thanked me for the missionaries that had meant so much to her. So news had traveled fast in the entire area: the son of former missionaries had returned! She talked too fast for me; I was unable to understand everything she said in her thick Jiangxi accent, but her smile and the inner peace she exuded spoke volumes!

South America is a different matter. I had been invited to hold evangelistic crusades and preach at a national youth congress in Argentina. First I didn't want to go. I was adamant; I just didn't want to go? Why?

The invitation was firm, and ever since receiving it, I had prayed for this event as I did with all other forthcoming events. However, there had been a problem—since the very first invitation, I had not heard from Argentina again, and that for months! Either all of my correspondence had not reached them, or my contact was too busy to answer.

Meanwhile I had been told by the American director in charge for the Buenos Aires Billy Graham Crusade: "We established our own network of people who disseminate our news through captains and sub-captains and so on down the line. That is the only way to get the information out to people! We simply don't depend on postal services here."

Years before I had lived in a South American country myself—in Brazil—and learned then that things there were not done the same way as a German was used to. Punctuality, orderliness, and efficiency, the way we understand those qualities are irrelevant there. In fact, I was told that sometimes officials just swept stacks of mail into waste paper baskets when the overload got too large. However, at the end things are getting done somehow, and it "all will come out in the wash."

But for this event I had waited so long—too long! I almost cancelled twice—the second time a few days before the day of my departure. Then and only then I received a frantic phone call from Argentina begging me not to give up now: "Please come! Everything is ready," he said.

So I went, telling the Lord, "Even if only one person will be blessed or finds the Lord, I want to be obedient to your call."

When I got down there, everything was in disarray, or at least it seemed so to me. Logistically and organizationally it was a disaster.

Amazingly, though, in meeting after meeting the "altars were filled!" Within five days some four hundred ten people had made commitments to Christ—some made first-time decisions, and others rededicated their lives to the Lord.

I was deeply humbled, yet thrilled. I stood back and marveled at how He had drawn people unto Himself. At midnight after my last meeting, someone slipped a letter into my hand.

> I thank God for His Word to me through you. I really had to thank God on Friday after your first message here. He had directly spoken to me and to my need to live like a "daughter of light." The same happened again on Saturday and Sunday. I want to live and do what He wants. Thank you for having been here!

This topped it off. This was the one person I had been praying about before leaving for that assignment, who in an unsolicited letter said, "I am glad you came!"

And besides that person several hundred others had been touched by the Lord. What a thrill to have seen God work again!

For my final assignment in 1991, I was in New Zealand. Wilbur Wright (he passed into glory-land in October 2011), a close friend and former president of New Zealand YFC, had invited me for meetings across the north and south islands. As I faced the super large crowd at Auckland's YFC rally, directed by Ian Grant, I felt so inadequate. But I depended totally upon the Lord for this important task.

This then I reported to my friends:

> Shortly before Christmas the large town hall in Auckland was filled with teenagers. Many young people walked forward that night to commit their lives to Christ. What an amazing evening! I had asked you to pray for me as I preached at that rally. I felt your prayers. There is nothing more thrilling than to see young people walk into the counseling room after having heard the preaching of God's Word and to be shown the way to the cross.

Ian Grant is a great communicator and preacher. However, he has one handicap—he stutters when he normally converses with people. Nothing serious, but people who know him as a stutterer are then surprised and thrilled to hear him preach fluently without any trace of this handicap. In fact I was told that a stutterer in the audience, who did not know him, once approached Ian after one of his sermons for counsel. It went something like this:

> "Pastor, I I-I-I have a pro-pro-problem. C-C-Can you h-h-help m-me?"

> "Wh-wh-what is th-the pr-pr-problem?" Ian inquired.

The counselee almost lashed out, hitting Ian, thinking that he was making fun of him. I do not know whether this actually happened, but as I said above, someone told me this story. The fact is that Ian as a stutterer did not stutter when he proclaimed God's Word. Amazing!

As the New Year began, I reflected on what had transpired the year before. With all the many ministry events, China stood out—this was very apparent. For me this was a sign that I was in love with China. China was the country of my birth and where I spent the first eighteen years of my life. I was drawn to it like nothing else.

Teaching and training emerging Christian leaders

We had trained Christian leaders from ten different provinces. All over China, churches were being reopened and new ones formed and built. Millions of Chinese had been attracted into the kingdom of God. The church in China was growing like nowhere else in the world.

However, they needed instruction! They needed biblical instruction! They needed encouragement! They needed Bible-based literature! They needed direction for their personal and corporate lives!

I was convinced that we had been successful in contributing to those needs at our first leadership training seminar in Nanjing. Christian leaders wanted us to come back and repeat the same in other seminaries and Bible schools across the land.

We had heard that the government was planning to revert back to their previous dealings with foreigners. Some western news commentators talked about them wanting to evict all Christian language teachers. Some western organizations had used Christian teachers as "missionaries." Missionaries, however, were not allowed by the Communists to operate in China. It was true that missionaries were *persona non grata,* but Christian teachers were welcomed as long as they were not proselytizing. When the authorities found out that those English language teachers were disregarding the government's regulations and misused their privileges by evangelizing, our own ministry was put at risk. *They might throw out the baby with the bath water*, I mused. And we might be the baby!

Our policy had always been to work within the framework given to us by the Christian church leadership in China. We refused to do anything illegal. We had decided to abide by the rules, regulations, and laws of the government.

On January 13, 1992, Ruth Graham called me. She wanted to see whether her son Ned could work with us. He headed up Eastgate, an organization that Doug Sutphen had started after a falling-out with "God's smuggler" Brother Andrew. Together with him they had raised US$ 10 million and planned to smuggle one million Bibles into China. Later I heard that this had ended in a total fiasco. When the rented boats with Bibles moved toward the shore, most of their "captains" got scared and just dumped their Bibles into the ocean. The rest were stacked up on the beach and burned, after law officials had confronted the Christians who were to transport them into the interior. I was told that only a few thousand actually reached their target. Praise God for those that benefited from them. But as a whole it was a massive waste of God's money!

Ruth Graham mentioned that her husband wanted to underwrite Ned's ministry with royalties of her husband's latest book. BGEA donated $5,000 per month. Ned planned with the help of the American Bible Society to purchase 200,000 Bibles from the Nanjing Amity Press and distribute them to Christians, also those in house churches, across China. She encouraged me to get in touch with Kitty Xia, a government lady in Shanghai. I shared with Ruth our need of $25,200 for Christian literature we wanted to distribute in China and asked whether BGEA might be able to help.

"Oh, I think I can help you with this," she responded. A few days later I received a letter from her with a personal check of $25,200!

All the ten years since my first trip to China we had stayed true to the principles we had adopted at the beginning of our China ministry, and we sensed that our Christian friends trusted us. So did the government departments. Later our son Erik, who succeeded me as president of China Partner, carried on in the same way. This resulted in further open doors across China. The next seminar was held in Guangzhou in the province of Guangdong.

Every morning our teaching team was picked up by a van provided by the Guangzhou Christian Council. Everything went well, however, after a wonderful farewell one week later we were given a bill for the usage of the van. This surprised us, because we had expected that this would be covered by our host. Furthermore, it would have been so much cheaper to have used taxis! We laughed and realized that Chinese Christians are also good capitalists—they know how to make money!

However, the fellowship with the students was outstanding. They wanted us to return quickly. This encouraged us to continue with our plans to teach in as many schools as possible. We eventually taught in Fuzhou, Beijing, Hefei, Jinan, Xian, Hangzhou, Nanchang, Changsha, and Chengdu, to mention just a few.

At YFC's Triennial Convocation in Nairobi, Kenya, in 1990 I met the national director of Guatemala YFC. He had invited me for evangelistic meetings in his country. Two years later I was there. Stephan Tchividjian, Jr., grandson of Billy Graham, put together a team of young people to help with this venture. I was greatly impressed with their willingness to pitch in wherever needed, from installing and tearing down a huge sound equipment for our singer—sometimes for three meetings at three different locations in one day—to giving testimonies, singing, or counseling with those who wanted to accept Christ.

Several of those team members were so blessed by what they had experienced that they wanted to further serve there. Seventeen meetings within seven days had left an indelible impact on them. To see thousands of young people come under the sound of the gospel, and then to see many of them make a commitment for Christ, is something one does not forget easily. And they did not.

I thought to myself, *if only the first evangelical missionary could have been present.* He had arrived in Guatemala on November 2, 1881. He faced insurmountable hurdles! What a thrill it would have been for him to see what God had done since those early and tough missionary years.

A century later, 20 percent of the population is considered to be evangelical Christians! And the church is totally run by nationals.

On September 1, 1984, one hundred three years later, a young Guatemalan couple started YFC. Their goal was to lead 100,000 young people to Christ.

At the final meeting I gave the challenge to totally surrender their lives to become God's channels in reaching out to those without Christ. So many came to the altar that I had to move my lectern back to make more room!

India is the second largest country in the world with 1.2 billion in 2011 and may overtake China with its one-child policy soon. 80 percent of Indians consider themselves Hindus. There is a strong move by some to make India totally Hindu, and persecuting Christians has already taken place in some areas. 52 percent of its population is illiterate, and the poverty is inconceivable! I had visited India many times, yet the vast poverty hit me each time afresh! In Calcutta alone there are still 3.5 million slum-dwellers, and 107 million in India beg for their living.

I was back there for meetings. As my taxi came to a stop at an intersection in Bangalore, I handed some money to a twelve-year-old begging girl. Literally, within a second, others came running, stretching out their hands into the car. One estimate said that 52 percent live below the poverty line.

"Your life is God's gift to you; what you do with it is your gift to God." I found this quote by Abraham Lincoln on the wall at a high school in South India. During the day I was teaching at a leadership seminar, and in the evenings I preached in evangelistic meetings. In spite of the offensive by a number of Hindus described above, the Christians are still making an impact in some areas.

CHAPTER 22

INGE'S HOMECOMING TO LITHUANIA

K LAIPEDA, A CITY on the Baltic Sea, has had a stormy history! Now it belongs to Lithuania, formerly to the USSR, and before that to Germany.

Klaipeda is a city close to our hearts, because Inge was born there. Toward the end of the Second World War, as a twelve-year-old, she had to flee the onrushing Red Army, but her interest and love for the people who now live there never waned.

We accepted an invitation to hold an evangelistic crusade in the only evangelical church left in that city. On the first day we had been invited for a *Friedhofsfest*—a festival in a cemetery. Such festivals were popular events for Christians during the Soviet occupation. Only in cemeteries were Christians permitted to speak freely in public about their faith—after all, a cemetery is a neutral place. "Even the Communists have to die," someone told us. Therefore Communist party members would attend such festivals as well. What an opportunity to evangelize.

After Lithuania's liberation in 1989, the Christians were still "celebrating" these festivals and we had the privilege to preach at one of them. People arrived from the surrounding cities and villages. Some sat on crude benches that had been brought in; most of them stood throughout the two-hour service.

It reminded us of the early Christians during Nero's days. Then they met in catacombs, now in cemeteries to profess their faith in Christ.

On the last morning in Klaipeda after our five-day meetings, we stood in the hotel lobby looking out, when Inge spotted a young man standing outside looking in. He had accepted Christ on the first day of our evangelistic crusade. He had his arm around a girl and apparently was searching for someone.

"Perhaps he wants to see us," Inge uttered.

So we stepped out and they immediately approached us. In broken English he asked us to pray for them.

"Bless us as Jesus did," he said.

The beautiful girl at his side was his bride-to-be. They wanted to get married that year. Therefore, they wanted to have a special blessing from God.

"I now have Jesus in my heart," he disclosed. "Please pray, please pray."

We moved away from the main entrance, then formed a circle embracing one another, and putting my hand on his head I prayed:

"Lord, here is a young couple that loves you. He just found you as his Savior. He now needs your guidance and help, your fortitude and benediction. Let them begin their new life together under your protection and blessing. Thank you for saving his soul."

Both of them smiled, and tears welled up in his eyes when he said, "Thank you, thank you."

As we drove off to the airport we saw them tightly holding each other, walking away into a new life—together with Christ.

This is what makes the many hardships of travel and labor so worthwhile. He was one of over thirty that had begun a new life with Christ during the crusade in Klaipeda.

CHAPTER 23

CHINA'S OPEN DOORS—
GOOD-BYE TO YFCI

MORE THAN ONE thousand worshipers overflowed what was the former Anglican cathedral in Hangzhou, at that time one of close to 10,000 churches that had reopened in China by 1992. It was said that every two days, three more churches were started or reopened at that time. The congregants even spilled over into the choir loft. After Ed Lyman had sung a gospel song, I preached to this large congregation. They had told me before that they expect a long sermon, so I preached for one hour. The central part of my message was the cross of Jesus Christ and the need to be born again. At the close I asked those who wanted to commit their lives to Christ to follow me in a silent prayer of repentance. To my astonishment I heard a host of them praying out loud. *God is truly in our midst,* I thought to myself.

One of the highlights of that trip was our visit to the home of Watchman Nee (1903-72). This famous Chinese preacher of the '20s and '30s of the twentieth century had started house churches all across the eastern seaboard of China. While traveling in England he had fellowshiped with the group known as Brethren. They did not believe in clergy and church buildings, but met in homes for prayer and exhortation. One of their laity expounded the Scriptures after they had celebrated the Lord's Supper. This was done every Sunday. Watchman Nee liked this idea and started a movement—similar to a denomination—known as Little Flock.

Under Communist rule he was incarcerated like a host of other pastors and Christian leaders had experienced. Rumors floated around in the western world that in prison his tongue had been cut out. Inquiring about this, the elders of the church (Little Flock) who had monitored his development until the end rejected such falsehood. "Nonsense," they said, "it is true that he was imprisoned for many years, but later he worked as an interpreter and translator in a local business establishment while still under arrest."

Now the house fellowship that he had started in the large home of his well-to-do mother had morphed into a good-sized church with four hundred seats. The government had even declared this a historic site. The edifice is located on a river island. Every year floods would cover the entire island, and the city authorities finally decided to resettle all the inhabitants off the island; only Watchman Nee's building was spared. In fact, later the entire island was prepared in such a way that floods were curbed and a Taiwanese businessman was allowed to build a super Walmart-type shopping center on that island. Also Nee's church was permitted to build a larger church on that island with a seating capacity of close to one thousand.

If I had a choice where to live in China, I would choose the city of Xiamen opposite and across from Taiwan. More and more Taiwanese, who had fled their original home country, and others are establishing businesses and beautiful homes in that city. I drove along the waterfront and was flabbergasted to see brand new and expensively built estates overlooking the gorgeous turquoise Taiwan Straits.

The first church ever reopened in China after the Cultural Revolution was in this city. It originally was established in 1848 and was later declared a historic site under the Communist government. It was here where Bob Pierce was challenged to start World Vision. He took the ferry across the bay to where German deaconesses administered an orphanage. He was appalled when the sisters refused to take in a little baby that had been found on the street while he was visiting there. "We cannot take the child," they declared. "We just don't have any more room!" Pierce was adamant: "You must take the baby in. Imagine what will happen to him without proper care." Thereupon one of the sisters thrust that baby into his arms. "Then you take care of him."

He did. He was told it would take US$10 per month to house, feed, and eventually educate one child. World Vision was born, which today has a budget of close to one billion dollars. Amazing how minor incidents like this develop into momentous, significant, and meaningful organizations.

In Fuzhou a young Chinese pastor interpreted for us as we were teaching at a leadership training school. He was thirty years old. I asked him how he found the Lord. "I wanted to improve my English and listened to radio broadcasts of BBC (British Broadcasting Company) and VOA (Voice of America)," he explained. On one of those programs he heard a Bible message.

This was the first time he had learned about Jesus Christ. He immediately searched for a church and found one that had just opened in Xian, where he lived. It was 1982, just after Deng Xiaoping had reopened China to the West. He could not believe what he saw—hundreds of Christians assembling and worshiping Jesus Christ. Hadn't his Communist Party stated that God was nonexistent? After having attended the church a few times, an elder approached him, saying, "I have seen you in church a number of times, but we don't come here only to listen to sermons and sing praises to God. We also want to lead people to Christ. Do you know Him?"

As he was so forcefully confronted with the gospel he accepted the challenge and turned his sinful life over to Christ. After that the elder exclaimed, "Now the angels in heaven said a loud hallelujah!"

At this stage I need to interject some correspondence I had with YFCI's leadership. I had wrestled for more than one year over what steps I needed to take in the future. I was getting older and thought, *if I stay with Youth for Christ, they will have to change their name to "Old Folks for God"!*

Furthermore, YFCI needed new leadership at the top, and I was glad when Jim Groen stepped down. I wrote him on August 20, 1990:

> I just want to thank you for having been so gracious when you relinquished the presidency to Gerry Gallimore. I believe you showed real stature at that time.
>
> I know it must have been very difficult for you, and as Dotti told me, you were deeply hurt. But never forget that all of us had to go through periods like that as Christ tries to mold us into His image. It is now my prayer that God will

give you courage to do what needs to be done and trust Him for the future of your life.

I can only tell you that I found wonderful peace and a tremendous ministry after having relinquished different posts in my life such as the presidency of Germany Youth for Christ, and the area directorship of Europe YFC, among others. God always has a job for us to do, and what a thrill it was when Billy Graham asked me to direct his conferences afterwards. So I know by experience that God will not let us down.

Please give my love to Dotti. She also was a courageous woman.

As ever your friend, and above all, your brother in Christ.

Then I wrote him on December 24, 1991:

Today I received the *World Perspective* from Singapore in which I read the news that you have chosen to step off YFCI's board and move into your own ministry.

As a friend—and tennis partner—I want to thank you for your and Dotti's friendship over the many years. I will never forget when we really met for the first time in Cyprus. It was fun to have known you.

May the Lord guide you into an expanded ministry that is close to your heart. May He sustain you and may you experience His everlasting grip on your life.

Finally, I also realized that the time for my departure from YFCI had come. I had established "Werner Burklin Ministries" for ministries I couldn't do with YFC. During a YFCI leadership conference near Zurich, Switzerland, on April 23, 1992, I handed the following letter to the president of YFCI, Gerry Gallimore:

> After many months of prayer and counsel with friends, I herewith want to ask you to accept my request for early retirement at the age of sixty-two. This can take effect at the close of our next Convocation in 1993.
>
> We are thankful to our Lord for having brought you to the presidency of Youth for Christ International. This was a dream of ours come true, and you are now well established. However, Inge and I both feel that we are no longer meaningfully needed by the organization. Thus we are very much at ease stepping out of the movement we will have served for over thirty-five years in one capacity or another, knowing that God will surround you with godly men and women who will help achieve your goals.
>
> In order to phase out properly we would like to do it over a period of one year. During that year we can notify our friends, make arrangements for an ongoing ministry, think through practical matters such as our pension plan and medical insurance, and do whatever is needed to make the transition as smooth and amiable as possible.
>
> I still have some engagements with YFC in India and would like to personally explain our new situation to our many YFC friends and other contacts around the world. It is extremely

important that the ministry we have done for YFC will go on unceasingly.

Gerry, you must know that we are always available in case you need our counsel or help. We want to stay as close to YFCI as time and resources permit. We will continue to pray for you daily, as we have done since you took over the presidency. We rest assured that the most spiritual ministries of YFCI are ahead as you give leadership to it in humility and with integrity.

Please convey our decision to the board, but permit me to personally make it known to my long-standing friends of the WLT [world leadership team].

On October 17 he graciously answered.

Your letter of April 23, 1992, requesting early retirement is hereby formally acknowledged in as much as it was already the subject of discussion and comment in your presence by members of the World Leadership Team and the Executive Committee of the YFCI board at our meeting in Zurich.

You have had a most distinguished career among us having served at the national level in Germany and for the last several years you have served the international family of YFCI in many roles. You have also done [made] us proud by outstanding service that you rendered the wider field of world evangelization through your service with the Billy Graham Evangelistic Association. Now for the last six years you have carried the flag of Christ and of YFC around the world as YFCI Evangelist-at-Large.

But it is not the titles so much that have given you credibility; it has been your solid devotion to the Savior, your strong passion for evangelism, and your sincere commitment to integrity. These things are what marked you out as God's servant.

It is therefore with joy and yet with a heavy heart that we will accede to your request for early retirement and release you as requested at the close of our YFCI Convocation on August 1, 1993. We will hold you to your promise to provide counsel and help when we need it and expect you to remain close to YFC until the Lord calls you home.

Already your name is being considered for membership on our international board when you move out of your current staff position.

We know of your great heart for China, the land of your birth, and will follow your ongoing ministry with our prayers, our love, and our support. We claim you as one of us always and will view whatever you do for the Lord as an extension of our heart for the Gospel.

We identify Inge and your whole family with every sentiment in our hearts for you and praise the Lord equally for their sterling contribution with you in the work of the Kingdom.

You have been an especially dear friend, mentor, brother, and colleague to me. It was through you that the Lord called me into the work of YFC 24 years ago. That day is enshrined in my mind forever. Thank you for helping me hear the call of God and helping me submit to the molding of His hands.

On behalf of the worldwide family of YFC we assure you of our love, prayers, and deep appreciation for your over 35 years of service among us.

Into China fulltime

As I was now on my own with my newly formed Werner Burklin Ministries (later changed to China Partner), I studied materials of other interested parties for events unfolding in China. I found an article in *Christianity Today*, written by Ralph Covell, former Dean of Faculty at Denver Theological Seminary. He had been a missionary to China from 1946-51 and then Taiwan from 1952-66. He expressed the same sentiments about foreign religious activities in China as I had held:

> When it comes to the Church in China, many American evangelicals [other Westerners as well] understandably know only one scenario, that of suffering Christians in a Marxist regime desperately needing outside help to survive. More specifically, they see the visible church in China as having fatally compromised with its Communist overseers; and the true church as being made up of underground Christians who conduct their lives secretly and thereby preserve the faith in its pristine purity.

> May I, however, suggest another scenario sketched only in broad strokes; one that, despite the severe problems and persecutions of the past, more accurately has today's Chinese government granting freedom of religion to all groups in China—albeit within the tightly regimented framework of patriotism and acceptance of its laws. And it is within these limits that the visible church in China has indeed grown remarkably.

Covell then described the advances that had been made by the China Christian Council, whose churches function with the approval of the central government. He asked:

> Why, then, are so many evangelicals pessimistic about the visible church in China? Granted, the severity of past terrors augments some of our negative thinking. However, the most critical reason for this pessimism, I believe, is that for the first time in well over 100 years we are faced with the reality of a strong Chinese government....

> Whenever there has been a strong central government, with firm sovereignty over all of China, a kind of state orthodoxy (be it Confucianism or Marxism) has produced a tight control and supervision over all religious groups. These groups, in turn, learned to live within these limits and to grow and prosper. The government viewed those not willing to submit to this type of surveillance with suspicion—as possible centers of dissidence and a threat to the government-sponsored orthodoxy....

> China's historic distrust of religions has been magnified by outside involvement with the so-called underground churches. Imagine, if you will, the confusion confronting a government official trying to understand these committed Christian groups. They meet secretly, even where there are public worship services at which the Bible is faithfully preached. They do not identify themselves publicly as Christians, even when promised freedom of religion. And they are often contacted secretly by outside groups (usually based in the West) who bring an assortment of written material which to officials is not familiar.

Covell concluded with an appeal to western Christians to use some common sense:

> Christians outside of China do well to think of using their professional gifts in helping in the development of this vast country. If done conscientiously, their activities will promote friendly relations with the Chinese people and make an excellent contribution to China's modernization....

And this is where I absolutely agree with his assessment:

> But the current task of evangelizing China rests not with these "outsiders" but with the body of Christ miraculously raised up within China's own borders.

Covell later became a board member of China Partner.

In October I met James Taylor III, great-grandson of Hudson Taylor, for breakfast in our hotel in Hong Kong following our ministries in Nanjing, Shanghai, and Fuzhou. Interestingly, even though we taught at the seminary in Fuzhou, we were not invited to preach on Sunday. The reason? We had a journalist, Ed Plowman, with us, who often worked for Billy Graham and the magazine *Christianity Today,* and who had been my communications director at Amsterdam '86. Our interpreter explained, "The old leaders of our churches here are still frightened because of what happened to them during the Cultural Revolution. Therefore they take extra precaution." Government officials were leery when foreign journalists traveled through China.

"You are doing the right thing working within the confines of the China Christian Council (CCC)," James Taylor told us over breakfast. "With my background as general director of

OMF (formerly China Inland Mission), I cannot do that, but you should."

He had totally reversed his opinion about a working relationship with the CCC. It was so good to see how prominent and thus responsible people were throwing off their previously held biased attitudes. Just as I had to, after having been told and been misled by so-called evangelical China-watchers to avoid the CCC. So many of them had been opposed to the so-called open churches (visible churches as Covell termed them) judging them wrongly as being subservient to the Communist Party. I personally found them believing in Christ and honoring Him. They were patriotic, yes, but their first loyalty belonged to Jesus.

The teaching ministry moved along so well that we decided to create a newly revised manual on Christian leadership, especially geared to Chinese culture and mentality. But the very foundation of it came right out of the Scriptures. That is what the Christian leaders needed.

In the coastal city of Fuzhou we had met a twenty-three-year-old girl that had just become a Christian. She had been attending a Bible study class run by believers that had not registered with the authorities. She wanted to have us visit their meeting, but I knew we had to be careful not to jeopardize their standing.

"Are you sure that it would be all right for us to visit your group?" I queried.

"No problem," she said.

But I have had my experiences in China. So I asked again, "Are you really sure? Would it not be better for you to check this out with your leaders?"

That evening the telephone rang in my hotel room and she was on the line.

"You are right," she disclosed. "My leaders think it wiser for you not to come."

Here again we encountered a dilemma we had faced over the years. We vowed to be sensitive in a country that was atheistic in its policies. We were grateful for the many open doors we found in China, but as our Chinese friends always had cautioned, "We only have relative freedom. But the freedom we do have we enjoy, and we want to make use of opportunities of service we have."

Starting October 1, 1993, our son Erik joined our ministry full-time. Youth for Christ graciously freed him. Inge and I were deeply moved that the grandson of my missionary father was willing to step into his shoes to continue the work he had started some seventy years ago. This was a big step forward for us.

In between, after a number of years waiting, Inge and I traveled to Meissen in East Germany. I had been invited to hold evangelistic meetings in the Protestant church *Sankt Afra* on top of the historic "*Dom am Burgberg.*" The city was known as the "secret capital of Saxony" (Sachsen) and it became famous for its beautiful and precious porcelain. Ed Lyman joined me and sang himself into the hearts of the people. It was a challenging, yet blessed crusade.

However, China was central stage for me. I was told by Bishop K.H. Ting, head of TSPM and CCC that the interest in Christianity among Chinese intellectuals developed into an all-time high since 1949. Religion courses were among the most popular at some universities. What a change! Nanjing Theological Seminary faculty members were teaching religious-study courses at the city's largest teachers college. The president of Shanghai's Theological Seminary, Rev. Su Deci, had been leading students at a teachers college in that city in a fifteen-session curriculum on "Introduction to the Bible"! A number of scholarly journals dealt with religion. The bottom line: No longer is Christianity seen as an "opiate for the people." Furthermore, groups of Christian students had begun to meet openly on some university campuses—and that without interference!

China was truly changing. Of late, there also had been a revival among older and retired believers, many of them well-educated. They had begun returning to the churches after hiding their faith for decades, some even joining the Communist Party, to protect prestigious jobs and social positions.

In early 1994 rumors were circulating that the Chinese government was taken a more belligerent posture again versus Christians. I wrote:

> Quite a number of you were concerned about reports in the evangelical press that the recent crackdown in China may hinder our ministry in that country. But we have good news!

I immediately had gotten in touch with the US State Department in Washington to inquire about the background of such crackdowns. I was informed that two decrees had been signed by the premier of China, Li Peng, prohibiting foreigners to proselytize and "establish religious organizations, organs for managing religious affairs or centers or schools for religious activities."

The State Department also told me that these decrees were not new, but were codified and had been newly stated in the official newspaper of the Chinese government.

The same had been confirmed to me in a telephone conversation with Bishop Ting. He said, "Please proceed with your ministry in China. What you do is legal and therefore does not cause a threat to the Chinese government."

While others had been detained and deported recently, we were allowed not only to continue with our ministry but additionally to accelerate with what we had been doing.

In fact, just at that time we had received another invitation:

It is said that you have taught in the theological seminaries in Fuzhou, Hangzhou, Shanghai, Nanjing, etc. Elder Lu Chuan Fan of the China Christian Council told us that you intend to teach at the Wuhan Theological Seminary this year. We are very glad to hear the news. Nanchang is not far from Wuhan. We would like to ask you to come to Nanchang and teach in our Bible school if you are teaching in Wuhan.

Though our Bible school is small, it is very important for the churches in Jiangxi. We are sorry that we have to ask a favor of you, with the hope that you will be good enough to help us. Our only hope is that you will come and teach in our Bible school this term.

We were overwhelmed at how the Lord kept opening doors in China! While other foreigners were being harassed, detained, and deported, we were allowed to freely minister the gospel in China! In spite of what the secular and evangelical press had been revealing and declaring; changing times and attitudes had brought the Chinese church to the threshold of its greatest opportunity for outreach in the history of its country!

In the West we were constantly confronted with this question, "How come you can do things in China others apparently cannot do?"

One of the evangelical papers stated, "A new wave of persecution rolls across China. More restrictions are being placed on those who minister in China."

I was stunned, because we never had experienced this. We never had been hindered in carrying out our mission in China. We taught, preached, lectured, held gospel concerts, and shipped thousands of evangelical study books into China. We were aware of bitter relationships between some house church and legal church leaders. However, even there positive and heartwarming things were happening.

Ned Graham, son of Billy Graham, experienced the following:

On a recent trip I met two young men after a house church meeting in Beijing where I spoke. I asked them about their background and how they came to attend a house church.

The two men had studied engineering together at a Beijing university. One was a Christian. However, since the two met shortly after the Tiananmen Square incident in1989, he never had told his friend about his faith in Christ. After graduation these close friends were placed at distant work sites and lost contact.

One night as the young Christian man attended a Three Self Church in central Beijing, he was astonished to see his friend from the University stand and give his testimony. He explained how he recently had come to know Jesus Christ at this Three Self church. Afterwards, the two embraced and shed tears together. They began to rebuild their friendship around the person of Jesus Christ, and attended church together. On Sundays, they attended a Three Self Church and Tuesday evenings, they attended youth nights together at this house church.

I asked if they ever encountered any restrictions from the government authorities in attending church. "Absolutely not," they both replied. They never faced any problem from attending either the house church or the Three Self Church. In fact, they never experienced any repercussions within their work units for being open Christians.

On our way to China we had stopped in South Korea. We felt that the South Koreans should get involved to minister among the more than one million Koreans that live in the northern part of China. While there, we had the opportunity to preach in four cities. Thousands attended our meetings, high schools and colleges opened their doors, and hundreds made commitments to Christ. Wherever we went, we also challenged Christians not only to pray for China, but to get actively involved. Yes, they had a burden for their compatriots in North Korea. Every South Korean church is getting ready to plant another one in North Korea, once the "wall" comes down. Wouldn't it be wonderful to have them do the same among their compatriots in China! The burden they have for their countrymen in North Korea must be extended beyond the Yalu River.

At the home front our daughter Linda was in charge of our finances. Ever since 1987 she had helped me in the office, often alongside with Inge. She enjoyed working for the Lord and buttressed it with her spiritual development. She said:

I grew up as a missionary kid—which by the way is the most wonderful thing to be! I accepted the Lord as my Savior when

I was five on my mother's lap. Since then my walk with the Lord has had its ups and downs, but I never abandoned the teaching of my youth. God always showed me that He was real.

In the fall of 1995 I had an amazing experience while holding an evangelistic crusade at the Korean Sa-Rang Presbyterian Church of Southern California. The church had been founded seven years before. The dynamic young Korean pastor, Rev. Oh, went all out to win his fellow countrymen to Christ. Within just a few years the church had grown to a membership of 1,200. But he wanted to see more.

Before the crusade started, special early morning prayer meetings (5:30 a.m.) were held for forty days. The day our team arrived, that very morning over five hundred members had been at the early morning prayer meeting. Their church building only seated seven hundred people, so they rented a hall with a seating capacity of 2,500! The first night the hall was overflowing and hundreds could not get in. Several hundred responded to the invitation during those three nights. The church choir was told that they would not sing during the crusade, because their responsibility was to go out and bring and sit with those they invited. The pastor had hired a professional choir to do the singing for them.

Monday morning, following the crusade, close to seven hundred members attended the 5:30 a.m. prayer meeting to give praise to God for what He had done. A few days later over one hundred had already joined the church. In a letter Pastor Oh expressed his impression:

Hallelujah! Greetings from Sa-Rang Presbyterian Church. We thank God for sending you to our church to share the Good News to lost people. It turned out to be one of the greatest historic events in our Korean-American community, because the crusade was one of the prominent bilingual evangelism rallies that happened in our community. We did our best to bring people from diverse ethnic groups. A number of our church members brought more than twenty people respectively, and many of those accepted Christ. Over one hundred of them already became members of the church. I believe God used your powerful preaching to shake the hearts of our people. Your messages penetrated the hearts of all those who came to the rallies.

We will pray for you, your family, and your ministry. Come back and visit us at any time. We would like to support your mission to China both by prayer and financial support. May God's abundant grace and love be with you."

I felt so humbled by this letter, because I knew it had not been my doing. In fact, I remember how weak and attacked I felt during that time. It truly had been God's miraculous way of working out His plan! The prayers of God's people released His power.

Meanwhile, the media continued to major on persecution stories in China. After a church service at which I had preached in Florida, someone gave me a *Miami Herald* newspaper clipping from December 15, 1994, headlined "China Christians struggle against Beijing crackdown." Having had the privilege and joy to minister in China unhindered and that for several years, I was both surprised and grieved; surprised, because in all of my many ministry trips to China I had never experienced this; and grieved, because if it was accurate, then our Christian brothers and sisters were going through another phase of suffering.

However, the same article with all its negative stories, also reported that a pastor had asked the members of his church "to stay home at Christmas, if possible." His explanation, "We are expecting more than one thousand people for each of our services. Many of them are young people coming to church for the first time and we would like to give them a chance as well. So if you can make room for them, we would appreciate it."

I wrote to my friends:

In spite of hardships some of the government people may inflict upon Christians, the Lord has given us tremendous opportunities of ministry. We are already making plans for four more pastoral training schools across China! We continue to ship good evangelical study books into China for all participants of our schools. We plan to hold gospel concerts and we will be preaching in many churches. We will continue our ministry aggressively as long as we can!

God allowed us to minister in China in an unprecedented way. Our pastoral training schools have been received with enthusiasm, and Ed Lyman's gospel concerts were always a great hit. The Chinese Christians loved to hear him sing.

We were touched by a letter from China which said, "We can never forget your wonderful teaching on evangelism last June. It all impressed all the teachers and students." Another letter, this time from Rev Peng, a thirty-two-year old professor at the Fuzhien Theological Seminary:

I would like to give my part-time or even full-time serving the Lord Jesus Christ with you. Beatrice [his wife] and I are praying toward that end.

With this in mind, he had made a special visit to counsel with Bishop Ting in Nanjing. However, the bishop told him, "Stay with what you are doing in Fuzhou, teaching at the theological seminary." He did, but many years later he migrated to the United States and pastored a growing church in New York City. Within a few years his church had grown to over 1,000 members. He stayed a good friend and Erik preached at that church a number of times.

Fundraising had been part of my entire life. To be honest, I never really liked it but I had to do it. Two of the most successful fundraisers I know were Bob Pierce and Billy Graham. What set them apart from others? Integrity.

I was shocked when I heard that a Christian philanthropic organization had gone bankrupt. It had collected over 100 million dollars from Christian ministries to invest and produce lucrative returns. All of them lost most of their money. I also had been contacted by them but had refused to enter into their scheme. For one, we did not have much, nor was I willing to go out on a limb. I had developed three principles gleaned from Billy Graham:

- Never spend money we do not have
- Always pay bills immediately
- Raise money openly and honestly

The lessons I had learned years before became important to me once again. First, to be deeply grateful for all sacrificial gifts made by committed Christians who want to see God's kingdom advanced.

Secondly, never succumb to the temptation of making shortcuts to raise money fast and easy. Our western culture is steeped in today's life philosophy of wanting things now and quickly. The easier and faster to success, the better it is! Take shortcuts whenever you can! However, this is not God's way. Every plant takes time to grow. It needs care, nurture, and pruning. Oak trees, for example, take years to mature.

Thirdly, we need to prayerfully think through every step of fundraising efforts. God looks upon the heart and He will give the increase according to His plan. He is the one who touches and moves hearts to give. Our trust should be solely in Him.

Ever since Erik joined China Partner (first known as Werner Burklin Ministries), he accompanied me on all China trips. While we were in Nanchang, the oldest pastor in town invited us for a farewell banquet. During the banquet he rose and made a short, yet significant speech. Erik recalled what this old man of God said:

> The old pastor, now in his eighties, rose and thanked us for continuing the work my grandparents had started. Then he turned to me, grabbed my hand, pulled it over to where three of the young Chinese pastors were sitting, and linked my hand with theirs. He turned to my father and said, "The two of us are getting old, but how wonderful to see young men taking our places. You from overseas and we here must link together to reach our people with the Gospel."

While teaching at the Beijing Theological Seminary, we visited one of the house church Christians, a professor, who also taught Greek and Hebrew at the seminary. When we were back home, he wrote us a moving letter:

> It is so precious for Christians to enjoy the sweet fellowship in the Lord. I appreciated the presence of the honorable guest in my humble home. Your lectures helped our students very much. You and your friends came and helped our students in the seminary to know something they had not heard before. For after liberation of China, nearly no one led special or revival meetings, and we have not taught that.

And then we received another letter, this one from a medical doctor:

> I admire your family very much; your father, you, and now your son are all pastors of the Lord, preaching the gospel around the world, being apostles of the Lord Jesus. You dedicated your entire family to serve the Lord with all your heart, your soul, and your mind. You set an example for all of our Christians.

> I heard the gospel when I was a medical student. His Spirit enlightened me and opened my heart. Jesus Christ is now my Lord. Now I work as an anesthetist, but I want to grow in the Lord Jesus. I am silently waiting upon the Lord to find my real calling in serving our Lord.

CHAPTER 24

MARXISM IN CHINA IS DEAD—OR IS IT?

I N NANCHANG, THE capital city of the province of Jiangxi, south of the mighty Yangtze River, where my parents had done missionary work half a century before, we were met at the airport by a young doctor. He had attended some of the sessions of our training school during the month of May in the previous year. He came from a city six hours away by train. He had been so overwhelmed by what he had learned that he had brought along one of his church elders to meet us. In our hotel room he literally begged us to come to his city to teach and preach. The doors for ministry kept opening up in an amazing way.

Later in the year we were teaching again at the Wuhan Theological Seminary. These repeat events became more interesting and challenging all along. The president of the seminary, Wang, had befriended officials at the prestigious Hua Chung University, one of the four most prominent and renowned universities in China. It had been founded in the fifties shortly after the "Liberation," as the Chinese label Mao's political takeover in 1949. President Wang approached me. "One of our universities here wants you to give a lecture on religion." While walking to the institution, he reminded me: "You need to explain sin. Most of the students don't understand the gravity of it. Please do not forget to emphasize this truth."

The university had 16,000 students at that time. The department of humanities sponsored the event. The sponsors had booked a magnificent lecture hall with a seating capacity of some three hundred, but when five hundred students jammed the hall, an additional hall had to be secured to accommodate the overflow of a further three hundred plus students.

It was very apparent that China was undergoing a massive change, not only economically but also culturally. Young intellectuals were extremely inquisitive about spiritual matters.

Following the lecture, our team did not get away until after 11 p.m. Students crowded around us wanting to know more about Christ. Our Christian hosts from the seminary were ecstatic! God had answered their prayers beyond expectation.

I also had been told that a number of government leaders now say, "Marxism does not hold the only truth—one must open another window." Furthermore, "the Chinese tend to go from one extreme to another. Confucianism gives stability, because it stands in the middle."

It was very noticeable that the search was on. Young people were eager to discuss any topic, even the one relating to God. They wanted to find the truth. Too long they had been misled. We sensed an excellent opportunity for Christians to make the claims of Christ known in China.

The chaplain of the seminary later explained:

We have to jump out of our little pond of the Christian community and jump into the big pond. We have to go where the non-Christians are. That is where we can make the greatest impact with the gospel. God has sent you to help expand our influence. You are the first western foreigner to be invited to lecture in that university about "God in Western Culture."

But this was not the end! A couple of weeks later they celebrated Christmas as millions do around the world. But read this. We received this amazing letter from the president of the Wuhan Theological Seminary shortly after Christmas:

We had a wonderful Christmas Eve service. It finished by 9:30 p.m. Most of our people had gone home. But after 10 p.m., many young people came and the chapel filled up again. All of them were students—both college and high school students. Most of them had never been to church before. Teachers and theological students greeted them and gave them a warm welcome. We then explained to them the meaning of Christmas, Jesus, salvation, and the Bible. We sang carols for them and taught them a few songs and taught them how to pray. They did not leave until 5 o'clock in the morning! Five hundred young people did not go to sleep—they stayed in our church the whole night and some of them received Christ. Praise the Lord!

What a thrilling letter! Most of those students had come from the university where we had given the lecture on "God in Western Culture." God had been speaking to many hearts. Rev. David Stillman from Great Britain had been part of our teaching team and had been so impressed with what he experienced:

The best way to correct any misunderstanding one may have is to go and see for yourself and find out firsthand what the situation is really like. My expectations of China were colored by my dealings with officials of the former Communist countries of Eastern Europe prior to the fall of Communist governments. My passport clearly indicated that I am an evangelist and an ordinary Christian minister. My next pleasant surprise was that no one in the consulate wanted to knows why I wanted to go to China. More pleasant surprises were to follow in Nanchang. As we arrived at the church for the Sunday morning worship service, the church building itself was already full to overflowing with people. Even more surprising was the number of people outside the church build-ing simply kneeling in prayer in preparation for the service. When the service began, there seemed to be as many people gathered around the building outside as seated inside, who knows how many more were listening to the message which could be heard in the street due to loudspeakers positioned in the courtyard of the church. All this in a country with a Communist government that is no friend to the Christian church! There was not a police officer to be seen anywhere to interfere with the service or keep the people away.

Then we continued to Wuhan. There were more pleasant surprises for the team: "Will you speak at the prayer meet-ing? Will you preach in chapel? Will you come over to the music conservatory and teach? Will you speak to high school students at the local high school close to our seminary? Will you lecture to students in the philosophy department at one of our universities in town? Would you be willing to preach in some of the churches in the countryside on Sunday?

I thought foreign Christians were not supposed to do those kinds of things in China.

Yes, you can, if you function sensitively and prudently!

My desire always had been to work closely with the Chinese leadership and to harmonize our activities with their plans, desires, needs, and their aspirations. Therefore I had called for an international mini-symposium, which was attended by twenty-three Chinese Christian leaders from seven provinces and three major cities of Beijing, Shanghai, and Nanjing and eighteen prominent evangelicals from ten countries of Pacific/Asia, Europe, and North America. We met from December 4-8 in Nanjing. This was only the second time since China had opened to the West that such a conclave had convened.

The purpose had been to listen to church leaders in China, and together with them search and pray for ways of better cooperation between the churches in China and evangelicals in the rest of the world.

The delegates from the West left with two major impressions:

- The growth of the church in China is attributable to the grace of God and the work of the Holy Spirit shown in the testimony of believers in word and deed. Christians have the reputation of being better workers, good citizens, honest business people, and willing to help and pray for their neighbors, especially when they are sick.

- The willingness of the China Christian Council to relate to overseas bodies who respect the selfhood of the Chinese church and who are ready to apply the rule that the responsibility that such bodies offer should correspond to the needs of the Chinese churches and be prepared to work legally, openly, and above board.

Tom Houston, former President of World Vision and member of the Lausanne Committee, summed up his sentiments following the symposium:

The registered and unregistered churches are all growing at a rate that is difficult for us in the West to comprehend. There are unresolved difficulties between the registered and the unregistered churches and we sensed this while we were there. It may take some time before much progress can be made towards reconciling these differences. What is not in dispute is that they are both growing in a way that outstrips the formation of leaders to disciple the converts and pastor the congregations.

The leaders of the churches are a mixed multitude in every country. But leading the churches in China is like trying to hold on to "a tiger by the tail." We know how that ends. The tiger is stronger than the one who is trying to hang on to it. Jesus said, "I will build my church and the gates of hell shall not prevail against it."

The final month of 1995 was probably one of the best months we have ever had! Our board members were overwhelmed to hear how God was continuing to use our ministry to reach into a difficult, yet so challenging country. China posed many riddles but she moved ahead with unabated speed. She, no doubt, is the most rewarding country to those who spread the gospel in those days. And we were deeply grateful to have had a small part in reaching out to a searching people.

Someone had said recently, "Prayer is for me the hardest of all labors." This is so true and I continuously encouraged our friends and donors to keep praying for our important mission.

Some years back I had been invited to be the main speaker at a missions conference sponsored by the First Presbyterian Church in Macon, Georgia. I was stunned seeing a huge banner announcing Dr. Werner Burklin. *What's that,* I thought. I didn't have a doctorate. I was amused but more than that, embarrassed.

Driving home after a very successful missions conference, Inge asked, "Why don't you get a doctorate?" I first shrugged it off, but then laughed and said, "Why not?" With that I started my doctoral studies and three years later traveled to Atlanta, Georgia, where I was awarded the Doctor of Ministries degree by the Luther Rice Seminary and now a University. For the preceding three and a half years I had spent evenings, weekends, and traveling times studying while working fulltime. It had been tough, very tough, but it had been a rewarding experience. My thesis or dissertation was "China by Faith, a Model of Training Christian Leaders in Atheistic Societies." May 17, 1996, was a major milestone for me when the doctoral cowl was put on me.

Pastor (*Pfarrer*) Wilfried Reuter, a Lutheran and at that time director of a large retreat center in Krelingen near Hannover, was our main teacher in Jinan, the capital city of Shandong and in Fuzhou, Fuzhien. At that time Shandong had a population of 80 million with about 600,000 Christians, who were being taken care of by sixty ordained pastors. Jinan had about 30,000 believers with eleven ordained pastors. One thousand baptisms had been performed in Jinan the previous year. Amazingly, even there, so close to Beijing, the churches were making great strides.

Bishop Wang in Jinan, then eighty-three years old, was a man of God who had gone through the dark days of the Cultural Revolution (1966-76). "We experienced the sacrament of suffering," he told us, "but it made us strong in the Lord."

When I returned home from that trip, I had a letter waiting for me from Bishop Wang, thanking us for teaching and ministering in his city. But he had one request: "Could you locate for me an old hymnal by Sankey (1840-1908)?" Well, Ira Sankey had lived in the nineteenth century and was famous for having been the song leader for evangelist Dwight L. Moody (1837-99). But where would I find such an old hymnal? I checked everywhere, because I knew that Bishop Wang was a great musician and had composed many songs himself. During the Cultural Revolution that hymnal had been destroyed and he so much wanted to have it replaced. But my search was unsuccessful until I casually mentioned this to Ruth Graham on the phone.

"Werner," she exclaimed, "I might have one in my library. When Bill and I were in London for the Harringay Crusade in the fifties, we found two of them in a bookstore for antique books. We bought them. Let me look."

That evening she called me back, "I found it; I'll have it mailed to you right away." Three days later is was on my desk with a lovely inscription from her and her husband Billy. On my next trip to China I passed it on to him. He was absolutely thrilled to have the hymnal by Sankey. Sankey to him was the greatest! Moody must have felt the same. When he was asked by a local pastor what he felt was the primary contribution that a gospel singer and song leader such as Ira Sankey brought to his meetings he replied, "If we can only get people to have the words of the Love of God coming from their mouths, it's well on its way to residing in their hearts."

No wonder a bishop in China was so captivated with Sankey!

In Nanjing I met another person who had to endure the hardships of the Cultural Revolution. He was an outstanding

Christian professor at the Nanjing Theological Seminary. He deeply loved his Lord, and this love was further purified during the harsh years of persecution during the "Anti-Rightest-Campaign" and the infamous Cultural Revolution. He had been sent to hard labor into the countryside and for eighteen years had to endure privations and agony. But he never lost hope. He told me, "One needs to see the suffering in history in the same way that one views suffering of childbirth. In the end, a child is born."

Taking a passage from the Song of Solomon (2:10-14), he had written three verses of a poem before his years in the wilderness, and only after his release he finished it with a fourth:

The winter is past, rain is done.
Flowers fill the earth, birdsong in the air
Why do you wait? Why do you hesitate?
My fair one. Come away with me.

Let me see your face, hear your voice,
For your voice is sweet, your face comely,
O my dove, come away with me.

My beloved, I'll follow you,
Away from the rocks and cliffs,
In the birdsong, among the flowers,
I'll follow your steps, I'll go with you.

Twenty years later, after having experienced the horror but gone through it with the help of his Lord, he found the unfinished poem among his papers. He wrote then the chorus pointing to the One who had sustained him and had given him hope, faith, and love:

My Lord Jesus, Source of my love.
My body, my soul, forever yours.
In darkest valleys, I long for you,
I will go with you, spring has come again.

On that trip I had taken my sweetheart along. Her last trip to China had been ten years before. She was anxious to see the fruits of our labor firsthand. We visited Hong Kong, Chengdu, Wuhan, Shanghai, Nanchang, Nanjing, Shenyang, and Beijing. It was a long and strenuous journey for her. She was overwhelmed with what she saw. She recorded the positives and negatives in twenty "Incredibles." Here they are:

First the Positives:

- Incredible need for teaching
- Incredible need for financial help in expansion projects in at least three cities we visited
- Incredible vision and faith of local leaders for future development against all odds
- Incredible openness and friendliness and warm reception for our international team
- Incredible endorsement of our type of teaching subjects: personal leadership, pastoral care, and evangelistic preaching
- Incredible appreciation for the thousands of books we have shipped in. This time alone: 2,800 books worth $28,000

- Incredible hunger for God of some new believers we met
- Incredible growth in some churches. In one church in the city of Shenyang they have had nine hundred baptisms this year
- Incredible reason for growth: the personal walk and talk of Christian family members, friends, and co-workers, i.e. lifestyle evangelism
- Incredible economic growth and development in many areas
- Incredible protection on all flights and travels from accidents, protection from serious illness (except Werner's cold, exacerbated by incredible pollution)

Now the Negatives:

- Incredible poverty, dirt, and pollution
- Incredible indifference to environment
- Incredible and indescribable squatting toilets in some seminaries and restaurants
- Incredible foods, most of which I did not have to eat, because I am a vegetarian. Good excuse when invited to big Chinese banquets with exotic and indefinable dishes
- Incredible masses of people everywhere, a veritable "sea of humanity." All airplanes, buses, trains are jam-packed
- Incredible traffic jams: kids, people, bicycles, cars, trucks, buses, pedicabs. Sometimes nothing moved
- Incredible noise level: everybody blows their car horns; nobody listens or pays any attention
- Incredible near-misses on the road. Sometimes you just had to close your eyes and trust the deftness of the drivers to avoid crashes

- Incredible dilapidated and run-down, dirty taxis. You wondered whether you would make it to the airport in those junky cars
- Incredibly many stairs to climb everywhere; sometimes up to the eighth floor in the seminaries (no elevators), in and out of airplanes, cars, buses, vans, airports—the whole world seemed to consist of stairs. At least it feels that way when you have arthritis in your knees
- China—vision of a huge ant hill. But they are not ants, but people—1.3 billion of them, created in the image of God. Needy people, desperate people, lost people for whom Christ died. You are overwhelmed by one point: the incredible, incredible, incredible love of God!

20,000 members in a single Chinese church

When Erik and I returned from the latest of our China trips, we spoke at the missions conference at the Patterson Park Church in Dayton, Ohio. I had been extremely impressed with the interest of its members in overseas missions. The senior pastor, Rev. Dale Kurtz, a former colleague of mine from Youth for Christ days, revealed a tremendous vision to reach the world for Christ. That is one reason why his church was growing rapidly at home, because he heard the groans of the world.

Over the years I had made the observation that whenever a church is actively involved in missions, a special blessing of God rests on it. The fastest growing churches are mission minded churches.

Members of this particular church thanked me again and again for sharing genuine facts about China. All of them had been unaware of what God is really doing in China. Their insights had been based on media reports that, as we all know, are mostly biased. They had never heard that we can go into China to preach and teach—and that openly and freely. They did not know that we can ship in thousands of evangelical books—and that legally. They were not aware of printing presses in China producing millions of Bibles each year—over 19 million at that time (In 2011 the number had mushroomed to close to 90 million). They were surprised to hear about evangelical seminaries, where hundreds of young emerging leaders are being trained for the ministry. They were astounded to hear of one church we had visited in northern China, where 900 converts had been baptized in one year alone.

In Shenyang, Liaoning, I had preached at the Dong Guan (East Gate) church jammed to overflowing with more than 2,000 people. When I marveled at the number, the pastor whispered while we were sitting on the platform, "This is only one of four services we have today, and all the others have as many attendants." Later I was told that a few years back the church had reopened with two hundred thirty people, while I was there it had grown to over 20,000. Within nine months of that year, they had performed nine hundred baptisms. The pastor said, "We can only accommodate half of our members, so we arranged a system, where on any given Sunday, one half of the believers have to hold meetings in homes, while the other half can attend the church. The following Sunday we reverse the order."

Wow!

For lunch the pastor had invited us to a quaint building on the church grounds, where John Ross, a missionary from the Church of Scotland, translated the Bible into the Korean language. It took him six years, from 1872-82, to achieve it. By 1887, 30,000 Bibles had been taken into Korea by him and twelve church leaders—from China!—which ultimately resulted in the establishment of the first Korean church in 1889.

Back to Dayton's missions conference. At the final meeting they took up a large offering for our ministry in China. They wanted our ministry to expand all over China.

Following that conference, I wrote to our supporters:

> Dear friends, I am more encouraged than ever. I wish I were thirty years younger to give all of myself to reach China for Christ.

I then understood what Hudson Taylor (1832-1905) once said: "If I had 1,000 lives, I'd give them all to China." He did not only say it, he meant it.

And then a new challenge was presented to us by the Christian leadership in Nanchang, Jiangxi—the construction of a Bible school. The school had been founded in September of 1992. This was the first and only Bible school in the province of Jiangxi, with a population of 40 million. It was known as an impoverished area, where 70 percent are farmers. It was also known as the Revolution province, where Mao began his first Soviet republics, and therefore it was closely controlled by the government.

We from China Partner got heavily involved. We not only started a scholarship program for poor students and gave financial aid to graduates who had become grassroots pastors in remote rural regions, but we also invested heavily in the construction of the campus.

During this time an astonishing new development took place: the emergence of a so-called "third group." Up until then the churches had been divided into registered and unregistered groups. For want of a better term a "third group" or "joint Christians" was evolving. Members of that group were made up of true believers from both groups, those belonging to the CCC and those belonging to house churches. It was well organized and financed, mostly from overseas. Members were mission-minded (sending missionaries into remote areas of China), had training programs, were Bible-centered, and had a strong sense of mission to build up the church of Jesus Christ.

The "third group" was profiting from the fact of the government's pressure on house churches to surface and thus legalize their activities. This was a positive result. This enabled them to work in greater freedom. Interaction between them and the CCC was facilitated. The "third group" profited from this phenomenon.

Some of the younger generation wanted to, and in fact were moving away from established and often fossilized structures. Leaders of the "third group" hoped that old structures would crumble and the central truth and the meaning of the gospel would regain preeminence.

However, this remained more of a yearning and did not convert into reality. For many more years the divide got even more critical. In fact, when the Lausanne Congress in Capetown convened in 2010, Chinese house church leaders threatened not to take part as delegates, if CCC leaders were admitted as delegates. The Lausanne leadership gave in to their demands. "This set back the then-improving reconciliation between the two groups in China for years," a Christian leader in China said. It is amazing how western evangelical leaders are to this day entrenched in their way of thinking.

This made me think. In fact, around that time I wrote the following to our supporting friends:

As I make plans to leave for China in about two weeks, my mind goes back to a conference I recently attended in Washington, D.C. China lovers met to discuss what can be done more effectively to reach out to the masses of that great land. One thing came through loud and clear: "The Lord is doing a mighty work in China today." However, after many years of "living in the wilderness," believers in China are hungry for fellowship with believers from across the world.

This is, I believe, where Bible-believing evangelicals come in. It is up to us to extend our hand of fellowship to *all* believers in China. This is a historic moment, and we need to seize it.

Historically speaking, China was reborn at the height of her deepest humiliation after the Opium War in 1839. From that moment on, China believed herself to have been "born anew" restoring herself to the glory she formerly enjoyed.

What does it mean for Chinese to be Chinese? They have always considered themselves to be the center of the world. To them, this is a cultural concept. They continually ask *what it means to be a nation. How can we as Chinese chart our own course? How can we be freed from foreign domination?*

She yearned to be strong, modern, and equal with other nations. She honestly believed that Communism was the answer. This resulted in cataclysmic developments from which she yet struggles to survive and break out.

My question, however, goes into a different direction. *What will be China's value system in the twenty-first century? Does the gospel offer a way out of her present dilemma? What can we do as western evangelicals to undergird our brothers and sisters in China? Where can we be most effective?*

Yes, we can do much. However, it must be done in harmony with the millions of believers in China. We must be willing to accept their counsel and follow their guidance.

I am convinced that we are on the right path. We from WBM [later China Partner] have a warm and close working relationship with them. This has gone on now for several years. And you, our friends, have made it possible with your prayers and gifts. Thank you, thank you!

In early February 1997, I was driving into Shanghai from the airport. I couldn't believe my eyes. The changes that were being made in the infrastructure were mind-boggling. I couldn't think of any other city in the world, including Berlin, where such mass construction was taking place on a scale unsurpassed in world's history.

The magazine *Hemispheres* wrote:

At any given moment, fully one-fifth of the world's high-lift cranes are at work in the city of Shanghai. In one massive convulsion, the urban city space is being erased and regrown. When the smoke clears in a couple of decades, China's largest city [now it is Chongqing, Sichuan, with a population of 31.4 million] will assume the position now occupied by Hong Kong as the nation's commercial center. The plan is to make

Shanghai China's first fully modernized metropolis, its pearl of the Orient for the 21st Century.

What *Hemispheres* did not say is that a more spectacular development is taking place in the hearts of the people. Men and women, boys and girls are being "born for a prominent new role." Hearts and lives are being changed for Christ like never before in China's history. They are being born again from above.

My confidant in Shanghai, Joseph Lu (*Lu Chuan Fan*), told me of his thirteen-year-old granddaughter wearing a cross on her jacket. When he asked her why she does that, she answered, "All of my classmates should know that I am a Christian." What a testimony. No wonder the church in China is exploding!

"*Diese Konferenz kommt fünfzehn Jahre zu spät,*" said one of the German mission executives following the China symposium we had sponsored in Germany. In English: "This conference should have been held fifteen years ago."

We had invited mission executives and friends from Germany and Switzerland to the retreat center in Krelingen (north Germany), to explore ministry opportunities in China. We also wanted to refute some of the misinformation spread by others concerning China. One hundred participants had signed up, and all of them were extremely interested. China was a hot topic at that time.

Hong Kong—again part of China

This took place shortly before Hong Kong's handover to the People's Republic of China scheduled for July 1, 1997. All participants were greatly encouraged with what God was doing in China, and most of them had positive expectations and aspirations for post-colonial developments in Hong Kong. Of course there were some diehards, who continue to follow the old John Foster Dulles (foreign minister in the Eisenhower administration in the fifties) hard lines of anti-Communism. All of the participants were anti-Communists; however, some could not see themselves working within the realities before us.

A survey conducted a few weeks before the handover in Hong Kong revealed that 73 percent confirmed that the territory would "continue to be" stable and prosperous after the handover. Business people saw the change as a new opportunity for doing more business with the world's largest country. New construction continued to accelerate throughout the metropolis. Hong Kong boasted of an only 2-3 percent unemployment rate at that time. Wilson Chow, president of the China Graduate School of Theology in Hong Kong said:

> Many pastors who had escaped from mainland China in the fifties and sixties are the ones who have a negative attitude toward the handover in July. Today the majority of pastors in Hong Kong are younger pastors who do not look at the handover as a negative. They are looking forward to new ministry opportunities.

> Even though a good number of the residents may have distrust in the Chinese communist government, as Christians that is not the most important factor. We believe in the Lord; He is in control. What is so exciting about being a resident of Hong Kong is the fact that Hong Kong will be part of China. With that we have a tremendous opportunity to reach China with the Gospel.

On July 1, 1997, I was in Hong Kong. The handover from the British to the Chinese was not a forceful takeover by the Chinese government. It was a peaceful handover from one sovereign state to another.

It was 10 p.m. I had left the hotel on foot; there was no other way to get to the harbor. All streets were overcrowded with people. It seemed like all residents of Hong Kong were moving toward the harbor to view the planned fireworks. It rained heavily. So I ducked into a store and bought an Italian umbrella. Hundreds of thousands of cheerful Chinese faced the rain. All they were interested in was the countdown at twelve midnight. The fireworks were something to behold. I had seen many over the years in different parts of the world. But nothing could compare with what I experienced on July 1. Amazing! It went on and on. Fireworks were fired from both sides of the harbor, and from special platforms in the harbor, high into the air. It was breathtaking!

Back in the hotel I watched Prince Charles shake hands with President Jiang Zemin on TV; the British flag was lowered and at the precise moment at twelve midnight the Chinese flag representing Hong Kong hit the top of the mast as the Chinese national anthem was intoned. An indescribable roar of millions of Chinese throats exploded across the waters. I had never heard such ecstasy of unbridled joy before—ever!

Even I was overcome with unrestrained emotion.

I did not know what made me so emotional about what I saw and heard. Perhaps it was the memory of the toppling of the Berlin wall in 1989, which for us Germans was an extremely poignant experience. Tears had rolled down my cheeks then. Or, having been born in China, I felt more Chinese than first realized. Or was it the awesome responsibility we as Christians must assume to help our Chinese brothers and sisters spread the gospel across their great land. Whatever the reason, it was an event I will cherish all of my life.

With the return of Hong Kong to China, the Chinese feel much more at ease with themselves, now being a true sovereign link within the chain of the world's nations. One hundred fifty-six years of humiliation had been wiped away with one stroke. With it a more relaxed attitude toward religious freedom may emerge. This may facilitate even more the spreading of the gospel and will bring it to new heights unreached before.

I then knew that China will not only become a world power politically and economically, but also a power house for God. Spiritually speaking, God apparently had chosen China to be the Korea of tomorrow. What a privilege to have been involved in China in times like these.

However at that time, it was common for some, in fact for many, to state that there is no religious freedom in China. All they talked about was "closed doors." "As a foreigner," they said, "you can only work effectively in China by going underground." But this was not true, at least not in my experience.

The Peoples Church in Toronto, Canada, was known as *the* leading church on missions in North America. As a young man I had read and been deeply influenced by the book *Glühende Retterliebe* (Passion for Souls) authored by Oswald Smith. His son Paul, who later succeeded his dad, had written me while I was directing the YFC rally in Frankfurt. He inquired whether he could preach at our rally on his way to Moscow. Now it was his church under the new leadership of pastor John Hull, which had asked me to preach in his Toronto church. The title of my message on March 16, 1997, was "Open Doors that Never Were Closed."

Why?

I felt I needed to set the record straight. Of course, there was and still are cases where Christians are harassed or even persecuted. This is happening in very few cases. However, there were and are vast opportunities of ministries. One of the goals of China Partner was and still is to educate the Christian public about the amazing developments in China.

So this is what I preached in Toronto:

So-called "closed-door countries" in Eastern Europe and Asia—China—were actually open. To God there are no closed doors. We must have a different perspective of closed doors

1. Closed doors to countries have always been open in God's perspective
2. Closed doors are only those of closed hearts
3. Closed doors are there to be opened by the preaching of God's Word

Such concepts were new to some people. What seemed closed to those who wanted to enter a country actually was wide open to the Holy Spirit. He did His work without using those who seemingly felt shut out. God often is doing His work in a way that we do not understand.

To clarify this further I wrote the following to our friends:

For several years now, I have had the privilege to minister in China. Most of you have been following this ministry since its inception and are amazed at what we are allowed to do.

Some of you, however, may have been confused by recent media reports. The China bashings on national TV and radio during the last few weeks seem to contradict many of the things you may have read in our publications.

This reminds me of what Billy Graham had to go through occasionally. For instance, when he first went to the former Soviet Union to preach, he was misunderstood. But far worse, he was severely criticized, sometimes even by his friends. These critics felt that by going to the USSR, Billy Graham was giving credence to the Communist system.

This, of course, is far from the truth. His only motive and desire was to preach the gospel.

Now back to our situation. A number of people have asked me, "How come you can do in China what others claim they cannot do? You are working with the registered churches, but by doing so, are you not compromising your Christian faith by working alongside the "government controlled churches"?

This, by the way, was the main argument evangelical critics had. They stated, and falsely so, that pastors were not allowed to preach on the Second Coming of Christ. Or those pastors were on the payroll of the government. Or, that Christians had to be allegiant first to the government and then to Christ. To sum it up, they were controlled by the government. So I continued in my letter:

My first response is to ask them what people mean when they say "government controlled." I have visited and ministered in China on thirty-four different occasions [up to that time].

Our team ministered in many cities—all the way from Shenyang in the Northeast to Guangzhou in the South; and all the way from Chengdu in the West to Shanghai in the East. I have yet to find one church that considers itself government controlled.

Whatever people may say, the truth is that the churches in China are not "controlled" by the government. They are, however, obliged to work within a framework set up by the government. For instance, they have to register with the government, and abide by certain government laws, rules, and regulations. It is the same with churches in western countries which have to abide by rules and regulations set up by its government.

Churches that register with the Chinese authorities have, as Christians in China say, "relative freedom." They cannot distribute tracts in public places. [When people in the West point this out, I ask "When was the last time you passed out tracts? You have the freedom to do so!"] They cannot buy radio or TV time. There have been times when Sunday schools for ages under eighteen in some places were restricted, although I have seen churches where they now have them. They cannot hold worship services in places that have not been approved by the government [however, this has changed also, because many meet in hotels and other buildings].

However, they can worship freely in registered churches (over 12,000 such churches are operating today [in 2011 this has mushroomed to close to 25,000]. Every three days, two new churches are opened. They can distribute Bibles that are now being printed by the millions in China [close to 90 million by

2011]. They can hold Bible study classes. A few weeks ago our team attended such a class on a Wednesday morning. Close to 1,000 people took up every available space in the church and its adjacent rooms. They can train emerging young Christian leaders in Bible schools and theological seminaries. They can witness to their friends and coworkers freely. They can pray publicly in restaurants before taking their meals [and they do it verbally by standing up]. They can print evangelical books (a few weeks ago I was given the Chinese translation of *Peace with God* by Billy Graham which had been printed by a secular press in Nanchang). They can print and distribute a Christian monthly with 120,000 paid subscriptions all across China.

So you see there are many things Christians are allowed to do. And they can worship freely in registered house churches also called meeting points—more than 30,000 of them.

Someone once told me, "I suspect the reason why quite a few executives of evangelical ministries major on the negative are to raise funds." People tend to give more to causes that highlight the sufferings of Christians with whom they empathize. Of course, *who does not want to help those that are in need!* I continued in my letter:

[But there is] the other side, the positive side of China. And although the government in China is run by the Communist Party, isn't it amazing that such a government, which adheres to an atheistic ideology, is willing to give the above mentioned freedoms to its citizens? That's why we can be involved in China with the mission to give help when and where asked.

For instance, as a foreigner I can be invited by a local church in any given city to minister. This gives me the freedom to co-labor with my Christian brothers and sisters in China. And that is what we do. My goal is to spread the gospel. However, in doing so, I do not compromise my Christian beliefs. So far, on all of my ministry trips to China, I have never had to change my sermons nor my teaching subjects.

Again and again I ran across people who were puzzled and bewildered by what we were permitted to do in China contrary to what they had heard from others. I was forced to set things straight. I closed my letter:

You may be amazed at what we are allowed to do in China. So are we! Knowing the situation in China firsthand makes us marvel at the many opportunities God has given to us. It is only by the grace of God that we have so much freedom to do what God called us to do in China.

Are Christians persecuted in China? Yes, there are some. Even in western countries this happens, although rarely. I met the wife of a Presbyterian minister who had been incarcerated for standing up for her beliefs re abortion right here in the US. Two men were put into prison for the same reason. Are Christians in China under pressure? Yes, many are. So are some in western countries. Are 60 million Christians in China being brutally persecuted today as was reported in an evangelical video recently? Absolutely not. Such [false] reporting can be detrimental to the cause of Christ in China.

A few weeks ago, a Christian leader in China said to me, "Yes, we do have problems in China, but let us not magnify them. All I am asking is to be fair in your reports." And fair we want to be. Also honest. And loving.

Do not get wrapped up in the culture of our time. I heard Gingrich [US congressman at that time] say today, "We seem to have a passion for the negative." Listening to newscasts, you can get the impression that what all people want to hear are sensational stories. And many of the stories you may have heard about China are sensational, distorted, and often untrue.

All true believers—whether they belong to unregistered and registered house churches, or to registered churches—belong to the body of Christ. In this we can rejoice!

CHAPTER 25

DIETRICH BONHOEFFER— MARTYR FOR CHRIST

I NGE AND I had visited the Nazi concentration camp in Flossenbürg to see the sight where the gallows stood that brought an end to Dietrich Bonhoeffer's life. This was the fourth concentration camp established by the Nazis in the spring of 1938. An estimated 73,000 victims died there before it was liberated by the 2nd US Cavalry on April 23, 1945. Bonhoeffer was not only an outstanding theologian—some say if he would have lived, he would have developed into the greatest theologian of the twentieth century—but he also was a spiritual hero.

He lived what he preached. You can read it in his book *The Cost of Discipleship.* His brilliant mind produced some of the deepest and most devout thoughts ever put on paper.

He was born in Breslau, Germany on February 4, 1906, was arrested by the Gestapo in April of 1943, and died a martyr's death on April 9, 1945. With his writings he left a legacy calling for supreme discipleship. Discipleship can only be lived when total obedience to Christ is part of a Christian's life. Bonhoeffer lived a life of discipleship. He lived in this world, and that fully, but his mind and heart were set on heavenly things. Someone said of him: "He, a giant before man, was but a child before God."

He hammered away at cheap grace. The death of Christ on the cross makes grace available, but it is costly. Costly grace demands discipleship. To encourage sin and rely on grace is blasphemy. He wrote, "The word of cheap grace has been the ruin of more Christians than any commandment of works."

Single-minded obedience makes a Christian stand out from the world. Bonhoeffer is so refreshing as he clarifies basic truths of the Bible. "Discipleship and the Cross," "The Visible Community," "The Hinderness of Prayer and the Devout Life," "The Simplicity of the Carefree Life," "The Decision," and "The Image of Christ" are all dealt with in detail and with deep conviction.

Bonhoeffer's life was cut off too soon. He was only thirty-nine years old when he was brought to the gallows. He should have lived longer!

I often thought of Bonhoeffer when I taught young, emerging Christian leaders in China.

It is so easy for foreigners to question the depth of the Chinese Christian's faith, as so many in the West do. When I looked into the eyes of those students and saw those taking copious notes as they absorbed our teaching, I knew that they understood discipleship and obedience.

Often it is not easy to live out the Christian life in China. But many do—millions of them. That is why they always ask for prayer. They understand that pitfalls can hinder their spiritual growth. Living in an atheistic society can be treacherous.

Christians have to be very careful how to proceed with their spiritual lives. However, in all of my ministry travels I never have heard any Christian complain. They know that they live in an antagonistic society and decided to live a life of love and compassion. If they are slapped in the face, they are willing to offer the other side as Jesus taught them to do.

I was convinced that all those whom we trained for gospel ministry must hear clear teaching on the validity, relevance, and effectiveness of God's Word, the Bible. Chinese Christians love the Bible. They know what it is like to have been deprived of such a valued book. For years, during the Cultural Revolution, they had to do without it. Bibles were banned, confiscated, and burned. How thrilling it was for them now to have them printed and distributed in their own land again.

I shared my convictions in a letter to my friends:

All open-minded readers of Scripture are amazed to find absolute harmony of thought in the Bible. From Genesis to Revelation God's intent is seen and felt. He had in mind to save man from sin. All Scripture is in logical sequence. Nothing contradicts God's plan and purpose. History moves in one direction. The beginning and the end are clear. All writings complement one thought, and that is redemption. Christ is the center of all activities.

This alone is proof of God's revelation. The Bible is God-breathed. He moved men to pen His deliberations. Books written by men living in different centuries, coming from different backgrounds, having gone through different schools of education or none at all, representing different nationalities, and coming from all walks of life—they all wrote driven by the inspiration of the one and only God.

The Chinese students understand and believe this, and we did not and still don't want them to fall prey to those who are out to mislead them through false teaching. I always reminded them of what happened to Germany after the Enlightenment had begun and swept through Europe in the eighteenth century. As a result it emptied the churches.

Of course, there were some noble concepts that came forth from this period, such as, "Human autonomy has to be honored" which means the individual has the right to think for himself. Also, that any individual should have the privilege to think rationally without giving up the right to express his faith in God! Furthermore, religion and politics should be separated, and one's method of worship should be a private matter. Under Mao Zedong people had been stripped of this privilege, and Christians suffered greatly because of this. However, the present generation was elated to now be able to worship as it pleases.

Three principles guided our ministry within China—we must work legally, openly, and honestly. We have to be sensitive to the situation facing the leadership of theological institutions in China. As time goes by, enlarged pressure was placed upon them due to the increased interest by foreign organizations to "help out." Chinese Christians strongly feel that God had called them and that they should do the work primarily themselves. Therefore, any assistance from outside should proceed in accordance and in harmony with those leaders.

The president emeritus of one of China's most prestigious universities invited me for lunch. As a young man, while studying at the Nanjing University, he had run across some Christians, but decided to become a Marxist. The teachings of Karl Marx had gripped the minds of the young intellectuals of his day. As he sat across from me at the lunch table, he confessed that through the years he had turned into a "liberal Marxist." Furthermore, he shared his conviction that the Christian faith had something to offer to Chinese society. He had started an "Institute for Studies on Christianity," and it already had over 1,000 students. The institute had been approved by Beijing. He asked me to help find lecturers from overseas to lecture on Christianity at this newly founded institute.

The government continued to upgrade their regulations. For foreigners teaching in China new guidelines had been established by the Department of Education. We wanted to be sure that we continued our work within the framework of Chinese laws. The situation in China continued to be volatile, and we did not want to do anything that might jeopardize our ministry. We always needed God's wisdom on how to proceed. One of the insiders in China, Rev. Jinglong Zhang, agreed with our policies:

> People tend to be too naïve in dealing with China in which things are so complicated, but the Spirit of God has never ceased to move and operate in an active way. The either/or of black/white logic, which works in many areas in the West, may not work in the same way in China. The reality is that there is no one-way traffic in China.
>
> Although China Partner (CP) is but a tiny part of God's whole plan for China and in China, it has played and will play a crucial role in getting the gospel to the Chinese at all levels. This is so because CP has used God's wisdom and

the gift of discernment. CP has transcended the man-made barriers of confusion, which has made it possible for CP to take big strides in China in the future, without minimizing the importance of other approaches.

Praise God for His wisdom in using this ministry to advance the gospel in China and to bear ever-increasing fruits of the Holy Spirit.

During that time I felt that our CP coworkers needed to get together for our first international consultation. Representatives from New Zealand, China, Canada, USA, Germany, and Switzerland met in beautiful Delray Beach, south of West Palm Beach in Florida, to strategize about our ministry in China. Our Hong Kong delegate, Hannah Miller, had been rushed to the hospital upon arrival in San Francisco and operated on for acute appendicitis. We greatly missed her with her fertile mind. Her parents came from China, and while living in Hong Kong she had married a Britisher.

At that time we were incorporated in five countries, however, only Germany besides the US had paid staff. Konrad Brandt, former director of Marburger Mission, a remarkable German mission organization, was CP's representative. He succeeded in elevating the stature of China Partner among evangelical leaders and paved the way for us to be included in Germany's Christian umbrella organization Arbeitsgemeinschaft Evangelikaler Missionen.

China, as many other countries in the world, was undergoing tremendous economic changes. One of the greatest threats to the burgeoning church in China became materialism. As the economy exploded, young people were being attracted to the pleasures of life that often accompany such rapid changes in society.

However, our representative from China had a moving testimony. As a teenager, he was sent to the countryside during the Cultural Revolution. He was a young Marxist at that time. Thus he was proud to be involved in helping poor farmers confront their hardships. However, he slowly saw that Marxism was not the solution to society's problems. Nor was Confucianism. Later he turned to the Bible and found true peace. He told us, "Christ became the rock on which I started to build my life."

The province of Jiangxi is known as the Revolution Province. It was there where Mao Zedong started his first Soviet republics. Our teaching team, consisting of Hans Wilhelm, my brother Fred, Erik, and I, were taken to a church in the countryside north of Nanchang. It was started by a lady who used to be a Buddhist. She found the Lord through someone witnessing to her. She started a church in 1990 with ten believers in her home. In just a few years her church had grown so large, it could no longer meet in her home. So she applied for registration and the purchase of some land to construct a church building. That building was completed in 1995, and when we visited there the membership had grown to six hundred. A graduate of the new Bible school we helped build now serves as a lay leader. The entire building, a nice structure by countryside church standards, was paid in full. The money had been raised by its members and one donation from a church in Taiwan.

This is just one example of how the church in China is moving ahead.

Chinese people are increasingly getting more interested in the Christian faith. *Here I Stand*, the book featuring the life of the reformer Martin Luther, had been printed by a secular publisher in China. It turned out to become a best seller, and in a very short time it headed into its sixth printing!

Xian, formerly known as Chang'an, in the province of Shaanxi, is one of the oldest cities in China with more than 3,100 years of history. It became famous to the western world as the home of the Terracotta Army in 1974, which had been created for the first emperor of the Qin dynasty (221-206 BC), Qin Shi Huang, who wanted to rule another empire in the afterlife. Beginning in 246 BC, 700,000 workers supposedly worked on this mausoleum. Only few foreigners have been allowed to walk through the pit with its thousands of warriors. President Reagan in 1984 and Queen Elizabeth later were two of those exceptions. It is now a famous tourist attraction with walkways around the pit.

Xian is also one of the four great ancient capitals of China along with Beijing, Nanjing, and Luoyang. It was the eastern terminus of the famous Silk Road.

One of the twenty-one theological institutes in China is located in this ancient city. While teaching at the school, we had the opportunity to visit this famous site. We were not allowed to take pictures, but as someone who never takes a "No" for an answer, I kept my video camera rolling while it was hanging on my side. I just did not understand why they were so secretive about it. The same was true when I visited the renovated ancestral home of Mao Zedong in Chaochan, Hunan province. But no one hindered me doing it, even the military guard looked the other way. He probably had seen so many other tourists taking photos that he finally gave up.

While teaching in Xian, we noticed that the pastors were under great pressure facing the many new converts who had emerged from heathenism. Especially the younger pastors had been overwhelmed with the enormity of pastoral care. Since all new converts had no background of Christian beliefs and convictions, it takes much patience to guide them into correct understanding of God's truth. Many of them had turned their back on Communism. Others had been disillusioned by their old religions. All of them had been drawn by the Holy Spirit to become true, yet inexperienced babes in Christ. They needed much help.

"The demands placed on pastors/evangelists in the church are constantly increasing," wrote Lin Zh'ien from Zhejiang province. That was true, as they also had to carry out substantial pastoral duties, preaching, leading worship at many different locations spread across a large area, meeting with individual believers to discuss matters of life and faith, and praying with the sick, housebound, and elderly. On top of this, they often find themselves burdened with the tasks within the church that nobody else will do. This could include cleaning and sweeping, changing light bulbs, plumbing and electrical repairs, financial management, and so on. Many congregations justify this by pointing out that evangelists receive wages from the church in order to work fulltime.

All the duties described above keep pastors busy all hours of the day and night. As a result, they hardly get any quiet time in which to read the Bible, pray, or attend to their own spiritual growth. Also their family life suffers.

We noticed some of these predicaments and addressed them openly in our teachings. We often used materials of The

Navigators to explain how those difficulties can be overcome. As an example we used the illustration of "the hand." I first had heard Dawson Trotman, founder of The Navigators, explain this to me in Shanghai. He taught:

- The little finger stands for hearing the Word of God;
- The ring finger stands for reading the Word of God;
- The middle finger stands for studying the Word of God;
- The index finger stands for memorizing the Word of God;
- The thumb stands for meditating on the Word of God.

Most Christians only hear the Word of God by attending church services as the Scriptures are expounded by the pastor. This is good, but not enough. When you make it a daily habit to read the Bible by yourself, you will learn so much more. However, if you really want to grow as a Christian, you need to take pen in hand with a piece of paper and study the Word of God. This, of course, takes much more effort. But meditating on Scriptures that you had listened to, or read, or studied and even memorized, is the key to real growth in Christian life!

When I was on my way traveling home via Hong Kong in 1998, I struggled to walk. I had noticed for months how my back pain had gotten worse from month to month. However, while walking to an assignment in Hong Kong, I had to stop in my tracks. The pain got so severe that Erik hailed a cab to take me back to the hotel. That night I called Inge. "Honey, please call the surgeon and tell him that he needs to operate on me."

Months before I had gone to Dr. Guesicke, a neurologist in Ft. Lauderdale, to see what could be done to eliminate my growing back pain. He said, "Surgery may be the answer, however, there are three reasons why I would not recommend having it done. First, there is no guarantee that it will help; second, it is extremely dangerous to remove the tissues pressing on the nerves inside your spine, you might end up sitting in a wheelchair for the rest of your life; and third, it is very expensive."

I took his advice and was willing to bear the pain. However, in Hong Kong I knew surgery was needed. When I got home, I immediately entered the Holy Cross Hospital in Ft. Lauderdale. Six weeks later I was back on the tennis courts and played like nothing had happened. The Lord had been very gracious to me. I learned to thank God for doctors with their skills.

And I was so glad for a family who prayed for me and stood behind me. In the Christmas greeting to my friends in December 1998 I wrote:

Merry Christmas. In our part of the world many people abandoned this greeting and use "Happy Holidays" instead. But we know what this holiday season is all about—we are celebrating the birth of our Lord Jesus Christ. Therefore, we boldly declare where we stand and whom we follow.

We are getting older, and we notice it. Inge was hospitalized twice this year, and I had to undergo back surgery. The Lord brought us through, but it did remind us how fragile our bodies are. We want to take this into consideration as we strive to do God's will in the years ahead.

And then I concentrated my remarks on our four children. They had grown up so often not having their father around. By then I had traveled between two and three million miles, most of them by air, ministering in one hundred twenty-six countries. Inge had had the added burden to raise them mostly by herself. I was eternally grateful for this. So I continued:

> Our children and grandchildren are a great source of joy. Our eldest son, Erik, lives in Denver, Colorado, and is Director of Operations of our China ministry. He is married to Tammy, and they have two daughters [Brittany and Briana]. Our second son, Heiko, lives in Berlin, Germany, where he, along with Kay, does missionary work. Their three sons [Stephan, Yannick, and Micah] now can say what the late President Kennedy declared while visiting Berlin: "Ich bin ein Berliner." Our third son, Stephan, is a businessman but also the chairman of missions of our local church. He resides with his Barbara and their three daughters [Stephanie, Katherine, Ashley] in Boca Raton, Florida. Our only daughter, Linda, is married to David Pervenecki, a detective (*Kriminalbeamter*), and they live in Wellington, Florida, where they are involved in a local church. They have a daughter and a son [Jerusha, Tilon].

I wished I had the space to include more letters we received from China. God is explicitly preparing many to become part of a great spiritual awakening yet to come. This, no doubt, will be unprecedented in China's—or possible the world's—history.

What a stark difference to what faithful missionaries had experienced decades ago! My parents worked for twenty-five years in China, and they only saw "as many as you can count on both hands" come to the Lord. They were so disappointed and often had thought during their sojourn to call it quits and return to Germany, their lovely homeland. They didn't. I only wished they could have lived to see what their faithful witness has done.

One Chinese seminary student wrote, "We are very grateful to God for all the provision and support this past year, a substantial part of which has been granted graciously through China Partner. May the Lord further open the gates for China Partner in China and bless you in ways beyond our expectation and prediction." This student had a prayer request about his future church involvement in China as soon as he had finished his studies.

CHAPTER 26

PERSECUTION OR PROSECUTION IN CHINA

B ACK IN THE US in church, a gentleman tapped me on the shoulder from behind and said, "This morning I thought of you, because I read an article about the persecution of Chinese Christians and that it is picking up again." *Oh, no,* I thought, "*not again!*" Soon after I received an email from Germany: "How is it possible for you to work freely in China whereas others are persecuted for Christ's sake?"

By then I was getting annoyed—really annoyed. Year after year people kept having the same concerns about so-called persecution and shared them with me. They were simply not getting it. What was going on? Why were they so slow to understand?

So I wrote another piece:

Why, then, are others hampered in their Christian activities? I think it has something to do with building relationships and trust. In China relationships are extremely important. [They call it *guang zhi*]. Only after relationships have been solidified over long periods of time—sometimes years—will Chinese accept foreigners who want to work in China. We have built relationships since 1981.

Furthermore, the term *persecution* has to be qualified. No doubt, there are incidents where persecution is taking place. Such incidents are minimal compared to the vast development of the church in China. On my forty trips to China [by 2011 I had made close to one hundred trips] I yet have to find a case where that happened. On the other hand, I have heard of those who have been prosecuted for breaking the law of the land. Therefore, prosecution would be a better term than persecution in most cases. The law in China demands from all religious [also secular] groups to register with municipal authorities. When certain criteria are met, believers can start a church. These include:

a)   There must be an existing congregation of believers
b)   The congregation must have a permanent place and name
c)   A proper organization with leadership must be established
d)   A qualified pastor must be available
e)   A proper constitutional organization must be set up
f)   Sufficient operational funds and proper accounting must be available

What then is the problem? Why do many groups face adversities and hurdles? Thousands of house churches had registered with the government. However, there are still many leaders of house churches who refuse to do so. The government interprets this as breaking the law and will prosecute. This does not mean that they are necessarily being persecuted for their faith in Christ. Christians in China today can live out their faith freely as long as they are willing to keep the laws of the land. They call it "relative freedom."

I further had explained this hazardous situation to my friends:

We can disagree with some of the laws and regulations, and many western Christians do. Unfortunately China does not have a democracy as we understand it; China is a dictatorship. I personally prefer democracy, but I do not propagate this in China. That is not our calling. Our mandate is to teach and preach the gospel "in season and out of season." And this we do. What a joy to lock arms with our Christian brothers and sisters in China to further the cause of Christ. Please keep praying for us to minister with conviction and sensitivity.

At that time our China ministry was moving ahead from strength to strength. In fact, the year of 1998 had been the best year yet. We had more teaching opportunities, sent more money to students and grassroots pastors, had more interesting, worthwhile, and meaningful encounters with Christian leaders, taught more students, and had all the financial support needed to enlarge our blessed ministry.

For instance, Inge had accompanied me when I preached at the prestigious Lake Avenue Congregational Church in Pasadena, California. Their mission pastor, Roger Bosch (who, by the way, was married to a German girl—how smart!) wrote as a thank you:

We can't thank you enough for your coming to Lake Avenue for our World Focus Weekend! It was an incredible time from beginning to end as we saw God do a wonderful work in the lives of our people through the two of you! We have received so many words of thanks from members of the congregation for having the Bürklins as our guests this year. It was so obvious that God had called you to be with us and anointed you with a special ability to touch our hearts with the needs in China. We'll never be the same again.

Wow, reading this, I blushed. There is no way we could have been able to rouse so much positive passion. We were just simply sharing with them what God had been doing in China! However, you must know that Roger had lived in Germany as a missionary, and we had known each other then. In fact, his wife was one of several sisters that, as teenagers, had been blessed in one of our YFC evangelistic crusades in the Ruhr area of Germany. I suppose he showed some bias in his letter.

Ted Engstrom, former president of Youth for Christ and World Vision, and Evon Hedley, former president of Canadian Youth for Christ, were members of that church. In fact, Evon had been so challenged during that weekend that he signed up as a team member for our China ministry the following year. You just can't keep down people whose passion is missions and who want to see the world reached for Christ!

It was in Karl-Marx-Stadt, East Germany, which, after the demise of the German Democratic Republic, was renamed Chemnitz, its former name, where I spoke at a youth conference *"Die Schritte"* (Steps). While having my breakfast in the hotel, I saw a foreign-looking gentleman who originally hailed from India. I introduced myself and found out that I had met his father in Bangalore when I directed Amsterdam '86. His son Ramesh Richard migrated to the United States and was a professor at Dallas Theological Seminary. He had been asked to give a greeting at the conference, and since there was no interpreter around, I was asked to help out. This started a friendship.

In March of 1999 he sponsored a conference in the Philippines for one hundred Christian leaders from around the world, who were involved in pastoral training. He had asked me to give a lecture on this subject. I traveled via Hong Kong, and when I checked in for my flight to Manila, the official at the check-in counter said, "I cannot let you through, because your passport expires within two months. You need a passport that is valid for at least six months." No argument could convince him to change his mind. "I will leave the Philippines after just a few days!" I maintained. However, no deal.

It was Saturday, and the German consulate was closed. In desperation I called their emergency number and lo and behold, the consul answered, "I will try to help you. Meet me at the consulate in two hours." Sure enough, he was there and within an hour I had my passport's validity extended. It was amazing; however, the next flight to Manila would not leave until the following day. But I just made it to the conference in time to deliver my lecture.

Those were some of the "pleasures" of travel!

Once again we had our international council meeting, this time in a Christian retreat center, "Männedorf," in beautiful Switzerland on the Züricher See. China Partner representatives from Canada, Germany, Hong Kong, New Zealand, Switzerland, and USA deliberated about and reviewed our ministry in China. We had invited a Christian leader from China, Rev. Guang Jien Guo, the dean of the East China Theological Seminary located in Shanghai, to advise us how best to do ministry in China. We were very sensitive to stay in tune with the actualities within China. Above all, it was our desire to work hand-in-hand with our Chinese counterparts. He turned out to be an excellent counselor.

Repeatedly our Chinese friend called for renewed and accelerated efforts to train theological students across his land. "The harvest is great, but few are the workers," he stressed. "Now churches are springing up everywhere, and there are far too few biblically trained pastors." He encouraged us to enlarge our vision to meet this tremendous need.

As we continued to make this need known to our constituents and churches in several western countries, we sensed a new awareness and interest about and for China. We also had been overwhelmed by the response to my booklet *Bridging the Gulf between Christians in China*. We had to order a special printing to meet the demand. We had been convinced that the message of reconciliation was desperately needed all over China and especially across the world.

Our friend Wilson Chow, president of the Graduate School of Theology in Hong Kong, said:

> I prefer to speak of serving China and God's people in China rather than doing mission to or ministry in China. It is not only a matter of terminology, but one of mentality and attitude. To serve China, one must accept her political reality and church situation. It requires a sensitive and responsible approach.

Hurdles to overcome—bombs in Belgrade and the bishop in Nanjing

And then the tragic bombing of the Chinese embassy in Belgrade happened during the Kosovo war. A firestorm of protests swept over China. China's President Jiang Zemin avowed, "The great People's Republic of China will never be bullied, the great Chinese nation will never be humiliated, and the great Chinese people will never be conquered." In Guangzhou we happened to stay in a hotel situated two blocks from the US consulate. Thousands of angry students demonstrators marched by our hotel on the way to the consulate. They shouted, "Get out of Yugoslavia!" and then shortened it to a vigorous chant, "Get out, get out, get out!" It did have a chilling effect on us. We were then asked by the hotel management to stay in our rooms and not to look out of the windows. At one time we had two of the students charge up the stairs to find us. Two days later everything was quiet again.

After that we encountered no more hostilities. Of course, even the Christians expressed their dismay about the pointless incident—yet they welcomed us warmly. So we moved on from Guangzhou to Xiamen, Shanghai, Nanjing, and Harbin.

In Harbin we preached to 1,800 worshipers. Harbin is located some 250 miles south of the Russian border in the province of Heilongjiang. In order to accommodate the crowds, that church had five services each Sunday: at 6 a.m., 8 a.m., 10 a.m., 2 p.m., and at 5 p.m. For a time it had been a small and struggling church, but in the eighties its membership doubled each year, reaching over 10,000 members. Several hundred new believers were baptized every year. Those were not people that moved from other churches to this one! Those were new

399

converts. All converts have to show their commitment to the Lord and their loyalty to the church for one year before they are permitted to be baptized. It is simply amazing to witness God's moving in that country.

In fact, in the province Heilongjiang the Christian community was growing so fast, we had been told that for the first time in China's history, the Christians had overtaken the Buddhists in numbers—at that time 540,000 vs. 180,000—three to one. Christianity had truly become a "Chinese religion." The Christian faith had finally put down its roots deep into Chinese "soil." Again I wished that my missionary parents would have been able to experience this for themselves. Their prayer and the prayers of countless other missionaries have been answered. Also, those who had supported them with their gifts and prayers will share in an equal amount of reward.

Buddhism originated in India (sixth century B.C.) and was brought to China in 67 A.D. Taoism, however, originated in China proper as far back as the fourth century B.C. For centuries, both religions had a strong influence on Chinese thought and life, and were considered to be indigenous to China. Confucianism is not a religion, but rather a system of ethics, even though some refer to it as a religion. When Protestant Christianity was first introduced to China as a result of modern mission advances in the early nineteenth century (Robert Morrison, 1807), it was seen by the Chinese as a foreign intrusion, and was therefore vastly rebuffed. Missionaries—and all foreigners—were called "foreign devils." This now had changed.

On that specific trip we had handed out four hundred seventeen sets of biblical study books worth over $10,000! They totaled 5,700 books!

And then we hit a snag—a big one!

In September of 1999 I had traveled to China, stopping over in Hong Kong, where I received a fax from our home office showing a stinging letter from my friend Bishop Ting:

> You surprise me greatly when I saw a copy of your September circular letter to your "Ministry Friends" which arbitrarily divides Chinese Protestant Christians as "evangelicals" (90%) and "liberals." The latter you define and vilify as those in our church who can only listen to government orders. So you turn a religious difference into a political one. This certainly was not the Mr. Bürklin whom I thought I knew and for whom I did much to start you off in what you now name WBM [later changed to China Partner]. Your letter makes me regret for having helped you establish connections with local theological schools after Nanjing led the way. I feel you are biting the hand that fed you.
>
> I thought you knew and supported the fact that the China Christian Council and the Three-Self Movement have all these years advocated and promoted Christian unity and upheld the policy of mutual respect in matters of faith and worship. It is no longer our habit to divide Chinese Christians into camps such as evangelicals and liberals. We stand for the unity of all those who recognize Jesus Christ as Lord, as Paul taught us in I Cor. 12:3. I supported you as an apostle of Christian unity, not as a sower of Christian division.

Even now as I write my memoir, I feel ashamed of having hurt my brother whom I had highly respected. Something had gone wrong and deeply so, but I did not have my circular letter with me and therefore did not know what had triggered such a response.

I immediately sent him an email expressing my apology:

> I was stunned reading your letter this morning which was passed on to me here in Hong Kong. I deeply regret that my September "ministry letter" went out the way it did. I never intended it to cause division among the churches in China. Please forgive if this is the way it came across.

> As you know, I always tried to be open and honest with all of our dealings in China. I am sure you are aware how often I have been attacked for my stance regarding China in the western world. My deep desire has always been, and still is, to build bridges wherever I can. I hope this unfortunate letter will not mar our warm and close relationship. I always trusted you as a dear friend and brother in Christ.

When I finally had my ministry letter in hand, I knew that I had made a big mistake. I took complete responsibility for it, even though my secretary had originally drafted the letter. I had been so busy that I had asked her to draft it, and this was the only time I had someone else write my circular letters. She was a strong proponent of the house church movement and loathed the TSPM. I saw the letter before it went to print and made a few changes, but did not go far enough. I had signed it. So I was the only one to blame.

What had I written?

> Based upon some recent reports we have received, it would seem that liberalism is trying to infiltrate one of the major seminaries. After the former assistant principal of the Nanjing

Seminary resigned so that she could join her husband who is studying in the West, a liberal was placed in that position. (I don't think I need to explain how critical this is—after all, look at the effect liberalism has had in this country and Europe. The Church is trying to maintain its witness in what is now called the "Post-Christian Era" in the West). Although there are thousands of godly, committed believers in leadership positions in the Chinese Church, liberals tend to be more concerned about implementing government policy rather than obeying the Lord's commands. This perspective can be fatal in such a setting as a seminary where the majority of students are from an evangelical background—in fact, over 90 percent of Christians in China are evangelicals.

When I finally had the chance to read my letter again, I immediately realized that I had made two mistakes; firstly, I had based my statement about the assistant principal of the seminary on reports that I had not verified nor properly vetted. Secondly, I had embraced the dispute of western evangelical leaders, who had propositioned that churches of the Tree Self Movement are stooges of the Communist Party.

No wonder the Bishop had responded the way he did in the third paragraph:

I hope you have not sunken to the level of rumor mongering. For example, from where did you get the information that Peng Cui-An has resigned or been denied a job? Was she not free to ask for a two-year leave of absence so that she and her husband could be enrolled in Fuller [Seminary] together, while maintaining her position in Nanjing Seminary? And does not Nanjing Seminary have the right to appoint a dean pro tem while she is away, whose theological view[s] are at least as sound as yours? I expected you to distinguish fact from fictions before you attack Nanjing Seminary or any other institution in China. I can understand your need to make your appeals to your "ministry friends" sound appealing, but you should not expect us in China to tolerate the way you distort facts.

Of course, his letter had grieved me deeply. I also was aware that our ministry was in jeopardy. In fact, when we landed in Changsha for our training seminar, we were greeted by the president of the Bible school who said, "Do you realize that Bishop Ting has sent a letter to all Christian institutions across China warning us about your position?"

I immediately decided to take the next plane to Nanjing to meet him in person to apologize. When I arrived in Nanjing, I was ushered into the office of Han Wenzhou, general secretary of the China Christian Council. After handing me the perfunctory cup of tea, he said, "The bishop cannot see you, but let me be your go-between. This again was very typical of the Chinese culture that prefers to have a third party mediate. He also had been a close friend over the years, and so I gladly accepted his offer. I explained my standpoint, offered my apologies, and traveled back to Changsha.

It turned out to be the right thing to do.

A couple of months later I honored the bishop with a banquet in Nanjing, which he reciprocated. Finally, several months later, he invited me and Erik into his home alongside with the right-hand man of Han Wenzhou, Wang Hao. After this momentous visit, Wang Hao told me, "I was pleased to see how the bishop has welcomed you back into the fold."

This irritable episode turned into renewed fellowship and an ongoing cooperation between the Chinese Christian leadership and China Partner's ministry.

In the bishop's closing remark in his September letter, he had written this:

> So, at this stage, the least we have to require of you is: in Changsha, Jiangxi, and anywhere else you go to in China, you declare to your listeners clearly that you honor the Christian unity advocated by the CCC, and that Christians need not all hold to exactly the same theological points of view as long as we hold to the Lordship of Jesus Christ as taught by the Bible. I hope this is acceptable to you.

With this I totally agreed.

On January 25, 2000, the hatchet was officially buried. He wrote:

> Thank you for yours of October 21, 1999, recent on 00-1-19, and for several previous messages. I am sorry for not answering you earlier. My excuse is that I was pressing myself to complete the version of a book of mine already published in Chinese [*Love Never Ends*]. Another excuse is that I was really tired of dealing with anti-China and anti-three-self utterances.

> I am pleased and want to assure you we are still friends since you are willing to show your listeners and supporters that you endorse the principle of mutual respect in matters of faith and worship as advocated by the Three-Self Movement and the China Christian Council and honor the principle in your activities related to China.

It was during this time that *World* magazine, a strongly evangelical periodical, ran a story with this headline, *Caesar's Seminary,* with a picture of Mao Zedong next to it and a cutline *MAO: No open door.* Mindy Belz started her article with: "Sweeping conservatives from China's best-known seminary may leave only foxes guarding the henhouse, but it may also strengthen China's underground churches." She continued:

> No preaching. No prayer. No hymns. Those are the restrictions Chinese officials recently imposed on campus meetings at Nanjing Seminary, the most prestigious of China's licensed Protestant theological training centers. Those prohibitions are different from the attacks on Nanjing thirty-five years ago during the Cultural Revolution, when "Red Guards"—Communist thugs—burned seminary books in the courtyard and doomed all who resisted to forced labor or death. But they represent one more attempt to strangle the faith that China's rulers most fear.

No wonder that Bishop Ting in his letter to me mentioned, "I was really tired of dealing with anti-China and with anti-three-self utterances."

On top of this, it was strange that *World* had refused to publish or acknowledge the counter information provided by an evangelical person, Faye Pearson, who had been living and teaching on the campus of the Nanjing Seminary for two years. She set the record straight:

> After reading the article "Caesar's Seminary" in *World* magazine I was quite distressed...I work, listen, pray, worship, laugh, and teach with the faculty, staff, and students on a daily

basis…The article began with the statement, "No preaching, no prayer, no hymns"…That has not been my experience.

I find a distortion of many of the facts in the *World* magazine article "Caesar's Seminary." I have pointed out only a few of them. There are many others.

I was also baffled with that same article. On May 12, 2001, I wrote a long letter to the editor of *World* magazine which included the following:

I understand your desire to keep Christians in the West informed about happenings in China. However, it is a shame that *World* magazine again printed wrong information about China mixed in with correct information. For instance, your statement: "No preaching. No prayer. No hymns. Those are the restrictions Chinese officials recently imposed on campus meetings at Nanjing Seminary…" is false. Sadly, the media, including the evangelical media, continues to put out wrong information.

I again realized how sensitive we have to be when reporting on the church in China. May God forgive us for placing wedges between Christian groups in that great country!

CHAPTER 27

REMINISCING ON FORTY YEARS OF MINISTRY

AT THIS JUNCTURE I need to reminisce on my past forty years of ministry. Some of it will be found in former pages, but I have to highlight selected events.

Forty years of ministry is something to be thankful for. In fact, the ministry started even earlier! It was 1949. Mao Zedong had just taken over China. All missionaries had been ousted, including us missionary kids. I returned to war-torn Germany. Most of the major cities lay in rubble. 80 percent of Kassel, a once beautiful garden city (and again now) in central Germany, was destroyed. It is here where I helped my uncle Friedrich shovel rubble day after day in order to rebuild his house and business.

As a young Christian I saw more than those mountains of crushed brick and concrete. I saw the despair in crushed lives of those who had barely made it through the devastating war. Young people everywhere were bewildered, confused, and did not know to whom to turn. Rubble needed to be cleared out of their lives!

Since I had become a Christian three years earlier, I now wanted others to find my Savior also.

I rented a newly built hall sitting in the midst of a vast pile of rubble, invited a YFC team from Canada, visited as many pastors as possible after my working hours, and set out with only one other young friend to hold the first major city-wide crusade in that town after the war. We had no money, housed the team in an air raid shelter, and started out with a handful of people in the first evening meeting. Within a couple of days, news spread around town about the crusade, churches began to notice what was going on and started to back us, the media covered the event, and soon we had the hall overflowing and people finding the Lord.

From then on I was involved in evangelism. Looking back I marvel at what God had done. God's faithfulness has proven true.

Some time later, after having graduated from the European Bible Institute, I was riding the train across France on my way back to Germany to continue my evangelistic ministry. I was young and inexperienced. The future was an unopened book, and I was frightened. But then I thought back to my graduation service where my professor Barnes had intoned the great hymn:

Great is thy faithfulness, great is they faithfulness!
Morning by morning new mercies I see;
All I have needed thy hand hath provided,
Great is thy faithfulness, Lord, unto me!

That gave me courage, and now looking back on those forty years I can say: To Him belong all the glory! His faithfulness sustained me.

The great Christian leader and Nobel-laureate John R. Mott had a battle cry: "World evangelization in our generation." This became my slogan as well, in spite of the obvious unachievability of it. It was an incentive nevertheless!

Inge and I started with nothing. We slept on a mattress on the floor in a small and shared apartment, and our first-born's crib was a dresser drawer. Already then we established a principle that we would not spend money we did not have and give 25 percent of our income to our Lord.

But we did have faith. We were willing to attempt the impossible. My life verse was: "Call unto me and I will answer thee and show thee great and mighty things which thou knowest not," Jeremiah 33:3.

Our first assignments were with Germany Youth for Christ traveling as one of their youth evangelists. Soon I found myself in leadership position. We started a radio ministry when radio was still called the "devil's tool." We produced the first evangelistic youth movie in Germany when the showing of a film in church was still anathema! We started youth rallies in several German cities, when anything out of the ordinary was frowned upon.

But God spurred us on.

With the help of co-workers our ministry expanded into other areas such as music, youth camps, evangelistic teen teams, and training through short-term Bible schools. Foundations for a strong ongoing ministry were laid. Those were exciting years.

All we knew about Jamaica was that it is a beautiful tropical island somewhere in the Caribbean, and that we had been called to serve there. Our responsibility was to prepare and then direct the eighth world congress of Youth for Christ International.

So our entire family uprooted and settled in that country. We had four small children, ages one to eleven. Our three boys had to learn English and attend Jamaican schools. The weather was hot and humid and the culture was different, but the co-laborship with Jamaican Christians was a heartwarming experience.

In the process of preparation, we traveled the length and breadth of that country and met with church leaders, pastors, and youth directors. In conjunction with the congress we laid plans for an extensive evangelistic outreach across the island, which was to culminate in a final super rally in the National Stadium of Kingston, the capital of the nation.

Three hundred thirteen meetings were held during a one week period, and thousands were confronted with the claims of Christ. Many were brought into the kingdom of God.

We re-established the ministry of Youth for Christ. I had been looking for a leader, and the Lord led me to Gerry Gallimore, an award-winning young man in the business world. I challenged him to move into full time Christian work and head up Jamaica Youth for Christ. And he did.

He became the foremost Christian leader of his nation. One year he was chosen "Man of Religion." He established YFC centers all across the island. He became the confidant of government leaders including the prime minister. And he was a humble servant of the Lord. So often we get lost in the events of mass meetings, but God also touches individual lives through our efforts and prayers. He ended up becoming president of Youth for Christ International.

Paul Overholt, veteran missionary to Brazil, had a dream. He wanted to train thousands of young people in evangelism. Thus Geraçao 79 (Generation 79) was born. He asked me to come and help him. Since I had directed other major events, I accepted the call. Once more our family had to move and get used to a different culture. We learned immediately that now we had to get adjusted to a "mañana" lifestyle. Only the traffic moved faster than we were used to.

After months of planning, the big event finally came. Thousands of young Brazilians and young people from other South American countries converged on São Paulo. 10,000 came to the final training session and 60,000 to a mass rally where Billy Graham spoke. Close to 3,000 came to Christ that day.

All the hard work, all long separations, all rough times, and all the tears were now overlooked and some even forgotten, for instance the heart-wrenching moments on our high balcony. Inge had written this moving account:

A mother's heart

As I stood on the balcony of our eighteenth floor apartment in one of those hundreds of skyscrapers in São Paulo, Brazil, looking down on that tiny figure below walking dejectedly to the waiting school bus, tears welled up in my eyes. I prayed a desperate, direct prayer, "Lord, we have come to this huge city not to seek an adventure, not to make money, not for pleasure; we have come because you called us to serve you, as we put together this training congress for Brazilian young people. I don't believe you will allow our little Linda to suffer emotionally, physically, or psychologically through our stay here. Help her right now to understand English better and loose her fears of that foreign school and the new kids in her class.

Every afternoon for several days Linda, then eleven years old, had come home from school crying, "I don't want to

413

go back to that school—I don't know anybody—I don't understand English well—I am scared to speak." Every morning she went reluctantly with tears in her eyes to the school bus. My mother's heart just bled for her.

But God heard my imploring.

Ten days later Linda celebrated her twelfth birthday. Presiding over her pizza birthday party and her six new friends, she was chatting away in English, with mistakes—yes, but no longer afraid or miserable.

And a week later at evening prayer she said, "I will never doubt again that there is a God. Because, look at all that has happened! I am no longer afraid; I speak English and like my teachers and my new friends. All that can't just happen."

A spiritual victory for a twelve-year-old—and a mother's heart rejoiced.

Amsterdam '83 and Amsterdam '86 were the other outstanding events. Here are some of the statistics of the latter one: Over 50,000 names amassed in our computers, 10,000 participants from 174 countries and territories chosen, 446 full-time and part-time staff, 900 stewards, 750 program/teaching staff, 500 media personnel, 143 technicians, 85 hotels used, 3,000 chartered bus trips, 61 airlines used, and 350,000 meals served.

No doubt, these international conferences for itinerant evangelists were highlights of our first forty years of ministry. And it was there where I renewed my commitment to preaching evangelism worldwide.

For years I had traveled the world and preached the gospel wherever a door opened. Whether it was Peru or Germany, the Philippines or Lithuania, India or New Zealand, Korea or Iraq, it was a thrill to see people walk forward as a public demonstration that they wanted to accept Christ and follow Him. But nowhere, it seems, I feel more at home than in China. China is the land of my birth, where I received my early education, where I found my Lord and received the call to serve Him full-time. China and its people are very dear to me.

The older I got, the more I wanted to be involved in China. I felt constrained to focus my attention on China.

Initially I made courtesy trips to get to know China and its Christian leadership. I often combined those trips visiting Korea as well. After the Second World War and following the Korean War, God had worked mightily in that country. Only there, it seemed, people by the thousands would assemble every time a meeting was arranged. I preached in then the largest church of the world, attended by 20,000 people. We crisscrossed the nation preaching in crusades, churches, universities, colleges, and high schools. At one high school 6,000 students attended and more than five hundred of them stood to accept Christ. Nowhere else had I seen such a spiritual harvest!

But China became the center of my attention!

Let me dwell on this.

CHAPTER 28

THE LAST DECADE 2001-2011

ON JANUARY 1, 2000, I wrote a letter to our ministry friends about matters I had felt deeply:

> As we move into a new millennium, it is only natural to look back and reflect once more on the many blessings received. I realize again how faithful the Lord has been. He, the perfect One, has never made a mistake nor has he ever let me down.

> As I look at the wonderful fellowship and relationships I have had with my many Christian friends in China, I marvel at the bond of love that unites us in Him. I constantly share this with those I meet in all the western countries I visit. To see an effort made for unity in the body of Christ, you have to go to China. Of course, not everything is perfect in the Chinese church, nor is it in the church in the West. We are all sinners saved by God's grace; however, we have observed that in China they are trying to build a **united** church. I have

417

seen this especially in the churches of the China Christian Council (CCC). As Bishop Ting wrote in a letter to me not long ago, "We stand for the unity of all those who recognize Jesus Christ as Lord, as Paul taught us in 1 Corinthians 12:3." For years they have been committed to promote Christian unity and to uphold the policy of mutual respect in matters of faith and worship. It is my prayer that this will also be a driving force in my life. Where I failed in the past, I want to confess it to the Lord and those I have hurt; and where I succeeded, I want to give Him the glory.

The last sentence, no doubt, referred to my September newsletter to our ministry friends of the previous year.

In order to facilitate some of those desires, we scheduled a staff retreat in Hans Wilhelm's house in Arnold, California, from January 13-16, 2001. We had finished ten years of ministry since 1989, the year of our incorporation. Erik had replaced me as president of China Partner. He had opened the retreat with a brief report of his vision titled: "Vision for China Partner in 2001 and Beyond."

In the report he first listed some accomplishments:

- In the ten years we had completed thirty-one pastoral training schools (PTS)
- We had taught in fifteen of the eighteen then existing theological schools
- We had legally brought in and distributed over 29,000 theological study books worth $310,000
- We had brought into China twenty-four pastors/para-church leaders representing eight different countries

- We had established a big network of close relationships with Christian leaders all across China
- We earned the respect of the CCC leadership
- Financially we finished the year 2000 stronger than ever before. At that time we had $250,000 in our bank accounts in Canada, Germany, Hong Kong, and the US
- All this was accomplished because of God's faithfulness and as it is recorded in Psalm 118:23, "The Lord has done this, and it is marvelous in our eyes

Then he shared his vision, admitting, "Over the last few weeks I have contemplated much on my new role as president of CP. Part of me is really excited; part of me is scared. However, one thing that has been a big encouragement is the overwhelming support I have witnessed the last two weeks."

- My vision goes beyond our present vision. I want to see that every person living in China is given the opportunity to respond to the Gospel of Jesus Christ
- Continue doing what we have done in the past
- Develop a third workbook [besides evangelistic preaching and pastoral care] on Christian leadership
- Improve evaluation and feedback
- Develop a website in English, German, and Chinese
- Host China conferences
- Acquire staff in Hong Kong
- Incorporate in New Zealand, Australia, and Singapore

Those in attendance were Hans and Alice Wilhelm, Ed Lyman, Bobbie Sartini, Jinglong Zhang, Erik Burklin, Inge, and I. We laid the foundation for the future ministry of China Partner. Brainstorming brought out amazing results. We also discussed and agreed on my role as someone who would work in the background helping wherever it was needed through friend- and fundraising, conducting fact-finding tours in China, and serving as chairman of the CP board.

At this time we were in full swing financially supporting the construction of a Bible school in Nanchang, Jiangxi. Our first installment was RMB 500,000 or DM 125,840 given from our German account (about $75,000 at that time's exchange rate). The total cost of the construction was $475,000. The school would accommodate up to one hundred sixty students. Later we raised an additional RMB 500,000, which Erik handed over at the groundbreaking service of the school.

I had traveled to Jiangxi to meet with Rev. Li Baole on January 12, when we discussed three specific projects: the Bible school in Nanchang, the construction of a new church in Linchuan, some 100 miles south of Nanchang, where my mother had started her missionary career as a single woman, and the construction of another church in Ningdu, where my parents had labored in their final missionary years. Liu Daochang, the ailing pastor in Ningdu, had revealed his final two goals before he would die: the installment of his successor and a new church building.

From Nanchang I continued my travels to Nanjing, where I met with Bishop Ting, Dr. Han, and Rev. Bao. The bishop had invited me to his home on the major day of the most important Chinese holiday—the Lunar New Year. It was an extremely cordial meeting during which we touched on his book *Love Never Ends,* the construction of the Jiangxi Bible School, his concern for Han's health, and my concern about Rev. Bao's overload of work.

Finally in Shanghai, Rev. Su Deci, president of the East China Seminary, met me for breakfast in my hotel. He was extremely interested to meet with me because he wanted to share from his heart about what was going on in the leadership of the CCC. He pleaded with me to be patient. "I don't know whether the future will get better or worse, but I know that God is in control," he said. "During the Cultural Revolution we never thought things would change for the better," he continued, "and, look, what God has done! Therefore, please be patient. I know your heart is pure, and you want to help the church. Please be patient."

We had some of the frankest interaction ever, and he asked me to keep the matters raised confidential. It had been a moving encounter and a blessing to sit in the presence of a seasoned man of God.

Later he told a group of western leaders who had visited the new seminary campus outside of Shanghai, "I have many friends, but Werner Bürklin is my bosom friend."

Wow, what a statement! I shall never forget it!

However, at exactly this time, the controversies between proponents of liberalism and fundamentalism began to erupt and fulminate not only in China, but what is worse, western evangelicals entered the fray with vengeance as well. I was getting concerned about the impact—that this might impede the effectiveness of our China ministry.

We had invited Jinglong Zhang, a former professor of the Nanjing Seminary, to attend one of our board meetings. We needed to get his insight on the matter at hand. So I sent him the following email on March 2, 2001:

> Since you know Nanjing from inside out, you are more qualified to read the trend of Nanjing than I am. I appreciate your giving us counsel how best to see through the fog that is so apparent.

> Interestingly, I received the English translation of the *National Theological Review* just a week ago, but, as I said, so far I have only been able to read one article. Therefore, I am glad that we have you to give us a better understanding, since we have not learned how to read between the lines, or are clouded with a western mindset. I am anxious to read the rest in order to get a more comprehensive view of things.

I wanted a Chinese theologian to help me unravel some of the complexities coming out of Nanjing.

> One thing we must be careful of, and that is not to fall into the trap of only seeing things black and white. Even though I am extremely concerned about the liberal trend at the Nanjing Seminary, I also know that many Christian leaders within the CCC stand firm on fundamental beliefs. This reminds me of the "battle for the Bible" that raged in the western world—mainly in the US—some twenty-five years ago. This battle was not so much between liberals and conservatives, but more between evangelicals and neo-evangelicals, or fundamentalists and evangelicals. Some even called Fuller Seminary to be neo-orthodox. Billy Graham was caught in the midst of these battles, but his wisdom and his balance (*Ausgeglichenheit*) saved the day for the Christian church.

I only hope that we don't get involved in the fray of such struggles, but that we as CP stay focused on helping the body of Christ wherever she is found. The Bible teaches us that the wheat and the tares grow up together, and only God can truly distinguish.

Working in a foreign country and with Christian leaders who had experienced persecution and setbacks during the infamous Cultural Revolution, we needed to be particularly sensitive about theological trends in China. Therefore, I concluded my email:

Furthermore, I pray that we don't get swayed by one group or the other as found here in the West. There are strong divisions between the two: The "underground group" and the "registered group." I believe that in some instances the divisions are cut stronger here in the West than in China itself. I see the body of Christ in both groups. We in CP chose to work with the latter, because we wanted to do things in China openly, honestly, and legally. We also felt that the part of the body of Christ found within the CCC had been shunned or even ostracized by my evangelical friends—and that for years! I learned from Billy Graham that nothing or no one will get us away from the centrality of the Gospel (cross) and from the Bible, but that on the other hand we are willing to work with anyone who respects and accepts our biblical beliefs. So far we fared well.

We heavily depend upon your counsel. We have much to learn from you. So please keep an open mind and heart and tell us frankly what you believe and experience.

These controversies came at a time when I noticed something was not right with my heart. While traveling in China, I noticed some pressure in my heart area. It was not real pain, but some uncomfortable feeling. When I returned home, I was sitting in my easy chair using my laptop to write a few letters. Again I noticed some pressure and told Inge, "Something seems to be wrong with me. I do not know what it is, I feel fine, play tennis, and eat the right things; however, I have these moments of pressure around my heart."

Inge encouraged me to see a doctor right away, which I did. I was stunned with his prognosis: "I need to do an angiogram on you, and you have to check into the hospital right away." "Well," I responded, "Let me drive home, get my stuff, and I will check in."

"No, sir," the doctor said. "My assistant will drive you to the hospital. Call your wife to meet you there. I will not allow you to drive." She did and strangely, after they had put me into a wheelchair at the hospital, she bent down and gave me a kiss on the cheek. At that time I noticed that something must be really wrong with me. I was taken to the intensive care unit and got hooked up with all kinds of gadgets. It was May 24, 2001.

The following day, a Friday, an ambulance took me to the Holy Cross Hospital at Ft. Lauderdale. Sure enough, they found that three of my heart arteries needed attention, one of them was more than ninety percent blocked.

I was the last patient to be worked on late in the afternoon. After he had done angioplasty on one of the three arteries, I heard him shout into the telephone, "You must not be serious! Why did the back-up team go home?"

"I will not be able to go through with the rest of the procedure," he explained to me. "I will have to do the rest next week. All the doctors have taken off for a long holiday weekend."

The following morning he came by at my hospital bed to see how I was doing. "I want to apologize for not finishing the total procedure last evening," he said. "I was so mad on the telephone, because the back-up team of doctors, who always have to stick around for emergency surgery when needed, had taken off without my permission. That's why I had to quit. It would have been too dangerous to continue without the team."

And then he declared with a subdued voice, "Last year the same thing happened, and the patient died because the back-up team had left prematurely."

God again had overruled something that could have gone wrong. I mended quickly, and six weeks later I was back on the tennis court!

Ministry in Europe and beyond

Heiko and Kay were missionaries in Berlin after he had worked as a youth pastor at the First Presbyterian Church in Lake Wales, Florida. It was a rough time for them, because most of the people living in what was formerly part of East Berlin were extremely hostile to the gospel. Therefore, Inge and I decided to visit and encourage them. We were amazed by the phenomenal construction that had taken place ever since Germany was reunited. The new political center of the city was something to behold! And also the area around the *Potsdamer Platz*, where Adolf Hitler's *Führerbunker* originally had been, was totally built up, and it looked gorgeous! So different from the days when I had my evangelistic crusade in the *Schwangere*

Auster, the famous Kongresshalle, so many years ago! Berlin truly had risen from the ashes of the Second World War. I was proud of my home country.

Inge and I love cruises. Kay dropped us off at the *Ostbahnhof* to take the train to Copenhagen, Denmark, where we were to embark on our cruise ship. We stayed at the brand new Hilton hotel near the airport, which I had gotten free of charge with American Express points. We spent many hours walking through Denmark's capital in absolutely adorable weather and ate pizza at the *Lange Linie*.

For one week we sailed around on the Baltic Sea (*Ostsee*), visiting Tallinn (Estonia), St. Petersburg (Russia), Helsinki (Finland), Stockholm and Kalmar (Sweden), and Warnemünde (Germany) before getting back to Copenhagen. St. Petersburg was, no doubt, the most impressive city we saw. The incredible Winter Palace, where the October Revolution took place, was amazing. And then the Hermitage, one of the most spectacular and largest museums of the world! In 1764, Empress Catherine the Great (1729-96), originally from Germany, purchased a considerable collection of Western European paintings, which was the foundation of the museum. Also, the St. Peter and Paul's Cathedral, where Peter the Great, Catherine the Great, and other Tsars are buried, including Nicholas II (1868-1918) and Alexandra, who had been murdered by the Communists on July 17, 1918.

St. Petersburg, however, as a whole with over five million inhabitants, is a dilapidated city. I figured it would take two generations to get everything fixed up. We were driven around in a bus. We stopped along the river Neva to eat our sandwiches that had been prepared on board the ship. Our tour guide admonished us, "Don't throw anything away you cannot eat. I will take it to my daughter." We were ashamed to be told by someone to be careful with food! There are needy people out there and they are hurting. We had to learn anew that food is precious.

As we walked off the ship in Helsinki (also known as the white city of the north), Inge fell and injured her knee. We immediately returned to the ship and consulted a nurse. Praise the Lord, nothing was broken, but she had to lie down and ice-pack her knee. Late in the afternoon she felt well enough to take a sightseeing bus ride through town. We sat on top of an open double-decker bus and enjoyed the interesting ride. Everything looked so peaceful under a sunny sky.

In Stockholm we had a little picnic in a park and were shocked to observe young people openly dealing with hard drugs. In front of our eyes they shot it into their veins. We had seen the same when we lived in Amsterdam, but we had thought this was unique to that city. Apparently not.

One of the highlights of the trip, however, was our trip to the *Lutherstadt* Wittenberg where Martin Luther (1483-1546) had nailed the 95 thesis on the door of the *Schlosskirche*. It was an extremely hot summer day. From the newly constructed train station (the train stations in East Germany were in total disarray) we had to walk about one mile to the Best Western Stadtpalais Hotel, a lovely four-star hotel, but they had given us a non-air-conditioned room—on this extremely hot day. Inge was devastated, and I did not like it either, so I tried and managed to get one for the same price and behold—even an executive room! We showered, then had a bite to eat at a sidewalk café.

Visiting the *Schlosskirche* was an awe-inspiring experience. Just to imagine that four centuries ago, one of the greatest reformers in history changed the course of the then-existing church right here! Inge and I looked with awe at the gravesites of him and Philipp Melanchthon (1497-1560), his close co-reformer friend. "They both had denounced what they claimed was the exaggerated cult of the saints, justification by works, and the coercion of the conscience in the sacrament of penance that nevertheless could not offer certainty of salvation" (Wikipedia). Then we sat down and enjoyed an organ concert that just started that very moment in the welcomed cool church. What a way to worship the Lord, and that away from the heat!

My mother had often told me about the famous evangelical "Allianz Konferenz" at Bad Blankenburg. Well known preachers would expound the Scriptures, and now I had been asked to give a talk about the Chinese situation in the session of "*Blickpunkt*" at that conference. Reinhard Holmer was the director of the convention. He had become famous for personally giving refuge to Erich Honecker, Communist leader of the German Democratic Republic, after he had been ousted by his own people. Christians in general had been delighted by this show of love, because so many citizens of East Germany had only hatred left for Honecker. But Holmer was a true follower of Jesus, illustrating love in a tangible and convincing way.

We greatly enjoyed the conference. The evening sessions were attended by 2,000-plus people—80 percent of them young people. This impressed us greatly.

One of the reasons for traveling in Germany that summer was to minister at the funeral of Inge's mother. She had passed away earlier. Finally on August 5, 2001, we held the memorial service in Bad Orb. Inge's siblings all came and I had the honor to conduct the service.

The following day good friends of ours, Walter and Lore Bühl from Frankfurt, took us out for a sumptuous dinner at the five-star Steigenberger Hotel in the *Kurgarten* of Bad Orb. He and I had served on the World Vision board for years. As the president of one of the largest banks in Germany, he was one of the very few who had steered his bank consortium successfully through a recent banking disaster. He had refused to get involved in speculative maneuvers that had sunk a number of banks. "You have to live within your means, even as a bank executive," he had told me. This came right out of my play-book. I agreed with him wholeheartedly.

Before heading back to the States, Inge and I once more walked through Frankfurt, the city where we had lived so many years ago. It had been totally rebuilt. I wrote in my diary, "So wonderful to be alone with my love—we live it to the fullest." We disembarked at the *Hauptwache* and strolled through the inner city—the *Römer, Dom* (cathedral), Main river, and had dinner at *"Zum Schwarzen Stern,"* a lovely and newly rebuilt restaurant, which had been destroyed during American bombing raids. Before the Second World War this building had more windows than any other house in Frankfurt, we were told. Anyways, the food was superb and I enjoyed the time so much with my love.

Back in the States, one of our objectives we had for some time at China Partner was to meet with some of the Chinese pastors who had moved to the United States and Canada. Some had come to advance their theological degrees, and others were in disagreement with the leadership of TSPM and stayed overseas. We invited thirteen of them to Billy Graham's *Cove* in Asheville, NC, for a time of reflection, consultation, and encouragement. Located on 1,200 acres, nestled in the Blue Ridge Mountains, the Billy Graham Training Center's (BGTC) property rises from 2,120 feet at the main entrance to 3,961 feet at the top of Cedar Mountain. It has a 70,000 square foot training center building, as well as two inns, and the Chatlos Memorial Chapel, which houses the BGTC visitor center.

We flew in from Boca Raton and rented an Avis car. While waiting for the car, we chatted with one of the attendees of the conference, and one of the Avis people overheard our conversation. When he handed me the key, he said, "I liked what I heard, therefore, here is the key to a Cadillac." Wow, I think this was the first time I had driven a Cadillac.

When we arrived at the *Cove,* I wondered what the folks at Billy Graham's resort would think. Having worked with him for years, I knew how he felt about extravagant or excessive gizmos. But no one nitpicked.

The times with our Chinese friends turned out to be "an extremely spiritual retreat," as I noted in my journal. Erik had told them that we did not have an agenda and that it was an informal meeting. They loved it, and we were thankful to the Lord to have led us that way. We also had given them enough free time to spend in the lovely woods, praying and sharing with each other. Wang Hao, formerly the right hand man for Rev. Bao in Nanjing and whose trip from Birmingham, England, we had paid for (he went to seminary there) wrote us after the retreat:

> Sharing with my wife all the beautiful things the Lord had done in our lives over the last days, I am feeling very much like waking up from a dream. I cannot believe, but praise Him that we met at the Cove, one of the places on earth I have longed for, and we so much enjoyed our time of fellowship together! I felt so blessed in spending time alone praying to

God, sharing His Word, and discussing our mutual concerns with you and my Chinese friends that I've really come away renewed in spirit and strength.

I want to thank you, pastor Werner, particularly for the private time you spent in counseling and guiding me. The time was short; your words were not many, but they are all part of your consistent love and care for me.

The icing on the cake for the Chinese was when Ruth Graham was driven from her home to meet "her Chinese." Even though weak and frail, she forced herself out of bed, and her daughter Gigi drove her to the Cove. She could not get out of the car, so everyone filed by her car window for a personal chat.

Following the retreat, Inge and I were invited by the BGEA staff to stay on for another two days. Inge had coaxed me to "storm up" the mountain, but it really was too much for an old man. It took us some four hours! Exhausted, we had a nice dinner in Ruth's favorite restaurant in Asheville.

The following day John Akers, the right hand of Billy Graham, invited us to dinner. We were seated in a far corner that had a plaque "for Billy and Ruth Graham." John shared with us that "Billy is very tired, has a hard time to sign letters, has no energy, and is in constant therapy to regain some strength in-between crusades."

September 11, 2001, is a day I shall never forget. In the morning I was on the phone with my travel agent discussing my next trip, when he suddenly exclaimed, "Turn on your TV! Something terrible is taking place in New York."

I watched in horror as two airliners crashed into two towers of the World Trade Center. In disbelief I saw them finally collapse and disintegrate in two massive piles of rubble. Close to three-thousand people perished on that morning. Terrorists instigated by Bin Laden had highjacked four planes; two plowed into New York, one into an open field in Pennsylvania, and a fourth into the Pentagon. President Bush happened to be in Florida when this happened, was taken to a safe place in the center of the nation, but then flew back to Washington that evening. As all of America looked on, he came through as a strong leader. His approval ratings soared to 91 percent, the highest any sitting president ever received.

Two days later he gave a rousing speech to the Congress and the nation. The nation was glued to TV sets. What a speech! "Great to have a president who believes in prayer and who lives up to the mandates and challenges of the presidency. What a difference between him and the former one," I wrote in my journal.

On September 14 at noon, the Washington Cathedral was filled to capacity for a special "Day of Prayer and Remembrance." All living former presidents were present, and Billy Graham spoke, so did President George W. Bush, but Billy was the only one who got a standing ovation. Amazing, how he is appreciated and honored—a true "nation's pastor," as he now is called.

Not only America changed that day, but also the world, as it viewed the Islamic faith in a new light. Never before had people world-wide taken a new appraisal on what Islamic fundamentalists might do to those who are not following their faith. It sent shivers up and down the spines of many. Something had to be done about it. However, the worry or even fear about being targeted by those fundamentalists was so great that government leaders were scared to openly speak out against them. Not so Mitt Romney, who as a candidate to dethrone Barack Obama in 2012 wrote the following in his book *No Apology:*

Violent jihadism: the fanatical, terrorist, and always threatening branch of extreme fundamentalist Islam. Despite the theological differences between radical Sunni Wahhabism and radical Shia extremism, both endeavor to cause the collapse of all competing economics and systems of government, and thereby, in a last-man-standing approach, become the world's leading power—in fact, its sole power. In the minds of Jihadists, there is only one legitimate government and it is waiting to be unleashed: a caliphate with the global reach and power.

Violent jihadist groups come in many stripes across the spectrum, from Hamas to Hezbollah, from the Muslim Brotherhood to al Qaeda, and from Lashkar-e-Taiba to Jais-e-Mohammed. Each espouses causes that are unique to its own branch of Islamism and to its own geographic region—independence for Chechnya, political dominance in the Sudan, hegemony over Kashmir, and so on. But without question, the jihadists also share a common overarching goal: violent holy war on America and the West, the destruction of Israel and the Jews, the recapture of all lands once held by the Muslims, the elimination of "infidel" leaders in Muslim nations like Jordan, Egypt, and Saudi Arabia, and ultimately, the defeat of all non-Muslim nations.

No one knows what the future holds and whether the Islamists will succeed to wipe Israel off the map and establish a "caliphate with global reach and power." I personally don't think so. I trust the Bible, the true Word of God, which promises the glorious return of Christ and the establishment of His Kingdom. However, until then many will go through tempestuous times as it is also taught in the Scriptures.

I am confident that we shall overcome.

Until then, our ministry had to go on. Many opportunities were awaiting us. On my next trip to China, I recorded into my journal:

> After a quiet breakfast with my love at a nicely set table [Inge always, on every Sunday, would set the most beautiful table for both of us to enjoy], we left for the Miami airport. It was hard for her to let me leave—she had tears in her eyes. During our forty-plus years of marriage we had to say good-bye so often, but it doesn't get easier.

Hefei is the capital city of Anhui, the province where I was born. This is also the city where I preached my first sermon in China. It always brings back many memories how my mother had to walk for a long while to the American Hospital in Wuhu, because the ordered rickshaw had not turned up on time. It was shortly after 4 a.m. and she almost did not make it. My father, who had helped her along, was very concerned but was overjoyed to assist Dr. Watters with the birth in "Dr. Mantel und Mütze" (doctor garb and cap) as he revealed in his diary. It was 8 a.m. on Sunday morning, the most important day of my life—the beginning of a marvelous and rewarding existence!

On October 5, 2001, in Hefei, I was up at 5:50 a.m. for my final sermon preparations. The worship service started at 8 a.m. and when we arrived we were overwhelmed with another incredible sight. People were sitting everywhere—inside and outside. Due to the rain, many were sitting under umbrellas. There was hardly enough room to squeeze through the throng of people to reach the platform. The building itself seats only eight hundred plus people, but over two thousand were present—possibly even three thousand! In the afternoon I preached once more at 2:30 p.m. and it was as crowded as at the morning service.

We were overwhelmed to experience again firsthand how God was moving in China!

We had come to teach at the theological seminary on biblical principles of Christian leadership. Rev. Chu, the principal of the school, was deeply moved, and when he thanked us at the end of our courses a week later, he had tears in his eyes. Seldom have I seen Chinese men show emotions like that. Students and teachers alike told us that they had never been taught on such subjects and therefore were deeply appreciative. The doors for future ministry were wide open.

On my seventy-first birthday I put this entry in my journal:

I don't feel any older. I do have some "aches and pains" and tire more quickly—I notice that while playing tennis, but otherwise I feel young. So thrilled that I can still be actively involved in the Lord's work! China is so much on my heart. What great opportunities we have! And what a thrill to see Erik develop into a real leader, taking on more responsibilities in our China ministry! He is so wise, prudent, forward thinking, and careful with finances. And then to have Heiko focused on his ministry in Berlin, which is one of the toughest mission fields in the world. And then have both of our younger children—Stephan and Linda—so committed to the Lord in their fields of ministry—one as a senior executive and the other as a home-schooling mom. The Lord truly has blessed my love and me with dedicated kids.

The following day we went on a cruise again. Vacation time is important for those who are busy in the Lord's work.

We love cruises. It always is a wonderful time of relaxation and getting closer to the Lord. Plowing through the majestic ocean and looking across it makes me marvel at God's miraculous handiwork. I then feel so close to Him. Many ideas for a more aggressive and meaningful ministry go through my mind. And it is thrilling to be alone with my love.

For instance, on November 8th I wrote in my diary:

Sitting on deck, I again had a marvelous "Quiet Time." I am in the Psalms right now; my goal had been to read through the Bible once a year. [By 2011 I had read through the Bible eighty-three times]. Was struck and blessed with Psalm 116:18, "I will pay my vows to the Lord now in the presence of all His people." I had to think back to the vows I had made years back. So blessed to know that I am on track!

The final big event of that year took place in Nanjing. The China Christian Council along with China Partner had invited over fifty well-known Christian leaders representing eleven countries to be part of a China symposium (Australia, Canada, China, England, Germany, Japan, New Zealand, Philippines, Sweden, Switzerland, USA, and of course Hong Kong). Originally Bishop Ting had wanted to take part, however, just before the conclave he had fallen out of his bed, had injured his spine, and was hospitalized. Also, Han Wenzhou had undergone heart surgery and therefore could not attend. But all other important CCC leaders from different parts of China were present.

The meetings took place from December 7-12 and went exceptionally well. My prayer in the morning of the first day had been, "May our Lord meet us in a special way. May He bind us in love and understanding—both us from foreign countries and those from China." God had answered my prayer.

Deng Fucun, one of the stalwarts and elders of CCC, and I gave the final discourses. He went on and on and finally I had to place my watch on the table to make him realize that someone else was waiting to give his final remarks. He sheepishly looked at me and said, "The watch tells me I have to hand over to Rev. Lin Mingdan"—which is my Chinese name.

In closing, CP hosted a fellowship dinner at TSPM Provincial Hostel, followed by the last prayer and sharing time. I sensed a beautiful spirit and, no doubt, most of the foreign participants were moved and challenged by what they had experienced. We were able to validate the motives for our ministry and demonstrate our genuine desire to serve the church in China. The friendships were significantly deepened.

The response from foreign participants was extraordinary. The executive director of the International Bible Society of Europe wrote:

> Greetings from Sweden! I just want to thank you very much for the privilege of having been invited to the China symposium. I really could not have got a better introduction to a part of the world which I knew only marginally about. You have been able to build all these valuable relationships over the years and in your very generous spirit you offer others to benefit from all your hard work. That shows the quality of China Partner and of its leadership!

The president of the Institute of Theological Studies in Grand Rapids, Michigan, wrote this:

The quality of your ministry was evident at every point—from all the logistics to all meetings. You provided us with an outstanding opportunity to learn about the Chinese church. This was one of the most inspiring weeks of my life.

Peter Conlan of Operation Mobilization, England, penned this:

I think I learned more on this trip than many other trips combined.

As we entered a New Year, someone sent me this hilarious commentary in German, which had been written on January 1, 1864 (sorry, it is in German):

Herr, setze dem Überfluss Grenzen und lass die Grenzen überflüssig werden. Nimm den Ehefrauen das letzte Wort und erinnere die Ehemänner an ihr erstes. Gib' den Regierenden ein besseres Deutsch und den Deutschen eine bessere Regierung. Schenke uns und unseren Freunden mehr Wahrheit und der Wahrheit mehr Freunde. Bessere solche Beamte, die wohl tätig, aber nicht wohltätig sind, und lasse die, die rechtschaffen sind, auch Recht schaffen. Sorge dafür, dass wir alle in den Himmel kommen, aber, wenn du willst, noch nicht gleich!

Preaching down-under

The New Year had started with a bang—Inge and I were on our way "down under." The twelve-hour flight on Air New Zealand from Los Angeles to Auckland in first class was superb—we never had traveled together in such luxury! All made possible with frequent flyer miles! Our entire cost was $40 for taxes.

Another first was having been sniffed out by a dog. Inge had to open her bag. Even though no fruit was found, the dog detected that she had carried a banana in the bag while in the United States. Amazing, how dogs can sniff out such delicate scents.

Wilbur Wright, my YFC friend and China coworker, drove us to the Hilton Hotel, a gorgeous hotel right on the harbor. He loaned us his car for a week of vacation on the northern island of New Zealand called Waitangi. It was here where on February 7, 1840, the treaty was signed between the Crown of England, represented by Hobsen, and chiefs of several Māori tribes. It kept the rights for Māori land ownership and gave them rights as British subjects. It is a gorgeous vacation spot.

A boat took us to the famous "Hole in the Rock," and because of good weather the boat slid right through the hole. Inge and I climbed a small hill on an island while others had their lunch. So glad we did, rejoicing in God's beautiful nature.

My real reason for our trip to "down-under" was exploring if and in what way we could or should establish China Partner in that region of the world. In Auckland we met with sixty Chinese Christian leaders, counseled with Ian Grant, formerly director of NZ Youth for Christ, who had read in the newspaper of my coming; preached at two Sunday services in the allegedly largest church of NZ—Greenlane Church—where a number received Christ and others recommitted their lives "to get spiritually involved in this new year of 2002"; gave an interview at NZ's largest Christian magazine *Challenge Weekly;* met with Rev. John Walton at Lake Taupo; stopped in Rotorua to view the geothermal springs, geysers, and mud pools, and to smell the faint sulphur scent lingering in the air, evidence of volcanic history; visited Rev. Graeme Birch in Napier, who encouraged me to form "an independent mission agency as a base for an effective ministry in NZ"; counseled with the chairman of the United Bible Society in NZ, David Harrison, and with Jimmy Chew, Asia director for the Navigators in Wellington, the capital city of NZ.

We then took the ferry to the South Island and met with Bishop Derek Eaton of the Anglican Cathedral in Nelson, who was formerly a missionary in Tunisia. He gave me some good pointers about the church situation in NZ and is for us the key Anglican contact in NZ. In the lovely town of Franz Josef we took a thirty-minute helicopter ride up to the Franz Josef Glacier—absolutely stunning—as part of the Southern Alps with Mt. Tasman and Mt. Cook! Being in a World Heritage Area, recognized as one of the world's foremost natural landscapes, gripped us with awe. At Arthur's Pass we had booked a room in the Chalet, a bed & breakfast hotel. It was the worst accommodation on our trip; however the surroundings made up for it. At 8:30 p.m. we could still see the spectacular sun-covered mountaintops.

The following morning I took a walk to the village chapel to pray. As I knelt in this small chapel, I thanked the Lord for a wonderful life and rededicated my life to the Lord as I gazed upon a rushing waterfall seen through the altar window. Then I walked up the mountain and sat on a rock amidst a sparkling brook. I just love to hear the gushing sound, and it reminded me of such brooks in Germany's Black Forest.

Off to Christchurch. Next to the beautiful huge park including a botanical garden, we found an elegant hotel—Chateau on the Park. I was deeply encouraged by the testimony of Rev.

Murray Robertson, the minister of the largest Baptist church in NZ, so I sat down in the hotel to write a letter to Billy Graham:

"Presently Inge and I are traveling through New Zealand, trying to encourage Christian leaders to get involved in China. As you know, all of them receive one-sided news about the situation in China. We try to balance this out, sharing with them the good with the bad. However, most are not aware about the phenomenal opportunities Christians have to minister freely in that country. One of the Christian leaders we saw is the pastor of the largest Baptist church in NZ. He faithfully served in the same church for thirty-two years! But what really thrilled me was to hear how he became a Christian.

As a teenager he heard you preach in Wellington and asked Christ to come into his life. He finished education, attended a theological seminary, and then was called as a young man to pastor a small dying Baptist church in Christchurch. Over the years he built a strong biblical church, even though he had to cope with a number of difficulties. However, he stuck it out, and now he can look back to a blessed ministry. And it all started in a stadium in Wellington under your preaching.

A four-hour drive away was Blenheim, where we checked into the Chateau of Marlborough Hotel. The evening sun blasted through the window into our room, and in spite of a moving fan, our room was very hot. We sought refuge at a Chinese restaurant, whose owner had emigrated from China with a Cambodian wife at his side, but it was hot wherever we went. Living in Florida with all the amenities including air-conditioning had made us vulnerable.

On our way back to the North Island we set sail from Picton, but it was a rough trip. It reminded me of the first trip I had taken across the English Channel from Calais to Dover many years ago. Then I had vowed I would never put my foot on a ferry again—I threw up all the way to Great Britain. This time Inge had that experience, moaning, "How long will it take us to arrive on the other side?" Due to bad weather, the trip took twenty minutes longer—some three and one-half hours altogether! Those were the longest twenty minutes we have ever experienced.

In Wellington Rev. Paul Jackson with his wife invited us to preach in their church at the town nearby, Upper Hut. They had bought a large factory/warehouse type of a building seating eight hundred people. The church services in NZ are mostly charismatically orientated with lots of singing during the first half of the service and all of it standing up. And this for thirty minutes! As a seventy-year-old guy I wondered why this was necessary. I was tempted to ask the congregation to keep standing throughout my preaching while I would sit! I did not.

Sydney in Australia is a beautiful city. The city was established in 1788 as a penal colony by Arthur Phillip, commodore of the First Fleet of England. We were immediately invited to meet with Gordon Moyes, pastor of a large Methodist church. His church was active all across the city with a staff of 3,100—yes, you are reading right—3,100! He had read about me in *Decision* magazine of BGEA and wanted to make a radio interview with me about China.

Then I was off to St. Andrews Cathedral to meet with Archbishop Harry Goodhew. He greeted me with, "I am Harry." His interest in China was immense because during the heydays of missions, Australia had sent many missionaries into China.

He had been my contact person in Australia when I directed the Amsterdam '83 and '86 conferences.

It was in Canberra where we heard the news that Sam Wolgemuth (1914-2002), former president of Youth for Christ International, had died on February 5. I immediately sent a letter to his wife Grace:

> Inge and I are grieving with you and the many of Sam's friends around the world. Like no other person, Sam has shown me how to walk like Jesus did. I never achieved His standard, but I tried. Sam was my mentor in this respect. I shall always be grateful for his example.

Once someone had told me, "If you would like to know what heaven is like, you have to live in the home of the Wolgemuths."

On our way from Canberra to Melbourne we drove through some dry and gray countryside. Such long hauls have always been a blessing to me, just being alone with Inge. We had so much to share, took hours praying together as we rolled along and enjoyed the many new sights. We stopped in the middle of nowhere and had a cup of cappuccino at the "first known bakery of Australia," opened in 1846 by William Bibo, a German immigrant (I'm sure his name actually was Wilhelm). The cappuccino was the best I have had since Switzerland.

In Melbourne we met with David Wraight, YFCI Pacific Area director and later president of Youth for Christ International. Ross Prout, editor of *New Life Press,* interviewed us and printed a well-balanced report on Christian ministries in China. We also had lunch with Rev. Sun Wai Kway, pastor for the Chinese congregation of Syndal Baptist Church. He had studied in Hong

Kong, USA, and Germany and speaks flawless German. I have never heard a Chinese speak German so well!

In Adelaide, Australia, we had an interesting encounter with a "bloke" (an Australian expression) and heard his remarkable story. Peter Daniels, seventy years old, picked us up for dinner with his Rolls Royce. He had planned to give one million dollars each to Youth for Christ, The Hour of Power, and BGEA. He told me his story (whether he ever did give his millions I don't know). Born into a poor family with a mother who had married four times, he was a poor student, failed all classes, was put into a special class for dumb children, and was a dyslexic. His teachers scolded him, punished and spanked him, but nothing worked. He started as a poor bricklayer. By accepting the Lord in a Billy Graham meeting, he changed his life and became a wealthy entrepreneur. He built a mansion so large that he could fit a huge portrait of his wife into the lobby. Another way of saying it, he built his house around the portrait! He lives on an estate about one hour from Adelaide. He lectures on business subjects around the world. He, of course, is quite proud of his achievements, but he also has straight morals and deep convictions about family and married life.

What an example of what God can do in a person's life!

Always anxious to learn from others how to improve our training materials for China, I sat in on a pastoral training session in Brisbane taught by Leigh Brown, director of Ambassadors for Christ and a board member of BGEA in Australia. Later we invited him to teach at our pastoral training schools (PTS) in China.

Brisbane, on the snaky river Brisbane, is one of my favorite cities. On July 17, 1799, Flinders landed at what is now known as Woody Point, which he named "Red Cliff Point" after the red-colored cliffs visible from the bay. In 1823, the governor of New South Wales, Thomas Brisbane, instructed that a new northern penal settlement be developed, and an exploration party led by John Oxley further explored Moreton Bay. German missionaries settled at Zion's Hill, as early as 1837, five years before Brisbane was officially declared a free settlement. The band consisted of two ministers, Christopher Eipper (1813–1894), and Carl Wilhelm Schmidt and lay missionaries. They were allocated two hundred sixty hectares and set about establishing the mission, which became known as German Station. More recently, the city played a central role in the Allied campaign during World War II as the South West Pacific headquarters for General Douglas MacArthur (Wikipedia).

But to really enjoy the city, you need to take the speedboat *CityCat* and race along the river. What a speed and what a sight! Brian and Moira Andrews had told us, "You need to take that ride—very exhilarating." It surely was.

He also had asked me to preach at his church, and I asked him to join us on one of our teaching ministries in China, which he later did. Amazing, the friends we were able to make across the countries "down under." In all, we had visited twenty-six cities, consulted with twenty-nine people about establishing CP, slept in twenty-two beds, and traveled 4,620 km by car. All major cities were founded as penal colonies except Adelaide.

However, one of the most unforgettable vacations we ever took was a trip to northeastern Australia around Cairns. We first stayed in the little town of Port Douglas north of Cairns in a beautiful hotel with a fifty-meter swimming pool, surrounded by a rain forest. It rained "cats and dogs." The highlight was a cruise on an air-conditioned catamaran to the Great Barrier Reef. The beautiful coral cay of Green Island is a protected marine national park, topped with emerald rainforest and surrounded by white sandy beaches and magnificent coral reefs. Green Island is fifteen nautical miles (twenty-seven kilometers) from Cairns. The Great Barrier Reef is Australia's greatest natural treasure, and the world's largest coral reef. This underwater wonderland stretches for 2,300 km (1,426 miles) from Bundaberg to Australia's northernmost tip. At its closest, it's only 30 km (18.5 miles) away from the Queensland coast.

We were told that the Great Barrier Reef encompasses almost 3,000 individual reefs. Their multicolored beauty is made up of 400 types of living and dead coral polyps, home to around 1,500 species of fish, 4,000 kinds of clams, 500 types of seaweed, 200 species of birds, 1,500 different sponges, and half a dozen varieties of turtles.

On the one-and-a-half-hour return jaunt from this gorgeous site, Inge and I were standing at the bow thanking God for His magnificent handiwork that we just experienced. The sun was shining brightly and the brisk wind was tussling at our hair. Holding hands we were thanking the Lord for the privilege to enjoy such marvelous tourist attractions, a sight we shall never forget!

CHAPTER 29

"JESUS NEVER LEFT CHINA"

ON THE OTHER side of the globe in Budapest, Hungary, the conference "Theological Consultation HOPE 21" convened from April 27 to May 1 with one thousand delegates. I had been asked to give a lecture at the theological track on "The Role of Theological Education for a Changing Church and Society in China." Erik had joined me for that event, and from there we traveled to Oslo, Norway, to meet with Chen Xida, a former professor at the Nanjing Theological Seminary.

He and his fellow teacher, Ji Tai, had been dissenters and activists against the theology of Bishop Ting. Years before, both of them had met with me at the Central Hotel in Nanjing for dinner and had warned me about the liberal streak that the bishop was embarking on. I had been well aware of this and had expressed my concern in a letter to our ministry friends mentioned earlier in my memoir. However, that fateful dispatch of mine had caused a firestorm in the halls of theological institutions across China. Only after my apologies, the former friendships and amiable relationships were restored. But Chen Xida had no appreciation for this—he remained a hardliner. He thought it had been wrong for me to apologize.

With the visit we wanted to show our admiration for his steadfastness in a controversial matter. But we also wanted to help him balance this with understanding and brotherly love. In my lifetime I had seen the corrosive aftereffects of harsh judgmental opinions. Billy Graham had shown me and others how to approach controversies with dignity and respect. He never abandoned his firm beliefs but made known his convictions with love and deference. This, I felt, Chen Xida needed to learn.

He never did, at least, not until then.

When Daniel Hsu, who had translated my book *Jesus Never Left China* into Chinese, asked him to promote it among his Chinese Christian constituents in Scandinavia where he then lived, he reacted violently against it. He had not been willing, as yet, to accept our counsel to disagree agreeably [with Bishop Ting]. I know it is a difficult proposition, but necessary to learn so that we can grow spiritually.

Many years later we finally had a chance to address this issue once more. God had done His work of grace and now we are looking forward to seeing each other with a congenial disposition, if not here on this earth, but then in heaven.

There was joy in Nanchang in 2002—great, unspeakable joy! "Today God is smiling on us," Lin Feng, president of the Bible school said. "Yesterday it rained all day long, and today we have this gorgeous sunshine." It had rained every day for three weeks straight before that. Firecrackers went off for five long minutes! The Chinese really know how to celebrate. Firecrackers are also used to scare evil spirits away. I remembered that from my youth, however, here it was an expression of heavenly joy.

The Bible school had been established ten years earlier. Teaching was first done on the balcony of a local church, then the school was moved a couple of times to other locations. Finally a sizable plot of land had been purchased where the first campus of the permanent theological institution would be housed. This was a great day.

All the students and faculty members along with members of the Christian community had gathered to celebrate. The dignitaries of the municipal government made their speeches. Erik, as the leading representative of China Partner, made a few remarks and handed over a red envelope—that's the Chinese way of dispensing presents—which contained a check of RMB 500,000 (about $75,000) as our first downpayment. CP had committed a total of $125,000 toward this project. All of us grabbed ribboned shovels for the perfunctory breaking ground ceremony.

Following the celebration we joined the dignitaries for a sumptuous banquet. "The future for you helping us to train young leaders in Jiangxi's Bible school looks bright," Li Baole, chairman of Jiangxi's Christian Council pronounced with the government leaders looking on. We were well on the way, becoming an intimate part of our Chinese friends.

Torrey Johnson (1909-2002), founding president of Youth for Christ, had been a close friend of mine. He was a world Christian and had supported my ministry when he was senior pastor at Bibletown, later renamed Boca Raton Community Church. He loved the work we were doing in China. He was the one who had hired Billy Graham as the first full time worker for YFC. On his first day of employment Billy was led into the YFC office in Chicago. "Where is my office?" Billy asked. Torrey shot back, "I sit on this side of the desk and you on the other side." There was only one desk in the room.

When I was a teenager in Shanghai I had first heard about Torrey. Bob Pierce had come to China as YFC evangelist, and under his ministry I had committed my life to full time Christian service. Torrey had sent him to China while he took Billy Graham to Europe. Torrey had been a beacon in my life and I had cherished his counsel from time to time. I had worked for YFC for more than forty years.

On May 15, 2002, he passed on to glory. His wife died on the same day! I thank God for Torrey and look forward to meeting up with him in heaven down the road.

Before going on an Alaska cruise, Inge and I decided to do something special for CP. We sent Erik an email:

While traveling in China [a few weeks back] the Lord had convicted me of making plans to raise money for CP without getting personally involved myself. I struggled with this for some time, but when I shared my thoughts with Mutti [Inge], we together decided to send some money from our savings.

Enclosed please find the check [$20,000]. The money should go to "wherever most needed" or the general fund. Have a good day.

In response Erik wrote:

I don't know what to say! I couldn't believe my eyes when I opened the mail today. I can't accept this! Are you sure about this?

I was so surprised, shocked, excited, happy, and overwhelmed, all at the same time. Thank you, thank you, and thank you—for your most generous gift. Is this really what you want to do right now? I didn't even know that you had so much money available.

So wonderful that we were able to do this! It must have been a real encouragement to him. He is doing such a fine job. We answered:

Yes, our dear son, it is our donation. When the Lord speaks, we have to listen. Even though humanly speaking, we possibly should not have done this, because I want to leave enough money for Mutti in case I should go home sooner than she, we still feel it was the right thing to do. It is hard always to ask others to sacrifice, especially so if oneself is not willing to do the same. We know one thing for sure—the Lord will take care of us.

So, please accept it with our love. We believe in you and in what you are doing.

Often I had been confronted with concerns of evangelical Christians in the West about the church in China. "Are those Chinese Christians truly biblical in their theology? What about their leadership?"

Well, as a typical example to answer those well-meaning critics, this is what happened on February 19, 2003, at the Nanjing Theological Seminary, as faculty and students celebrated the ordination of eight new professors. The candidates made the following pledge in front of God and the congregation:

I am willing to receive the sacred title of *Minister of Word and Sacrament.* By doing so, I pledge to dedicate myself to deny myself, to carry the cross, to serve the flock whole-heartedly, and to serve the Lord. I believe that the Scripture is inspired by God, and thereby contains all doctrines sufficient for our salvation, and that Scripture as such is authoritative for our faith and morality. I pledge to be diligent and loyal in teaching biblical truth, in preaching the gospel of Christ, in rightly administering Sacraments, in abiding by church constitutions and rules, and in safeguarding the Church with the true Word.

What a testimony to their faith in God!

Then the epidemic SARS (Severe Acute Respiratory Syndrome) struck in China in early 2003. Within a matter of weeks, it spread from the southern province of Guangdong to Hong Kong and thirty-seven other countries. We had been advised by the church leadership in China to postpone our trip that had been scheduled for May. We did, but then continued our ministry in China a couple of months later after the epidemic had run its course.

While teaching in Nanchang, God provided a Chinese English professor from the Jiangxi University of that city to be our interpreter. She had a remarkable testimony, which I must include; Susan Zou is her name:

In June of 1989, which was a hard time because of the Tiananmen Square Incident, I asked for a leave of absence to go to Xiamen, a small and beautiful seashore city in Fujian province. One day I saw my house keeper reading a very thick book. It was a Bible. I was surprised because I thought

452

only philosophers and scholars would be able to understand the Bible. How someone with little education like her could understand such a book was a mystery to me. In college I had been told by my literature professor to understand European literature one had to read the Bible.

I then borrowed a Bible from the library. I was able to recognize individual words using a dictionary, but I did not understand its meaning. It was hard to believe. It took me two months to get through Genesis but then conceded that only God could understand—and I stopped reading it.

My maid then said, "Only those who believe in God can open the book, unbelievers cannot." *Without much education she must be a philosopher* I thought. Later she asked me whether I would like to accept Jesus as my Savior. She was embarrassed when I confessed that I did not know who He is. I felt ashamed that I must have hurt her. So I asked, "What must I do to accept Jesus?" She appeared happy and then asked me to kneel. Then I felt awkward, but being afraid to hurt her again, I pretended to agree.

From then on my life took a turn. I was accused to have been part of demonstrations against the government following the Tiananmen Incident. They tried to force me to confess that I had joined the students' activities in Xiamen. I refused and felt helpless. I lost my friends and was afraid to share my anxieties with my parents and siblings. But I started reading the Bible my housekeeper had given me. I didn't know how to pray, but whenever I read the Bible I felt a peace in my heart.

Since I would rather die than compromise my innocence, I was challenged by my accusers with three conditions for punishment: publically make a self-criticism; accept a lower salary; and give up lecturing. If I would have agreed to those stipulations, I knew that they would conclude that I had conspired against the government after all. I knew that they were setting me up for a trap. So I refused.

On that special cold night of January in Nanchang, with the open Bible on my knees and in deep thought I heard a voice saying, "Why don't you ask them to show evidence to prove they are right?" They had claimed that I was being investigated by the Xiamen State Security because they had a photo showing me in those students' demonstrations.

The following morning I told them I would accept the three conditions once they could show me the evidence of their accusation. If they could not, I would file a suit against them. A miracle happened that afternoon. A guy came to me, stating they had made a mistake and asked me not to be angry. Three weeks later their accusations were dropped and I was asked to resume lecturing. Without their apologies I refused. Having nothing to do, feeling alone, I began talking to God and reading the Bible. I spent the whole year reading the Bible and at the end of 1990 I returned to Xiamen. One night I made a decisive choice to kneel and to confess my sins and then accepted Christ as my personal Savior. I saw His precious blood dropping for me from the cross and then wept for a long time.

He opened my heart to understand His Word of Life. He taught me how to love Him and people around me—even my enemies.

My conversion upset my family. They tried to force me to give up my belief. This brought me closer to the Lord. Six months later, my mother accepted Christ; two years later, my dad; and another four years later, my two brothers did. I saw many others saved by simply sharing the Word with them. Even though I am weak and weary, it says in 2 Corinthians 12:9, "My grace is sufficient for you, for my power is made perfect in weakness."

While we go to China to be a blessing to them, we in turn are being blessed by people like Susan Zou. There is so much that we in the West can learn from our Chinese brothers and sisters in Christ.

As the year 1990 came to a close and the New Year loomed before me, I reminisced how the Lord has blessed us. I confided this in my journal on December 31:

The New Year has come! Looking back on this past year I'm again thankful and amazed at God's sustaining power. He helped us in our ministry; we were able to lead people to Christ; plans for 1991 were finalized; we are trusting Him for another year of service for Him. If only I could get closer to Jesus, walk in His footsteps, do the things that are pleasing to Him, be considerate and kind to others, but ruthless toward sin, always being upright, honest, pure, and holy! For this I need God's presence and power!

CHAPTER 30

CHINA—SHORT OF THEOLOGICAL INSTITUTIONS

CONSTRUCTION IN CHINA goes fast! Everywhere high-rise buildings are shooting out of the ground. That's why we were not surprised to receive the invitation to attend the dedicatory service of the Nanchang Bible School several months later. A clear blue sunny sky greeted us on a breezy October morning as we met on top of "God's Mountain," as the local Christians call the tallest "hill" outside of Nanchang, where the campus of the new Jiangxi Provincial Bible School is located. As we were being led to our seats, Lin Feng, principal of the JPBS, said, "God is smiling on our school today."

The school grounds had been ornately decorated with red Chinese balloons, and a huge blow-up arch welcomed everyone who attended. Fluttering from the dormitory building was a red banner with white Chinese characters which read "Jiangxi Provincial Bible School New Campus Celebration Ceremony."

As I looked over the two buildings—one serves as a dormitory, the other includes a small library, classrooms, and offices—I

noticed a red cross crowning the classroom building. It looked
so beautiful against the rich, blue sky. I couldn't help but smile
inside as I remembered what Rev. Li had told us several years
earlier when he had showed us the hillside where the new Bible
school was to be built. He had said, "When our buildings are
completed, we will put a big cross on top so that everyone in
the area will know that this is the place where young people
are being trained for Christian ministry." They surely were
not hiding behind bushes as so many in the West had claimed
Christians in China needed to do. They openly confessed that
Jesus is their Lord.

Inge had joined me on this specific trip. We had traveled
to Shanghai, Nanchang, Linchuan, Ningdu, Nanjing, and
Guangzhou.

But Linchuan stands out. Years ago, before my mother had
passed on to glory, she had told me on a walk we took together
outside of Zwingenberg in Germany, "Linchuan was the first
city after language school, where I began my practical missionary
work before I was sent on to Nancheng." Now we were back
there to attend the groundbreaking ceremonies of a 1,800-seat
church. Our team was greeted on the open street with loud,
blasting trumpets before entering the old church, where my
folks had ministered so many years ago. Even here in the back
country, the Christians didn't go into hiding. They were out in
force. It was a Tuesday morning, but the church was packed with
hundreds of Bible-carrying believers. Followed by a sumptuous
meal that had been prepared by the women of the church we
moved to the site where the new church was going to be built.
We were overwhelmed seeing the faith of those Chinese believers.

Ningdu was our next stop. This was the last city in which my parents had labored before being sent home in 1950. The local pastor wanted to build a 500-seat church, but the director of the government's Religious Affairs Bureau said to me, "No, that would be too small a church; the church should hold at least 1,000 people!" I marveled at the Lord's doing in using secular officials to build His church in China.

2003 had again been a blessed and prosperous year. Erik and I reflected on what God allowed us to accomplish during that year.

1. **Pastoral training**

   This year we had strategized afresh how we can best help the leadership in China train their emerging young Christian leaders. Some changes had been made. We were thrilled with more short-term lectures given in Nanchang and Guangzhou. One of the top church leaders in China had told us, "What is acceptable at secular universities should also be permitted at religious institutions. We desperately need help from overseas." CP will continue to be involved with this and do what is possible and appropriate. We will help with expertise and finances.

2. **Literature**

   CP shipped over one hundred sets of theological study books to Jiangxi Bible School. Since 1991 CP has legally shipped over 30,000 theological books worth hundreds of thousands of dollars into China.

3. **Construction of a new Bible school**

   CP has financially supported the construction of the new Bible school in Nanchang, Jiangxi. So far, two five-story buildings have been completed—one for dormitories accommodating up to one hundred sixty students, which also includes a kitchen and dining hall and the other for offices, classrooms, a small library, and a chapel. The second phase will include a church seating one thousand people.

4. **Building of new churches in the province of Jiangxi**
   CP had been asked to help with the construction of churches in two cities—one in Linchuan seating 1,800 people and the other in Ningdu seating up to 1,000 people.

5. **Scholarships**
   CP gave thirty partial scholarships to needy students. Similarly we helped support forty poor, local pastors in Jiangxi, who cannot subsist on the meager salaries they receive from their churches.

6. **Support of Chinese students who study abroad**
   Currently CP is partially supporting a pastor from Taiyuan, Shaanxi, who is working on his M.Div. degree. CP is interested in helping Chinese receive solid, biblical education in theological institutions overseas.

7. **Study trips**
   CP took a group of pastors and Christian leaders from Germany, Switzerland, New Zealand, and the U.S. to China to allow them to get to know the church situation first hand. CP uses such trips to help educate foreign Christian leaders about the church in China

As we were traveling this summer to Shanghai, Nanchang, Linchuan, Wuhan, Hangzhou, Tianjin, Beijing, and Hong Kong, we were delighted to see pastors in some cities like Wuhan give open invitations to receive Christ. Coming from a German background, I know that this is not being done in

Europe very much. This usually is more done in Baptist and non-denominational churches in the US. So we were surprised to hear Rev. Wang encourage people to come forward after I had preached. Over thirty walked forward that morning! While they came, the rest of the worshipers were celebrating by clapping and singing, "I need Jesus, I need Jesus." After the pastor had prayed for these new believers, counselors passed out brochures explaining "the next steps" for their newfound faith. Here was a pastor who used his evangelistic passion by giving open invitations! Over five hundred new converts had been baptized in his church during the previous two years.

One morning I received word that a church had been bulldozed in Hangzhou. Christians in the West were enraged that the government in China would allow this to happen. Persecution seemed to be in full swing. One western Christian ministry organization announced in its news bulletin: "A new wave of persecution is sweeping across China."

Since I had heard of such disturbing persecution stories before that later had turned out to be bogus, I immediately contacted my friends in China to check this out. "Leaders of the house church movement had built a church without abiding by municipality's zoning regulations," I was told. To be sure, I also called the US consulate in Shanghai to check this out for me. The consul sent his representative in charge of monitoring human rights issues to Hangzhou to investigate. "Zoning regulations were disregarded," they reported back to me. But to convince myself of what really had happened and that the reports I had received were correct, I personally visited the pastor of a church in Hangzhou on my next trip to China.

One of his church workers drove me to the outskirts of the city where the event had taken place. She pointed to an area where she used to live. "The authorities tore down whole sections in order to replace them with high-rise buildings," she explained. "I was one of those affected, but they offered to resettle me in another place. The same offer had been made to the church, but the leaders refused to accept the resettlement. This had nothing to do with persecution."

Joseph Gu, senior pastor of the largest church in Hangzhou, told me, "I feel for those church members who had sacrificed so much to build that edifice, but regrettably they had been misled by their own church leaders who had refused to accept the existing municipal regulations."

Once more I learned that Christians in the western world easily jump to assumptions that persecution is the order of day when in reality it is that Chinese house church leaders often defy existing rules and regulations that had been formulated by political leaders of municipalities.

Here I have to include something in German. It was the time when George W. Bush was president of the United States. He successfully had removed Saddam Hussein from Iraq with the help of Tony Blair of Great Britain and forty plus other countries such as Denmark, Norway, Australia, New Zealand, South Korea, and Japan, among many others. The notable exceptions were France and Germany. Understandably Germany was reluctant due to her history, but it was unusual for France to sit on the sidelines.

The German magazine *Stern* published an article that was so outrageous and despicable that I felt compelled to write them a letter. Here it is in German. Sorry to those who do not know German. My answers to the correspondent are in italics:

Only for German-speaking folks

Ihr Bericht im letzten *Stern* ist ja schlimmer als die Hetzkampagne zu Hitlers Zeiten. Sie haben damals sicherlich noch nicht gelebt, ich aber. Deshalb kann ich mir erlauben dies zu sagen. Als Deutscher schäme ich mich von Deutschen solch eine Hasstirade zu lesen. Sie schrieben unter anderem:

Der kleinlaute Rückzug. Vom Großmaul zum Bittsteller. *Sie sollten sich schämen, so einen Ausdruck zu wählen. Journalisten sind dafür bekannt, ihren Mund voll zu nehmen, oft zu voll, und das leider jetzt auch auf vulgäre Art.*

Präsident Bush steht vor einem Scherbenhaufen. Er wollte eine Weltordnung schaffen, aber seine Kriege führten ins Chaos. *Wo ist das Chaos? Wo ist der Scherbenhaufen? Saddam und sein Regime sind weg, die Iraker sind befreit, sie erhalten die in den Massengräbern verbuddelten Angehörigen zurück und das Land ist im Wiederaufbau.*

Jetzt muss er die verprellte UNO um Hilfe bitten. *Wie schön können Sie das verdrehen und als Lüge den Menschen vermitteln. Gerade umgekehrt war es. Deutschland und Frankreich mit einigen anderen europäischen Ländern (Gott sei Dank nicht allen) haben die USA, England mit ihren Koalitionsländern verprellt. Ja, es stimmt, die UNO ist dabei schlecht weggekommen.*

Bush sagte nichts „von den vielen toten GIs". Nur vier Monate später ist Bush im eigenen Land so unbeliebt wie nie zuvor. *Dies besagt gar nichts, auch Churchill war nach seinem großen Sieg über Hitlerdeutschland nicht mehr so beliebt. Jetzt wird er allerdings als einer der Großen eingestuft. Dies werden sicherlich auch Bush und Blair erfahren.*

Niemals in der Geschichte war das Ansehen Amerikas so miserabel.
Sie haben wohl auch noch nicht zu Reagans Zeiten gelebt. Was ist er von der deutschen Presse fertiggemacht und verunglimpft worden. Und heute dankt ihm die Welt für den Sieg über den europäischen Kommunismus. Auch zu Carters Zeiten ist die USA wegen der Raketeninstallierung in Deutschland von der liberalen Presse verdammt worden.

Canossagang zu den von ihm so ungeliebten Vereinten Nationen.
Dies ist kein Canossagang, sondern er versucht nochmals die UNO vom Makel der Irrelevanz zu befreien, indem er hofft, sie mit einbeziehen zu können, so wie er es monatelang vor dem Irakkrieg schon versucht hatte. Hoffentlich ist die UNO jetzt schlauer und lässt sich nicht wieder von Schröder und Chirac unterbuttern.

Bush der meistgehasste Mann auf diesem Planeten.
Was für ein Unsinn verbreiten Sie da. Ich weiß nicht wer der unbeliebteste ist; vielleicht sind es die Journalisten! (Denkt nur an die Episode Völler).

Überheblichkeit, Großmäuligkeit, Verachtung für die internationale Gemeinschaft. Es war der Beginn einer Kette von Halbwahrheiten, Lügen, und überzeichneten Szenarien.

*Das muss erst noch bewiesen werden. Das Gegenteil scheint sich
abzuzeichnen. Siehe die letzten Erkundigungen über Kelly.*

Das Nein der Welt war nicht nur ein Nein zum Angriffskrieg,
sondern ein Nein zum American Empire, ein Aufbäumen
gegen zu viel Arroganz und Rambo-Politik. Die Niederlage
im Sicherheitsrat ist die größte Schmach, die die USA in der
Geschichte der Völkergemeinschaft erlitten haben.
*So sehen Sie das, aber schon wieder falsch. Bush und Blair mit
vierzig plus Nationen haben das getan wonach sich 30 Million
Iraker gesehnt hatten, und damit den Betonköpfen zu zeigen,
dass das zwölf Jahre lange Debattieren in der UNO nichts
genützt hat.*

Mit etwas mehr Clintonischem Charme
*(den kennen viele in unseren Breitengraden nur als
Hosenschlitzhampelmann—schön, dass er wenigstens in Europa
noch beliebt ist)*
und Carterschen Weltgewandtheit
*(und den nur als einen inkompetenten Präsidenten—nun gut,
er war ein guter Sonntagschullehrer und hat Gutes für arme
Menschen getan, dies aber erst nach seiner Präsidentschaft)*
hätte Bush vielleicht gesiegt.
Er hat ja gesiegt.

Der Krieg, den Bush im Irak führte, war der erste Angriffskrieg
in der Geschichte der USA.
*Wiederum falsch; er war die Fortsetzung und Vollendung des
ersten Golfkriegs. Der Waffenstillstand war xmal gebrochen
worden, und Blair und Bush mit vielen anderen hatten es satt
von Saddam weiterhin an der Nase herumgeführt zu werden,
(übrigens, Sie werden es immer noch). Und wie war es mit dem*

Balkankrieg? Da wurde ohne UNO-Erlaubnis ein Angriffskrieg geführt, und die Deutschen haben sich daran fleißig beteiligt.

Er verstieß gegen das Völkerrecht und verprellte langjährige Alliierte.

Das Völkerrecht ist Menschen vor Exekutionen, Folter, KZs, und den Barbarentum zu befreien. Langjährige Alliierte sind nicht verprellt worden, sie müssen nur umdenken.

Die Supermacht fleht um Hilfe.

Sie fleht nicht um Hilfe, sondern fordert alle auf, wenigstens beim Aufbau Iraks jetzt mitzuwirken. Wenn viele von ihnen schon nicht dazu bereit gewesen waren, Irak vom Schlächter Bagdads zu befreien, so darf man doch annehmen, dass den Irakern jetzt geholfen werden sollte. Hier könnte sich auch Deutschland vom Makel der Lieblosigkeit und der Absonderung befreien.

Well, I ended my remarks or rebuttal with a scathing rebuke which, no doubt, must have shocked the recipient.

Na ja, zu viel darf man von Ihnen nicht erwarten, wenn man schon so viel Unsinn schreibt, dann wird es wohl schwer fallen auf den Boden der Realität zurückzufinden. Aber hören Sie bitte damit auf, Menschen verdummen zu wollen. Göbbels hat es auch versucht, und was ist daraus geworden.

I am sorry for those who are not fluent in German, but I thought it would make more sense to leave the above in the original text. Find someone to translate!

On the right track

Erik had been a great asset in our China ministry. However, during the year 2004 he became discouraged with the attitude of some in the China Christian Council leadership. The battle of Bishop Ting's "Reconstruction Theology" was raging across China, and some Chinese leaders were endorsing his conclusions. Others did not. We of China Partner had honest reservations with some of his interpretations. This put us somewhat at odds with them. Erik wondered whether we could or even should continue our ministry in China. Perhaps the time had come for us to redirect our focus, he felt.

I had also noticed a shift in some of the new leaders' attitude toward us. But I was convinced that we should move ahead trusting the Lord with the mandate he had given us. So I wrote him the following memo:

I can identify with your feeling of disappointment and even anger after hearing what you heard from Mike [he was a coworker of ours at that time]. In my many years of working for the Lord, I had to learn some things the hard way. The major thing I learned is the way in which the service for my Lord steers my thinking and my actions toward *how* I do this service for Him. I learned that foremost everything I do is based upon *His divine calling.* Therefore, when things get rough, or when people disappoint me, or when I feel not wanted or needed, then I ask myself, "Why are you in the service of the Lord after all? What is the basis for your work? Are men's opinions or their arguments driving your work, or is the Lord giving the orders?" Once the foundation for the reason of my service is clear and solid again, then I can wrestle with the problems in such a way that it does not blur my focus or my call and task any longer.

Then I continued:

Now to the matter at hand. First of all we need to see that what you heard had been filtered through several layers. These are: Pastor Yang, who checked things out with "lower" national CCC people who had heard from someone in Nanchang and finally Mike. A lot of "filtering" was done—people with different understandings, agendas, perceptions, etc.

Secondly, it is true that ours is a "below average relationship" with the present national CCC leadership. The "above average relationship" [for them] is with World Council of Church groups, such as mainline and ecumenical organizations and those who are totally devoted to the principle of TSPM. Wickeri was one of those in the past and even Oblau. Their status has somewhat changed lately, because of their disagreements with the bishop [Ting].

Thirdly, it is true that there had been a rift between the bishop and me. However, this has been overcome, even though the scar remains.

Fourthly, we know of some grievances that some provincial TSPM/CCC leadership [now] have with the national TSPM/CCC leadership. This does play out in some way, and sometimes negatively. CP may get some fallout from this.

I concluded this long memo:

> Let me come back to the beginning of my email. Erik, what you are now experiencing is what I and other Christian leaders had to go through as well—even Jesus. Remember, 20 percent of His disciples turned against Him: Peter, who denied Him and then repented; and Judas, who betrayed Him and then hanged himself. I also think of Billy Graham, how he had been criticized by some of his friends and even his own staff besides the many who did not agree with him and his ministry. But once he refocused on what God had called him to do, he pressed on. And then I think back to my leadership position as German and later European YFC director. Also, the thorn in my flesh—Bob Williams—during my Amsterdam conference leadership! All of these experiences were tough, and only with the help of the Lord and also other friends I had—including Mutti—was I able to pull through.
>
> When we get to China, we will delve into the problems mentioned. I am sure once we confront them—not the people involved—things will not look as bad as they seem to us now. So let us go into the battle with heads high, knowing that we are under God's command wanting to do the right thing: openly, honestly, and legally. Our task is to serve the church in China.
>
> Love you much, Papa

Amazing things then happened. God reinforced our ministry and later some of the younger emerging leadership of CCC encouraged us to move ahead. "The future of CP looks bright," some said. Later Erik called me from China: "I love my job."

The year 2005 was a banner year for us. Our CP ministry teams continued to teach in seminaries and Bible schools all across China. However, the dedication of the largest church in China with its 6,000 seats was one of the highlights. Arriving as special guests that Sunday morning at the Chong-Yi Church in Hangzhou, we were given a brochure with the number 050505 printed on it. This stood for May 5, 2005. When we entered the huge church, I was startled by its immensity. 10,000 people were jammed into the church and its many interior rooms and halls—even the underground parking space was used for this occasion. Policemen were seen on the streets around the church, not to keep an eye on this undertaking but to direct the massive traffic surrounding this event. A 400-voice choir directed by an eighty-nine-year-old lady, Lyna Tsai, sang *To God be the glory, great things He has done.* It was a moving experience to see her in full action! I had first met her when I visited Hangzhou in the early '80s. She and her husband had taken me then on a boat trip on the beautiful West Lake. Hangzhou is one of the seven ancient capitals in China and is a garden-like city famous for its scenic splendor.

Elder Ji preached on *The Holy Temple of God.* "It is not so much about this newly erected temple of God we now dedicate," he stated, "but about us Christians who as temples of the Holy Spirit have to be a testimony in our society."

Bishop Ting was assisted to the pulpit to give the benediction. He hardly could walk. This was the last time Erik and I were able to see and speak with him. From then on he faded into the background, suffering for several years with dementia. He truly had been a prodigious leader of the Chinese church. Rev. Joseph Gu, in his forties, the senior pastor of the largest church in Hangzhou, encouraged us to keep on doing our ministry. "You have a bright future in China," he said.

This turned out to be true.

For years I had been contemplating to write a book on China. Many books had been written about China, but with my background and present involvement in China, I felt that I could offer an additional and unfamiliar aspect about God's doing in that vast land. By that time I had crossed the ocean close to two hundred times. I had seen and experienced China differently from other "one-time visitors," who had concentrated primarily on the negatives.

When the western world talks about China, two subjects are mostly discussed: economy and persecution. These represent glitter and gutter. However, next to a booming economy there is poverty. Besides the horror of persecution there is freedom—in China they call it relative freedom.

Let me reveal some of the sentiments I had also expressed in the preface of my book. I struggled to find an appropriate title. Humanists and human rights activists among Christians rightly exposed the dark side of the communist regime as told in multiple stories on persecution. However, another side to the evolving political establishment in China exists. This is not only reflected in China's economic boom but also in the government's aggressive steps to advance the legal system. Eventually this will affect the interpretation of the religious freedom article of the Chinese constitution in a positive way. The effects are already being felt. The latter had not been adequately reported. I wanted to reflect this in the title of this book.

Ruth Graham, in a letter to me regarding China, gave me an idea. She quoted Paul Harvey's motto, "And now the rest of the story…" from his famous radio show. The western media circulated so many controversial news stories—some of them true, but the majority of them misleading or even false—that I felt compelled to relate "the rest of the story." What had annoyed me most? The never-ending flow of stories of persecuted Christians left the impression that every Christian in China is being persecuted or under siege, and that is not so. On the contrary, millions worship Christ freely. Of course human rights violations do exist. But have we forgotten the government's effort to implement policies of religious freedom?

I wanted to focus on Jesus and His true followers in China.

A pastor in Shanghai told me a story that clinched my search for a title. Overjoyed by this pastor's invitation to perform in his church, members of a singing group from overseas composed a song specifically for this occasion. They stood in front of the congregation and enthusiastically sang, "How wonderful for Jesus to have returned to China." The pastor appreciated their enthusiasm but then pulled them aside after the service and said, "Thank you so much for your gusto, but listen—Jesus never left China." This led me to the title I used. Indeed, Jesus had never left China!

In the preface I wrote:

Let me take you on an exciting journey. The supposed death rattle of the church in China has been transformed into a dynamic force of an emerging faith that has swept across a land formerly blocked to the spreading of the gospel of Jesus Christ. On October 1, 1949, when Mao Zedong declared on Tiananmen Square, "China finally stood up," this became true for the church in China as well. The so-called "Opiate for the people" turned into a pulsating life-blood for the nation.

The book was published in English and in Chinese and was enthusiastically received by some and condemned by others. A reader in Hong Kong wrote, "I fear he is being used by the Communist authorities to promote their agenda, as many people who have aligned themselves to the Three-Self Church have become either willingly or unwittingly over the years." The President of Fuller Seminary in Pasadena, CA, had a different viewpoint: "Dr. Bürklin dispels the myths and misconceptions so many in the West have about God's wonderful work in China." And Ruth Graham had this to say: "… Werner always endeavored to paint a true picture of God's mighty work in China and succeeded again." Another one penned, "This is one of many recent books that tell the amazing story of the survival of the church in China—not "somehow," but "triumphantly"! Another one from Hong Kong was so enthused that he ordered seventy books. "I have been reading your book … and cannot put it down … your scholarly and practical research makes it compulsory reading … I can almost tangibly feel the Lord's anointing on this book. As a starter we want to order twenty hard copies and fifty soft-cover copies."

God's amazing provision

Over the years we have spent several million dollars to carry out our ministry in China. As we approached the end of the year we were rejoicing how the Lord had provided in spectacular ways. For instance, as I related earlier in my book, in Linchuan I was asked by Elder En Ai of the church we had helped build whether we could assist in eliminating the rest of the building cost to the tune of $114,000. I had told him that we have a policy that we do not spend money we do not have in hand.

"I cannot guarantee any help but I can guarantee our prayers," I told him. But his plea so burdened my heart, that following our meeting I knelt in my hotel room saying, "Lord, you see this great need, but we don't have any money to give. Please do something unusual." While traveling through China this burden would not leave me. Again and again I knelt and prayed for the Linchuan church and its needs.

A few days later I boarded my flight in Shanghai for San Francisco. I sat next to a Chinese lady from Taiwan—now living in California—who turned out to be a devoted Christian. She was so interested in what China Partner is doing in China that all we talked about was—guess what—China! Parting in Frisco she said she would love to do something for us. Five days later I received a letter from her with a check of $100,000. This is another one of those incredible and miraculous experiences I had with my Lord.

"We wept when we received your assistance," Elder En Ai wrote from Linchuan after receiving our check.

Year after year we continued our China ministry. Our motto remained the same, "To serve the church in China as they fulfill the Great Commission." 2008 was another exceptional year as the eyes of the world were fixed on the Olympics in Beijing. We had been constantly asked what we thought about chances the Chinese government would pull off a successful event. We knew of their expertise as had been displayed by their phenomenal economic growth and therefore we were optimistic. However, we were more interested in how this would influence the church in China. Erik wrote, "[We hope] the media will report more on what God is doing there; more positive reporting on what China and its church situation is like, instead of only concentrating on human rights violations."

I wrote, "[I hope that the media] will give a more inclusive report about China—not focusing only on athletic events, swipes against the government, or harping on the negative, but also being more positive." In our *CP China News* we informed our readers that "The Chinese church is making use of the Olympics as an outreach to the world by printing an Olympic logo Bible in English which will be handed out as a 'welcome gift' to all incoming athletes and media personnel."

Another big event happened during that year. China became one of the greatest Bible producers in the world—later we found out that China actually had become *the* world's greatest Bible producer! The yearly Bible production doubled from six million to twelve million per year—or twenty-three Bibles per minute! At that time there were over seventy official Bible distribution points in China, and people were able to buy Bibles in close to 50,000 churches spread across every province.

Ever since my first visit back into China in 1981, I have made numerous trips to the city of Ningdu, Jiangxi, where my parents toiled as missionaries from 1946-50. Throughout the following years I had the desire to help the Christians build a new church to replace the old chapel where my father had ministered. In fact, I had wanted to have this accomplished as one of my last projects before my death.

On March 2, 2009, Sister Honghong Lai sent me a letter with the architectural drawings for the new church:

Often, when I am in my quiet time [devotions], I am reminded of your kind voice, "I am a Jiangxi lao biao" ["I am a Jiangxi old uncle"—a Chinese saying which always prompts hilarious laughter]. Each time my heart is being stirred anew. When I saw you off to Nanchang on the mini-bus, you

475

extended your right arm out of the window and waved and waved. I know you have a deep love for Ningdu. I sincerely wish our loving heavenly Father to care for you and hope you can live in Ningdu for a period of time. That for us would be a great, great satisfaction and joy!

Since traveling with Sister Jujua Liu to Nanchang to meet with Rev. Lin Feng and Rev. Li Baole, we have been working hard on the church construction project. Through many twists and turns, the relevant government office has made a clear decision to permit the Ningdu Christian Church to rebuild on the original church site. The size of the property for the Ye Su Tang [Jesus Hall] is 454.85 square meters. It is obviously narrow and small. However, we do not have any other option to change the decision of the government. Apparently, God has His own will. We trust that where God puts His hand of blessing, the location will be beautiful.

Presently the Ningdu church members have established a seven-member church building project committee with the members being Taifu Jie, Aichang Liu, Camin Xiao, Ying Huang, Shuixiu Rao, Na Zou, and Honghong Lai. With our hearts and minds unified, we are working on plans to construct a new church building on the original church site. The drawings have been produced, making wise use of the available space for worship. It has an expanded area of 420 square meters that can accommodate up to 800 people. It will also include functional rooms for Sunday school, training, guest accommodations, etc. We are now focusing our attention on completing good relations with our surrounding neighbors. We anticipate that within the next two months we will be able to tear down the current building and then start the new [building]. We eagerly look forward to the early erection of the new sanctuary. According to the preliminary budget estimate by brother Ying Huang, the designer of the drawings, the cost for construction will be approximately RMB 1,500,000 [about US$ 230,000].

The entire membership will continue to work hard. May God show His favor so that we will be blessed on both the church building project and the church ministry. May both sanctuaries be glorious before God!

Greetings to all staff members of China Partner. Emmanuel!

This, of course, brought boundless joy to my heart. During my visit to discuss the possible construction of a new church building on June 23, 2008, I had met with some of the leadership of the church and handed over $25,000 and 20,000 (totaling $53,500) to be kept in trust by Rev. Lin Feng from Nanchang until the actual commencement of construction. At that time the church leaders of the Ningdu church had agreed to following stipulations: A competent architect and a builder need to be found, a proper bank account for the construction project had to be set up, one specific person must be chosen for overseeing the project, and church volunteers must be available to help with the construction.

I also had reminded them that only through their trust in God and with His help the project could be brought to a successful conclusion. Psalm 127:1 states: "Unless the Lord builds the house, they labor in vain who build it."

Now the construction could begin.

I was back for the ground breaking ceremony. Our daughter, Linda, with her two children, Jerusha and Tilon, along with Erik had made the trip to Ningdu for this occasion. As the cornerstone was laid with its inscription in Chinese characters "Jesus is the cornerstone" (Eph. 2:20), the choir sang the well-known song "Majesty." After the service an older lady came up to me with tears in her eyes and said with a quivering voice, "*Feichang ganxie nimen lai, ganxie zhu*"—"thank you so much for coming, thank the Lord." Her late husband, the elder of the church, had been the one who had asked me to help with this church project—it was his dying wish. Now his wife was able to see with her own eyes how the groundbreaking stone was laid. Her husband's wish had come true even though he did not live to see it.

The construction was finished one year later in June of 2010. As I got up to give my sermon on that hot June day of dedication, I was so overcome with emotion that it took me three minutes before I could speak. The congregation sensed what was happening and started to clap. This enabled me to regain my composure and I began with, "I am so moved because many years ago my father stood here and preached the gospel. Now I am privileged to preach on the same spot, however in this new church building. Great is His faithfulness." My friend Ed Lyman had sung that hymn just before I had entered the pulpit, and this had stirred my emotion. To me it was absolutely amazing that the church had survived the vicious Cultural Revolution and that formerly conceived enemies of China were allowed not only to visit China, but also were invited as honored guests to give the dedicatory address.

In the meantime the Communist Party remained true to her ambiguous principles, even though not as devoted and fanatical as under Mao. The party professed three basic ideologies:

- Being representatives of advanced productivity
- Being representatives of advanced culture by reintroducing Confucianism
- Being representatives of the broad masses of the people to further their basic interests to the highest degree (e.g. protect the interest of the common people rather than themselves)

Fortunately, and thankfully for the Christians, the party no longer pursued their former vendetta against religions. Unfortunately this threw open the doors for false teachings to flourish all across China, especially in the countryside where many of the uneducated populace lives. To show the extent of this dilemma, let me mention only the known heretical groups: Born Again Movement; Shouters or Yellers; Thunder From The East (led by a woman Christ); Wilderness Church [specializes in suffering]; Branch Church; Foot Washer's Church; King of "Billi"; Food From the Holy Spirit Church; Eastern Lightning; Ling Ling Church [Spirit Spirit] Church; New Testament Apostle's Church; Appointed as King Church; Lord God Church; Changzhou is Lord Church; Three Level Servant Church; Discipleship Group; Cold Water Group; Desert Group; Yi Guan Dao Group.

In the western world, members of these bodies were often included in the statistics of how many Christians live in China. I once talked on the phone with the spiritual leader of one of those heretical groups who claimed to have over one million followers. He was a barber by profession, had no theological training, and itinerated throughout China. He had been incarcerated a number of times for not registering with the government. These truly are strange people, and innocent people fall for them. Even in the western world! This man was a specimen of so many house church leaders. My interpreter just shook her head as he harangued on the phone against the churches not under his control and against the government with their rules and regulations. These people are adamant, unyielding, obstinate, and stubborn about their way of doing things. No wonder the government is afraid and troubled about them.

However, we praise God for many other house churches that are true to the Word of God. Once they register with the appropriate authorities they can worship freely and reach out to their fellow citizens. Let us undergird them and pray for their endeavors.

CHAPTER 31

THE LATTER YEARS FULL OF BLESSINGS

HAVING LIVED IN the United States over thirty years, Inge and I felt we should become citizens of that country. We always had hesitated, because we did not want to give up our German citizenship. For many years Germany did not allow dual citizenship. But then their laws changed so that we could take the step.

On my many trips all over the world, I had noticed that the German passport had been a great asset. For most countries I did not need visas as a German, whereas the Americans did. And we wanted to vote to help those who desired to bring back Christian values to America. So in the spring of 2011 we became American citizens. Before reciting the oath of allegiance to the United States, the official said, "When you come to the portion to renounce all allegiance to your former country, just don't say those words." Well, I was glad that we did not have to and we didn't. Now we carry both passports.

Inge and I had been members of Boca Raton Community Church, also formerly known as Bibletown. We had enjoyed numerous godly pastors, but Don (or Dick) Hubbard was my favorite. In my book he is the best expository preacher I have ever heard, and that consistently so. Amazingly, he never uses notes. However, as of late Bill Mitchell has done a phenomenal job of bringing the church to new heights.

The church is located close to the Florida Atlantic University (FAU) with many students from mainland China. In an outreach to them I befriended Ming Ming from Changsha. We invited him for meals, sat with him in church, and talked to him about the Lord. Several months later I asked Charlie Li, another Chinese who also had studied at FAU, to join me for lunch along with Ming Ming. Charlie had become a Christian and I wanted him for counsel, if needed, when sharing Christ with Ming Ming. I asked Ming Ming, "Do you now understand the gospel?" He said yes. "Would you like to accept Christ as your Savior and Lord?" I continued. Without hesitation he said, "I would." He prayed the sinner's prayer and when he looked up he blurted out, "Something just happened."

And it surely did. A few weeks later he led his roommate, Alex from Wuhan, to Christ. Ming Ming then married his high school sweetheart back home, and when both returned to Florida, she found the Lord. Sometime later Alex's wife made a commitment to Christ. What a wonderful chain reaction!

For thirty years we had been members of Boca Raton Community Church but then we were drawn to a more European styled church, the First Presbyterian Church. Later they changed their name to Grace Community Church. We loved the powerful music emerging from the pipe organ and appreciated the candles up front, which modern churches do not have any longer. Its pastor was previously the youth pastor in John Huffman's California church. Kirk McCormick is a deep thinker, and his sermons challenged us to the point that we decided to join his church. Since prayer had been a growing interest and burden in our lives, we were asked to head up the prayer ministry. I was reminded of what Billy Graham had told me when I visited him in his home in May 2010, "I am turning blind and have to use the wheel-chair. I would like to preach one more time. But all I can do now is pray." When I saw him again in September 2011, he still wanted to preach one more time. But all he can do now is pray. At our age we also wanted to be used by the Lord in this way.

Finally the day arrived when I retired from all activities with China Partner except being available as a consultant. This happened on my eightieth birthday on November 2, 2010. Erik threw a cherished party at the Embassy Suites in Boca Raton on November 22. My dear friend Larry Rybka paid for the event. He had been one of our most faithful supporters coming forth with gifts of $5,000 or $10,000 again and again.

All our children gave tribute, and what a joy to see some of our eleven grandchildren enjoy this extravaganza. My brother, Fred, and my sister, Joy, also spoke. For my brother it was one of his last speaking events before passing on to heaven on May 13, 2011, only nine days before his eighty-second birthday.

To express my feeling at that time let me disclose my farewell article in CPs *China News.* I wrote it on my farewell trip in China:

Today is my last day in China. What a phenomenal three weeks' journey it has been! However, I shall never forget yesterday's Sunday.

My farewell trip to China took me to Shanghai, Nanchang, Linchuan, Zishi, Ningdu, Nanfeng, Chongren, Wuhan, Changsha, Nanjing, and Hangzhou. In all of those cities I preached my farewell sermons. Also, everywhere I went, I was feted for my eightieth birthday—interestingly, for the Chinese I am already eighty-one years old—they start counting the years from the actual day of birth.

I look back to almost thirty years of ministry in China. During that time, I made close to one hundred trips to the land of my birth. China Partner is now known from Harbin in the north to Guangzhou in the south; from Hangzhou in the east to Urumqi in the west. Over the years, we ministered in countless cities, teaching and preaching the Word of God. We invited pastors and Christian mission leaders to help us train thousands of emerging Christian leaders in cites all across China. We shipped in tens of thousands of Christian study books worth hundreds of thousands of dollars. We helped build a Bible school and churches in five cities.

Yes, looking back I still marvel at the close to two hundred trips I had made over the Atlantic and Pacific. A number of times I traveled around the world, first from Germany and later from the United States. China became incessantly dearer to me.

We had made hundreds of friends over the years. I wish I could have said farewell to all of them in a personal way, but

I could only do that to a few. But I shall never forget the warm reception everywhere received and I will never forget my brothers and sisters in China.

On the final day, yesterday, I worshiped with the believers in the largest church of China in the city of Hangzhou. Years ago, the senior pastor Joseph Gu had invited me to come and preach in his church, and it finally came to pass. Ed Lyman, who accompanied me throughout, sang my favorite song, "Great is thy faithfulness," as he had done in the other cities. Our coworker Daniel Hsu interpreted for me. The church seats 6,000 people and it looked like every seat was taken. I preached on "The relevancy of Jesus in our world today." Seldom have I experienced a more attentive crowd. Most of them seemed to be younger than in other churches I had seen. At the invitation, an incredible number—over two thousand—stood to commit their lives for service in God's kingdom. Following that, I asked those to stand who wanted to accept Christ as their personal Savior. More than two hundred fifty stood. What a sight! The Chinese are hungry for the Word of God—Christians and non-Christians alike.

The pastor had always impressed me as a [great] spiritual leader. He was competent, loving, and hardworking and a true shepherd of the flock. He is an evangelist at heart and has always been eager to reach out to unbelievers.

Now this church plans to build a sister church on the site where several colleges are located. The groundbreaking ceremony is scheduled for July 7. They already have one-third of this in cash. This dynamic pastor is moving ahead.

Of course, the most memorable and moving experience I had on my farewell trip was in Ningdu, Jiangxi province, the last city where my parents had labored as missionaries. As I faced the congregation that had come from near and far, I thought to myself, *if only my parents could have been present!*

After thirty years of ministry in China, I was deeply grateful to my family who had stood behind me all those years. So I continued in my article thinking about the future:

> What is next? I am glad that our son Erik is continuing the ministry. Everywhere we went we were asked to return. The teaching ministry on subjects such as evangelism, pastoral care, biblical leadership, and discipleship is so needed. Erik will concentrate our efforts in the rural area of China—where the forgotten people live. Tourists and even other Christian ministries flock to the major cities, but the masses live in the countryside. And this is where we want to go.
>
> Thank you so much for your prayers and support all these many years. God is doing a mighty work in China and we have had the privilege of having a small part in it. Please keep on doing what you have been doing all along. We need your prayers very much. And the Chinese church needs your prayers.

My overarching feeling came through in my final paragraph:

> China is the land where I was born. It was there where I had my early schooling and where I found my Savior. In Shanghai I dedicated my life to the Lord's service under the preaching of Bob Pierce, evangelist with YFC and later founder of World Vision. Yesterday's commitments of those

in Hangzhou reminded me of that day [of my surrender to Him]. China is the land to which I returned some thirty years ago and where the ministry of China Partner was born. I lost my heart there. It is there where I would like to be buried—if that would be possible.

Please pray for China and its burgeoning—even exploding —church.

I was ready to release my responsibilities but I never will cut my ties with China—the land where I was born, where I was schooled, where I found my Savior, and where I taught on close to one hundred trips—China, the land I love!

The time had come to say farewell to active ministry I loved so dearly. The way I felt at that time highlights how I had felt all along on my life's journey. As a paragon to show what I mean, let me echo what I had penned in my journal more than a decade earlier on December 31, 2000, the day before Erik took over the presidency of China Partner:

[Today is a] good time to reflect back; but the older I get, the less reflecting I do. Nor do I make resolutions for the future. My life is safely harbored [and anchored] in the peace of God. How wonderful to have a constant in life! Through the now apparent ups and downs, not much really changes. As the Bible (Ecclesiastes) says, "Generations come and go ... The sun rises and sets ... The wind blows south and north ... The rivers run into the sea, but ... never full." History merely repeats itself. It has all been done before. And then Solomon continues in chapter 3, "There is a time for everything." And all of it has to take place! The year 2000 went to bed, and so did I—serenely and quietly. I am at peace with myself.

God is in control. He directs my path. He is my light as promised. Nothing will throw me off kilter. There is stability, straightforwardness, clarity in a life dedicated to Him—even if not fully, wholly, completely—for how can a mortal be perfect! But dedicated I can be—and have been ever since I surrendered my life to my loving God and heavenly Father so many years ago. And how wonderful to be yoked together with someone who is a woman of God! Her dedication to Him made it so much easier [for me]. I could always depend upon her—the way she raised our kids and the way she cared for me. No greater love can be expected from anyone! Her being is rooted in Him, who is the center of our focus and the stronghold of our lives.

To God belongs all the glory; great things he has done. This book is just a little footnote of what I experienced in my eighty plus years. As long as I live, I will be forever grateful to a God who had chosen me, along with many others, to execute His will—and that before the foundation of the world. Amazing!

Yes, Hitler, the cruelest of all dictators, shocked and devastated my trust as a German patriot. Mao, in whose land I was born and lived, and under whose regime millions perished, and where most of the others slid into poverty, disillusioned me. However, I will never lose my love for China.

Yet Jesus is the only one I learned to trust. He saved me and then sustained me throughout my life! What a magnificent Savior and Lord He was, and still is to me and forever will be! That says it all.

MINISTRY CALENDAR
SAMPLE OF SIX YEARS OUT OF MY LIFE-LONG WORLD TRAVELS:
1982, 1984, 1985, 1988, 1996, 1998

1982

01-06 Jan	USA
07-10	Egelsbach, Germany
11-15	Amsterdam, Holland
16	Egelsbach
17-18	Nyon, Switzerland
19-22	Amsterdam
23-26	Egelsbach
27	Neuhausen, Germany
28-30	Pliezhausen
31-05 Feb	Washington, DC
07	Atlanta, GA
08-11	Asheville, TN
12	Atlanta
13-17	Amsterdam
18-21	Egelsbach

22-26	Amsterdam
27-28	Egelsbach
01-04 Mar	Amsterdam
05-06	Egelsbach
07-09	Zürich, Switzerland
10-11	Amsterdam
12-22	Africa
24-26	Amsterdam
27-30	Egelsbach
01-02 Apr	Atlanta
03-07	Paris, Lamorlaye; EBI Alumni
08-12	Amsterdam
13-16	Amsterdam
17-22	Panama City
23-24	London, World Vision Board
25-30	Egelsbach, Evangelization
01 May	Linz, Austria, BGEA board
02	Egelsbach
03-07	Amsterdam
08-09	Egelsbach
10-14	Amsterdam
15-20	Egelsbach
21-25	Amsterdam
26-11 June	Far East: Tokyo, Taipei, Manila, Hong Kong, Singapore, Jakarta
12-16	Egelsbach
17-18	Amsterdam
19-20	Egelsbach
21-25	Amsterdam
26-04 July	Boca Raton (Boca)

MINISTRY CALENDAR

05	Wheaton, IL
06	Amsterdam
07-08	Montreux, Switzerland
09-11	Egelsbach
12-16	Amsterdam
17-18	Egelsbach
19-22	Amsterdam
23-25	Egelsbach
26-27	Amsterdam
28	Atlanta
29	Los Angeles
30	Atlanta
31-02 Aug	Minneapolis, MN
03-04	Atlanta
05-06	Amsterdam
07-08	Egelsbach
09-10	Neuhausen
11	Egelsbach
12-13	Amsterdam
14-16	Egelsbach
17-19	Titisee, Germany
20-22	Egelsbach
23-02 Sep	Amsterdam
03-05	Bad Orb, Germany
06-07	Amsterdam
08-12	Boca
13-14	Colorado Springs, CO
15-16	Amsterdam
17-20	Valence, France
21-23	Amsterdam

24	Frankfurt; World Vision Board
25-26	Bad Orb, Germany
27	Neuhausen,
28-01 Oct	Amsterdam
02-06	Boca
07-15	Kingston, Jamaica; Cuba; Mexico; Guatemala; Costa Rica; Panama
16-17	Boca
18-20	Chicago, IL
21-24	Amsterdam
25	Frankfurt
26-27	Amsterdam
28	Zürich
29	Pliezhausen, Germany
30	Linz; BGEA board
31	Vienna, Austria
01-11 Nov	Amsterdam
12-24	Bogota, Quito, Lima, Santiago, Buenos Aires, Sao Paulo, Rio
25-27	Amsterdam
28-29	Bad Kissingen, Germany
30-01 Dec	Heilbronn
02-05	Lausanne
06-12	Amsterdam
13-16	Atlanta
17-31	Boca

1984

16-18 Jan	Denver, CO
19-21	Boca

22-28	Germany: Frankfurt, Schramberg, St. Georgen, Königsfeld
29-30	Amsterdam
31-02 Feb	Boca
03-06	Orlando, St. Petersburg, FL
07-12	Boca
13-19	Chicago
20-02 Mar	Boca
03-04	Lake Wales, FL
05-08	Atlanta
09-01 Apr	Boca
02	Oakland, FL
03-05	Nashville, TN
06-08	Chattanooga
09-11	Birmingham, AL
12-13	Lake Wales
14-24	Boca
25-26	Los Angeles, CA
27-29	Honolulu, HI
30-01 May	Tokyo, Japan
02-14	China
15-16	Hong Kong
17-18	Singapore
19	Bangkok, Thailand
20	New Delhi, India
21-25	Frankfurt
26	Seeheim, Germany
27-31	Uelzen
01-04 June	London
05-21	Boca

22	Atlanta
23-25	Macon, GA
26-17 July	Boca
18-21	Liverpool, England
22-25	Boca
26-27	San Francisco, CA
28-04 Aug	Hong Kong; YFCI convocation
06-08	Guangzhou, China
09-11	Jiangxi, Nanchang, Nanfeng, Ningdu, Linchuan
12-14	Hong Kong
15-25	Boca
26-29	Atlanta, Macon, GA
30-04 Sep	London
05-11	Amsterdam
12-16	Stuttgart, Germany
17-18	Berlin
19	Linz, Austria
20	Zürich
21-25	Germany
26-29	Boca
31-05 Oct	Minneapolis, MN
06-07	Boca
08-11	Lake Wales
12-18	Boca
19-26	Germany
27-06 Nov	Boca
07-09	Atlanta
10-11	Nashville
12-16	Carefree, AZ; Billy Graham Team Meeting

17-18	Birmingham, AL
19-30	Boca
01-17 Dec	Boca
18-19	Jamaica
20-31	Boca

1985

01-05 Jan	Boca
05-06	Antigua, Caribbean
07	St. Kitts
08	St. Lucia
09	St. Vincent
10	Granada
11-12	Guyana
13-14	Trinidad
15-16	Barbados
17-21	Boca
22-25	Amsterdam
26	Frankfurt
27-29	Gwatt, Thun; Switzerland
30	Lausanne/Gland
31	Valence, France
01 Feb	Geneva, Zürich
02	Freudenstadt, Germany
03	Amsterdam
04-06	Washington, D.C.
07-10	Boca
11	Haiti
12	Dominican Republic, Puerto Rico
13-14	Virgin Island, St. Croix

15-18	Boca
19-20	Ft. Lauderdale
21-26	Boca
27-06 Mar	Amsterdam
07-17	India
18-21	Amsterdam
22-24	Uelzen
25-30	Amsterdam
31-03 Apr	Charlotte, NC
04-11	Amsterdam
12-15	Caracas, Venezuela
16	Maracaibo
17	Barranquilla
18	Bogota, Columbia
19	Quito, Ecuador
20-23	Lima, Peru
24-26	Amsterdam
27-02 May	Harare, Zimbabwe, Victoria Falls
03	Nairobi, Kenya
04-08	Amsterdam
09-11	Lakeville, MA
12	Dalton, PA
13-16	Boca
17-18	Upland, IN
19-20	Hartford, CN
21-23	Boca
24-06 Jun	Amsterdam
07-11	Helsinki, Finnland
12-13	Frankfurt
14-17	Amsterdam

18-19	Nicosia, Cyprus
20	Damascus, Syria
21	Aleppo
22-23	Damascus; Patriarch Syrian Orthodox Church
24-26	Amsterdam
27-30	Sheffield, England
01-05 Jul	Amsterdam
06-08	Chicago
09-13	Seoul, Korea
14	Suwon
15	Seoul
16	Tokyo
17-18	Shanghai
19-23	Nanjing, China
24-26	Tokyo
27-10 Aug	Amsterdam
11-12	Paramaribo, Suriname
13	Belem, Brazil
14	Recife
15	Rio de Janeiro
16	Porto Alegre
17	Curitiba
18	Sao Paulo
19	Asuncion, Paraguay
20	Santa Cruz, Bolivia
21	Cochabamba, Bolivia
22	La Paz, Bolivia
23-24	Miami
25	Boca

26	Atlanta
27-02 Sep	Amsterdam
03-05	Copenhagen
06-07	Aarhus, Denmark
07-15	Amsterdam
16-17	Johannesburg, South Africa
18	Lesotho
19	Durban, South Africa
20-21	Johannesburg
22-23	Botswana
24	Windhoek, Namibia
25	Johannesburg
26	Mauritius
27	Reunion
28-29	Seychelles
30-06 Oct	Amsterdam
07	Oslo, Norway
08	Trondheim
09-10	Stavanger
11-21	Amsterdam
22	Stockholm, Sweden
23-24	Wetzlar, Germany
25-26	Frankfurt
27	Kassel, Germany
28-02 Nov	Amsterdam
03-06	Singapore
07	Sydney, Australia
08	Melbourne
09-10	Auckland, New Zealand
11-12	Nuku'alofa, Tonga, Oceania

13-15	Apia, Samoa
16	Suva, Fiji
17	Port-Vila, Vanuatu
18	Nueme, New Caledonia
19-20	Singapore
21-02 Dec	Amsterdam
03-05	Patmos, Germany
06-08	Uelzen
09	Amsterdam
10	Mulhouse, Strasbourg, France
11	Zürich
12	Amsterdam
13-17	Boca
18	Wheaton, IL
19-31	Boca

1988

01-12 Jan	Boca
13-16	San Diego, CA
17-20	New Port Beach, CA
21	Boca
22-24	Palmetto Bay, FL (Miami)
25-29	Boca
30-05 Feb	Denver
06-09	St. Petersburg, FL
10-16	Boca
17	Frankfurt
18	St. Goar, Germany
19-21	Bickenbach
22	Langen

23	Bergen Enkheim
24	Mörfelden
25-29	Pune, Maharashtra, India
01-05 Mar	Madurai
06-08	Chennai (Madras)
09-12	Visakhapatnam
13	Hyderabad
14-17	Damascus, Syria
18-19	Lanarka, Cyprus
20-25	DDR (East Germany), Dresden
26-27	Erfurt
28-30	Uelzen, Germany
31	Bergen Enkheim
01-15 Apr	Boca
16-21	Milwaukee, WI
22-25	Wayland, Iowa
26-29	Boca
30-08 May	Iquitos, Peru
09-17 June	Boca
18-19	Macon, GA
20-23	Atlanta
24	Indianapolis, IN
25	Arlington Heights, IL
26-27	Wheaton, IL
28-03 July	Kitchener, Canada
04	Pittsburgh, PA
05	Lancaster, PA
06	Charlotte, NC
07-09	Charleston, SC
10	Orlando, FL

11-07 Aug	Boca
08	San Francisco
09-11	Hong Kong
12-14	Beijing, China
15-16	Taiyuan
17-18	Nanjing
19	Wuhu
20-21	Hefei, Anhui
22-23	Shanghai
24	Nanfeng
25	Ningdu
26-27	Nanchang
28-29	Guilin
30-02 Sep	Hong Kong
03-13	Boca
14-17	Frankfurt
18-25	Rüsselsheim, Germany
26-02 Oct	Uelzen
03-06	Lünen
07-09	Bad Laasphe
10	Bickenbach
11-24	Chicago
25-15 Nov	Boca
16-18	Tokyo
19-23	Manila
24-27	Bacolod, Philippines
28-30	Tokyo
01-10 Dec	Boca
11-14	Jacksonville, FL; Mayo Clinic
15-31	Boca

1996

01-29 Jan	Boca
30-02 Feb	Washington, DC
03-08	Boca
09	Chicago, San Francisco
10-18	Sydney, Australia
19	Canberra
20	Narooma Eden
23	Paynesville
24	Geelong
25-27	Hobart, Tasmania
28-29	Geelong
01-03 Mar	Auckland, NZ
04-08	Paihia
09-10	Auckland, Chicago
11-24	Boca
25-28	Denver
29-11 Apr	Boca
12-16	Toronto, Canada
17-21	Boca
22	San Francisco
23-26	Hong Kong
27-03 May	Jinan, China
04-09	Fuzhou
10-11	Hong Kong
12	San Francisco
13	Boca
14-18	Atlanta; LRS Doctorate
19-23	Düsseldorf, Germany
24	Köln

25-28	Uelzen
29-30	Wölmersen
31	Wetzlar
01 Jun	Weiterstadt
02	Mörfelden
03-05	Rüsselsheim
06-08	Korbach
09	Bensheim
10	St. Chrischona, Switzerland
11-16	Klosters
17-19	Krelingen
20-21	Uelzen
22-23	Berlin
24	Frankfurt, Düsseldorf
25-22 Jul	Boca
23-25	Naples, FL
26-30 Aug	Boca
31-02 Sep	Panama City
03-08	Boca
09	San Francisco
10-13	Hong Kong
14-16	Chengdu, China
17-18	Wuhan
19-20	Shanghai
21-23	Nanchang
24-28	Shenyang
29-02 Oct	Hawaii
03-10	Boca
11-14	Dayton, OH
15-17	Boca

18-19	Vancouver, Canada
20-21	Edmonton
22	Calgary
23	Winnipeg
24	Steinbach
25-27	Toronto
28-30	Cambridge
31	Toronto, Chicago
01-15 Nov	Boca
16-23	Cruise
24-28	Boca
29-02 Dec	Uelzen
03	Walsrode, Krelingen
04-05	Uelzen
06-07	Frankfurt
08-10	Dahle
11-12	Korntal, Aidlingen, Königsfeld
13-16	Berlin
17-21	Uelzen
22	Frankfurt
23-31	Boca

1998

01-30 Jan	Boca
31-02 Feb	Phoenix, AZ
03	Boca
04-06	Washington, DC
07-08	St. Petersburg, FL
09-15	Boca
16	Los Angeles

17-19	Sydney, Australia
20-03 Mar	Tasmania
04-08	Melbourne
09-11	Auckland
12-15	Wellington
16-23	Paihia
24	Auckland
25	Los Angeles
26-12 Apr	Boca
13-14	Rüsselsheim
15-16	Berlin
17-20	Uelzen
21	Wölmersen
22	Herzhausen
23-34	Lennestadt
25	Lünen
26-27	Lünen, Dahle
28-01 May	Boca
02-03	Elyria, OH
04-08	Hong Kong
09-10	Nanchang
11-13	Shanghai
14	Nanjing
15-17	Fuzhou
18	Nanjing
19-22	Fuzhou
23-24	Hong Kong
25-21 Jun	Boca
22-23	Jacksonville, FL; Mayo Clinic
24-18 Jul	Boca

19-23	West Palm Beach, FL
24-27 Aug	Boca
28-31	Sagharboo, Long Island, NY
01-06 Sep	Boca
07-08	Rüsselsheim
09-11	Berlin
12	Rügen
13-20	Eastern Germany, former DDR (German Democratic Republic)
21-25	Uelzen
26-27	Solingen
28	Wetzlar
29-01 Oct	Singapore
02	Hong Kong
03-05	Xian, China
06	Shanghai
07-09	Nanjing
10-14	Hangzhou
15-28	Boca
29-01 Nov	New Port Beach, CA
02-05	Los Angeles
06-09	Pasadena, CA
10-19	Boca
20-24	Canada
25-12 Dec	Boca
13-20	Cruise
21-31	Boca

MINISTRY OF CHINA PARTNER

C HINA PARTNER WAS founded in 1989 to help meet the spiritual needs in China.

China Partner conducts evangelism, pastoral training, and lay leadership courses in major cities across China.

China Partner sends short-term teaching teams to China conducting pastoral training seminars (PTS) in seminaries, Bible schools, and Bible training centers.

China Partner gives free workbooks and notes to pastors and lay leaders in China.

China Partner provides pastors and theological schools mini-libraries at no charge, including reference Bibles, concordances, Bible handbooks and dictionaries, commentaries, etc.

China Partner uploads to the internet training sessions focusing on the following seminars: evangelism, discipleship, Christian leadership, and pastoral care, covering such lessons as

507

"Communicating the Evangelistic Message—Presentation," "Maintaining Spiritual Freshness Through a Devotional Life of Prayer and Study," "Principles of Discipleship," "Marks of a Disciple," "Practical Wisdom for Pastoral Leadership," and lessons on various pastoral issues.

China Partner ministers to Chinese scholars who are studying in North America, with the ultimate goal of reaching them with the gospel of Jesus Christ and discipling them. When they return to China, they are potential Christian leaders and influencers of China's future.

China Partner supports Bible school students and grassroots pastors in poverty-stricken parts of China.

China Partner assists in the construction of new churches and Bible school campuses in China.

China Partner builds bridges of friendship, understanding, and communication with the church in China.

China Partner conducts China Symposiums and China Insight Seminars to educate and inform Christians in the West regarding the current church situation in China. The goal is to encourage Christians to pray more effectively for China and to help them participate with their Chinese brothers and sisters in the efforts to reach China with the gospel.

Our Vision: We envision Chinese with the love for Christ, an understanding of the power of God's Word so they can spread the gospel throughout China and the world.

Our Mission: To serve the church in China as they fulfill the Great Commission.

MINISTRY OF CHINA PARTNER

China Partner, Inc.
mail@chinapartner.org
www.chinapartner.org

* * * * *

China Partner has contacts in these countries:
Canada, canada@chinapartner.org
Germany, germany@chinapartner.org
Hong Kong, hongkong@chinapartner.org
New Zealand, newzealand@chinapartner.org
Switzerland, switzerland@chinapartner.org
United States, info@chinapartner.org

INDEX OF NAMES AND PLACES

THIS INDEX IS A COMPILATION OF NAMES AND PLACES
THAT ARE PERTINENT TO THE STORIES IN THIS BOOK

INDEX OF NAMES AND PLACES

WinePressPublishing
Great Books, Defined.

To order additional copies of this book call:
1-877-421-READ (7323)
or please visit our website at
www.WinePressbooks.com

If you enjoyed this quality custom-published book,
drop by our website for more books and information.

www.winepresspublishing.com
"Your partner in custom publishing."

CPSIA information can be obtained at www.ICGtesting.com
Printed in the USA
LVOW040610030812

292707LV00002B/2/P

9 781414 122212